# Claims Handling Principles and Practices

D1289779

# Claims Handling Principles and Practices

Edited by

Martin J. Frappolli, CPCU, FIDM, AIC, AIS

2nd Edition • 1st Printing

**The Institutes**
720 Providence Road, Suite 100
Malvern, Pennsylvania 19355-3433

2nd Edition • 1st Printing • October 2018

Library of Congress Control Number: 2018957146

ISBN: 978-0-89462-289-2

# Foreword

The Institutes are the trusted leader in delivering proven knowledge solutions that drive powerful business results for the risk management and property-casualty insurance industry. For more than 100 years, The Institutes have been meeting the industry's changing professional development needs with customer-driven products and services.

In conjunction with industry experts and members of the academic community, our Knowledge Resources Department develops our course and program content, including Institutes study materials. Practical and technical knowledge gained from Institutes courses enhances qualifications, improves performance, and contributes to professional growth—all of which drive results.

The Institutes' proven knowledge helps individuals and organizations achieve powerful results with a variety of flexible, customer-focused options:

**Recognized Credentials**—The Institutes offer an unmatched range of widely recognized and industry-respected specialty credentials. The Institutes' Chartered Property Casualty Underwriter (CPCU®) professional designation is designed to provide a broad understanding of the property-casualty insurance industry. Depending on professional needs, CPCU students may select either a commercial insurance focus or a personal risk management and insurance focus and may choose from a variety of electives.

In addition, The Institutes offer certificate or designation programs in a variety of disciplines, including these:

- Claims
- Commercial underwriting
- Fidelity and surety bonding
- General insurance
- Insurance accounting and finance
- Insurance information technology
- Insurance production and agency management
- Insurance regulation and compliance
- Management
- Marine insurance
- Personal insurance
- Premium auditing
- Quality insurance services
- Reinsurance
- Risk management
- Surplus lines

**Ethics**—Ethical behavior is crucial to preserving not only the trust on which insurance transactions are based, but also the public's trust in our industry as a whole. All Institutes designations now have an ethics requirement, which is delivered online and free of charge. The ethics requirement content is designed specifically for insurance practitioners and uses insurance-based case studies to outline an ethical framework. More information is available in the Programs section of our website, TheInstitutes.org.

**Flexible Online Learning**—The Institutes have an unmatched variety of technical insurance content covering topics from accounting to underwriting, which we now deliver through hundreds of online courses. These cost-effective self-study courses are a convenient way to fill gaps in technical knowledge in a matter of hours without ever leaving the office.

**Continuing Education**—A majority of The Institutes' courses are filed for CE credit in most states. We also deliver quality, affordable, online CE courses quickly and conveniently through CEU. Visit CEU.com to learn more. CEU is powered by The Institutes.

**College Credits**—Most Institutes courses carry college credit recommendations from the American Council on Education. A variety of courses also qualify for credits toward certain associate, bachelor's, and master's degrees at several prestigious colleges and universities. More information is available in the Student Services section of our website, TheInstitutes.org.

**Custom Applications**—The Institutes collaborate with corporate customers to use our trusted course content and flexible delivery options in developing customized solutions that help them achieve their unique organizational goals.

**Insightful Analysis**—Our Insurance Research Council (IRC) division conducts public policy research on important contemporary issues in property-casualty insurance and risk management. Visit www.Insurance-Research.org to learn more or purchase its most recent studies.

The Institutes look forward to serving the risk management and property-casualty insurance industry for another 100 years. We welcome comments from our students and course leaders; your feedback helps us continue to improve the quality of our study materials.

Peter L. Miller, CPCU
President and CEO
The Institutes

# Preface

*Claims Handling Principles and Practices* is the assigned material for the AIC 30 course in The Institutes' Associate in Claims (AIC) designation program. This course reflects the belief that there are principles and practices of good claims handling that can be applied to any type of claim.

*Claims Handling Principles and Practices* explains the vital role that claims representatives serve in keeping the insurer's promise to pay for covered losses and how the actions of claims representatives can improve the insurer's bottom line. This course examines the activities in the claims handling process. It explores various types of investigations, fraud detection, negotiations, and litigation management techniques. The material stresses good-faith claims handling, ethics, and professionalism. This combination of topics is designed to give students the claims foundation they need to become successful claims representatives and to pursue additional career opportunities.

The Institutes appreciate the contributions of the following individuals, who reviewed the curriculum, provided subject-matter expertise, and offered valuable suggestions for improvement:

James A. Franz, CPCU, AIC, ARM

James Jones, CPCU, AIC, ARM

Richard Litchford III, CPCU, AIC

William McCullough, CPCU, CLU, AIC

Donna J. Popow, JD, CPCU, AIC

James Sherlock, CPCU, CLU, ARM

Robert D. Stevens, Sr., CPCU, CLU, AIC

Christine A. Sullivan, CPCU, AIM

I am grateful for their expertise, dedication, and perseverance, which made the finished work possible.

For more information about The Institutes' programs, please call our Customer Success Department at (800) 644-2101, email us at CustomerSuccess@TheInstitutes.org, or visit our website at TheInstitutes.org.

Martin J. Frappolli

# Contributors

The Institutes acknowledge with deep appreciation the contributions made to the content of this text by the following persons:

Richard Berthelsen, JD, CPCU, AIC, ARM, AU ARe, MBA

Pamela Brooks, MBA, CPCU, AIM

Doug Froggatt, CPCU, AINS

Beth Illian, CPCU, AINS, AIS

Kevin Kibelstis, CPCU, AINS, AIS

Laura Partsch, JD

Christian Schappel

Christine A. Sullivan, CPCU, AIM

# Contents

# Segment A

**Assignment 1**
The Claims Function and Professional Ethics

**Assignment 2**
The Claims Handling Process

**Assignment 3**
Setting Case Reserves and Investigating Claims

# The Claims Function and Professional Ethics

## Educational Objectives

**After learning the content of this assignment, you should be able to:**

▷ Illustrate how an insurer's claims function supports these primary goals:

- Keeping the insurer's promise
- Supporting the insurer's profit goal

▷ Examine how Claims Department results can be optimized by:

- Department structure
- The types and functions of claims personnel
- Claims performance measurements

▷ Justify how ethical and professional behaviors are the backbone of good-faith claims handling.

▷ Illustrate the ethical and professional concerns of claims representatives.

▷ Explain how each of the following promotes high ethical and professional standards: codes of ethics, quality claims practices, and compliance with laws and regulations.

▷ Given a claim, explain why a situation presents an ethical or a professional dilemma.

# The Claims Function and Professional Ethics

## GOALS OF THE CLAIMS FUNCTION

Claims representatives become more valuable and can provide better service to both the insurer and its customers when they understand the two primary goals of the Claims Department and know how to support those goals.

People purchase property-casualty insurance policies to protect against financial losses. When policyholders make claims under their insurance policies, the insurer is called on to honor the promise made in the policy—namely, to indemnify the policyholder for financial losses. This does not imply that the insurer should or will pay every claim that is presented; rather, it implies that the insurer's Claims Department will conduct a good-faith investigation of a claim and pay only legitimate claims that are covered by the policy.

An insurer's senior management establishes the goals for the claims function. In doing so, managers must equally consider the needs of the insurance customer (the policyholder) and the needs of the insurer. The claims function helps an insurer meet these two primary goals:

- Keeping the insurer's promise
- Supporting the insurer's profit goal

### Keeping the Insurer's Promise

The first goal of the claims function is to satisfy the insurer's obligations to the policyholder as set forth in the insurance contract. In a property insurance policy, the insurer's promise is to pay for direct physical loss to covered property by a covered cause of loss. In a liability insurance policy, the insurer's promise is to pay on behalf of the insured any damages for which the insured is legally liable because of bodily injury, property damage, or other specified types of injury caused by an accident, up to the applicable limit of insurance. The insurer also agrees to defend the insured against claims or suits seeking damages covered by the policy.

The insurer fulfills its promise by providing fair, prompt, and equitable service to the policyholder either directly, when the loss involves a **first-party claim** made by the policyholder against the insurer, or indirectly, when the loss involves a **third-party claim** made against the policyholder by someone to whom the policyholder may be liable. See the exhibit "First-Party Insurance and Third-Party Insurance."

**First-party claim**

A demand by an insured person or organization seeking to recover from its insurer for a loss that its insurance policy may cover.

**Third-party claim**

A demand against an insured by a person or organization other than the insured or the insurer, seeking to recover damages that may be payable by the insured's liability insurance.

---

### First-Party Insurance and Third-Party Insurance

Insurance coverage is often referred to as either first-party insurance or third-party insurance.

Property insurance is considered first-party insurance because the insurer (second party) makes payment for covered losses directly to the policyholder. Liability insurance is considered third-party insurance because the insurer makes payments on behalf of the policyholder (first party) to a claimant (third party) who is injured or whose property is damaged by the policyholder.

[DA00038]

**Claimant**

A party that makes a claim and that can be either a first-party claimant or a third-party claimant.

**Claims representative**

A person responsible for investigating, evaluating, and settling claims.

The insurance contract is marketed not only as a financial mechanism to restore policyholders and other **claimants** to a pre-loss state, but also as a way for policyholders to achieve peace of mind. For a claimant, a loss occurrence and the consequences are not routine and can be overwhelming. A **claims representative** should handle claims in a way that promotes peace of mind for the policyholder who has suffered a loss and that quickly restores a claimant to his or her pre-loss condition.

## Supporting the Insurer's Profit Goal

The second goal of the claims function is to support the insurer's profit goal. Achieving this goal is generally the responsibility of the marketing and underwriting departments; however, the claims function serves a role in generating underwriting profit by controlling expenses and paying only legitimate claims.

By managing all claims function expenses, setting appropriate spending policies, and using appropriately priced providers and services, claims managers can help maintain an insurer's underwriting profit. Similarly, claims staff can avoid overspending on costs of handling claims, claims operations, or other expenses. Finally, by ensuring fair claim settlement, claims representatives prevent any unnecessary increase in the cost of insurance and subsequent reduction in the insurer's underwriting profit.

Policyholders and other claimants are likely to accept an insurer's settlement offer if they believe they are receiving fair treatment. Parties who believe they have been treated unfairly may seek to settle their differences with the insurer by filing lawsuits. Litigation erodes goodwill between the parties and generates increased claims expenses, reducing the insurer's profitability. Additionally, dissatisfied policyholders or claimants may complain to their state Insurance Department, and, if the state regulatory authorities find fault, an insurer may be subjected to regulatory oversight or penalties. Costs associated with regulatory action can further erode an insurer's profits.

An insurer's success in achieving its profit goal is reflected in its reputation for providing the service promised. A reputation for resisting legitimate claims can undermine the effectiveness of an insurer's advertising. Consequently, the two goals of the claims function work together in support of a profitable insurance operation.

# CLAIMS DEPARTMENT STRUCTURE, PERSONNEL, AND PERFORMANCE

Information generated by a Claims Department, including about loss payments and expenses, is essential to marketing, underwriting, and pricing insurance products. In this way, the claims function is crucial to fulfilling an insurer's promise to pay covered losses, creating an accompanying need for an insurer's Claims Department to operate efficiently.

The results of a Claims Department can be optimized by its structure, personnel, and performance measures. Let's look at all three.

## Claims Department Structure

An insurer's Claims Department can be organized in several ways. Usually, a senior claims officer heads the Claims Department and reports to the chief executive officer (CEO), the chief financial officer, or the chief underwriting officer. The senior claims officer may have staff located in the same office. This staff often makes up the home office Claims Department. Within this area, any number of technical and management specialists can provide advice and assistance to remote claims offices and claims representatives.

The senior claims officer may have several claims offices or branches countrywide or even worldwide. Staff from remote claims offices can all report directly to the home office Claims Department, or regional/divisional claims officers may oversee the territory.

Regional claims officers may have one or more branch offices reporting to them—for example, in both Boston and New York City. And a branch office in New York City may have smaller offices in Albany, New York, and Erie, New York, reporting into it. Each branch office could have a claims manager, one or more claims supervisors, and a staff of claims representatives. Similar department structures are adopted by **third-party administrators (TPAs)**.

## Claims Personnel

Claims personnel are among the most visible employees of an insurer and must therefore be able to interact well with a variety of people.

A claims representative fulfills the promise to either pay the insured or on behalf of the insured by handling claims when losses occur. People who handle claims may be staff claims representatives, independent adjusters, employees of TPAs, or **producers** who sell policies to insureds. Public adjusters also handle claims by representing the interests of insureds to the insurer.

**Third-party administrator (TPA)**

An organization that provides administrative services associated with risk financing and insurance.

**Producer**

Any of several kinds of insurance personnel who place insurance and surety business with insurers and who represent either insurers or insureds, or both.

## Staff Claims Representatives

Staff claims representatives are employees of an insurer and handle most claims, usually while working from branch or regional offices rather than at the insurer's home office. They may include inside claims representatives, who handle claims exclusively from the insurer's office, and field claims representatives (also called outside claims representatives), who handle claims both inside and outside the office. Field claims representatives handle claims that require such tasks as investigating the scene of the loss; meeting with insureds, claimants, lawyers, and others involved in the loss; and inspecting damage. If the branch or region covers a large territory, the insurer may set up claims offices in areas away from the branch office to enable the claims representative to serve insureds more efficiently.

## Independent Adjusters

**Independent adjuster**

An independent claims representative who handles claims for insurers for a fee.

Some insurers may find it economically impractical to establish claims offices in every state in which insureds reside. In such instances, insurers may contract with **independent adjusters** to handle claims in strategic locations.

Some insurers employ claims personnel in their home or branch offices to monitor claims progress and settle claims but use independent adjusters to handle all field work. Other insurers hire independent adjusters when their staff claims representatives are too busy to handle all claims themselves.

For example, if a disaster strikes, staff claims representatives may need assistance to handle the large number of claims quickly enough to satisfy the insurer and its insureds. Insurers may also use independent adjusters to meet desired service levels or when specialized skills are needed, such as to investigate aircraft accidents.

Some independent adjusters are self-employed, but many work for adjusting firms that range in size from one small office with a few adjusters to national firms with many offices employing hundreds of adjusters.

## Third-Party Administrators

Businesses that choose to self-insure do not use agents, underwriters, or other typical insurer personnel. However, they do need personnel to handle losses that arise. Self-insured businesses can employ their own claims representatives or contract with TPAs, which handle claims, keep claims records, and perform statistical analyses. TPAs are often associated with large independent adjusting firms or with subsidiaries of insurers. Many property-casualty insurers have established subsidiary companies that serve as TPAs.

## Producers

Producers can also function as claims representatives for certain claims. The term "producer" includes agents, brokers, sales representatives, and intermediaries who place insurance with insurers.

Insurers may allow producers to pay claims up to a certain amount, such as $2,500. Those producers can issue claim payments, called drafts, directly to insureds for covered claims, thus reducing an insured's wait time. In this capacity, producers function like inside claims representatives.

## Public Adjusters

If a claim is complex, or if settlement negotiations are not progressing satisfactorily with the insurer, the insured may hire a **public adjuster** to protect his or her interests.

Some states have statutes that govern the services public adjusters can provide. But in general, the public adjuster prepares an insured's claim and negotiates the settlement with the staff claims representative or independent adjuster. The insured, in turn, pays the public adjuster's fee, which is usually a percentage of the settlement.

Public adjuster

An outside organization or person hired by an insured to represent the insured in a claim in exchange for a fee.

### *Apply Your Knowledge*

A natural disaster just struck a large number of homes and businesses insured by Watkins Insurance Company. The company is receiving more claims than its staff claims representatives can handle in a timely manner. Which kind of professional would Watkins Insurance Company look to hire to make sure that it can satisfy its insureds?

a.   Independent adjuster

b.   Third-party administrator

c.   Producer

d.   Public adjuster

*Feedback*: *a.* Watkins Insurance Company would hire independent adjusters, which are independent claims representatives who handle claims for insurers for a fee. Some insurers hire independent adjusters when their staff claims representatives are too busy to handle all claims themselves.

# Claims Performance Measures

Because Claims Department members have diverse roles and are spread over a wide geographic area, insurers face special issues when it comes to evaluating and measuring the performance of their Claims Department staff.

Insurers are businesses, so they must make a profit to survive. Claims departments play a crucial role in insurer profitability by paying fair amounts for legitimate claims and providing accurate, reliable, and consistent ratemaking data. Because paying claims fairly does not conflict with insurer profit goals,

**Loss ratio**

A ratio that measures losses and loss adjustment expenses against earned premiums and that reflects the percentage of premiums being consumed by losses.

an insurer measures its claims and underwriting departments' performance using a **loss ratio**, which is a profitability measure.

In addition to reaching profit goals, an insurer strives to ensure that its Claims Department meets quality performance goals. Internally identified best practices, claims audits, and customer-satisfaction data are tools that provide measures of quality.

## Profitability Measures

A loss ratio is one of the most commonly used measures for evaluating an insurer's financial well-being. It compares an insurer's losses and **loss adjustment expenses (LAE)** with its collected premiums and reveals the percentage of premiums being consumed by losses. An increasing loss ratio could indicate that the insurer is improperly performing the claims function. Increasing losses could also mean that the Underwriting Department elected to cover loss exposures that were more costly or occurred more frequently than it estimated or that the Actuarial Department failed to price the insurer's products correctly.

**Loss adjustment expense (LAE)**

The expense that an insurer incurs to investigate, defend, and settle claims according to the terms specified in the insurance policy.

When an insurer's loss ratio increases, the Claims Department, along with other insurer functions, is pressured to reduce expenses. Claims representatives could quickly reduce LAE in the short term by offering the settlement payments insureds and claimants demand rather than spending resources on investigating claims and calculating and negotiating fair payments.

However, to reduce LAE in the long term, inflated settlement demands should be resisted; researched; negotiated; and, if necessary, litigated. LAE can also be reduced by making sure that claims procedures are always properly performed by claims representatives.

---

### *Apply Your Knowledge*

An insurer's CEO is analyzing the organization's profitability. He sees that three years ago, the insurer's loss ratio was 0.67, while two years ago, the insurer's loss ratio was 0.70. Last year, the loss ratio was 0.75. Further analysis indicates that the Actuarial Department is pricing the insurer's products correctly and that the Underwriting Department was selecting appropriate loss exposures. This leads the CEO to focus on the Claims Department as potentially undermining the organization's profitability. Which of the following are measures the Claims Department could employ in an attempt to reduce LAE long term?

a.   Immediately offering the settlement payment insureds and claimants demand.

b.   Resisting; researching; negotiating; and, if necessary, litigating inflated settlement demands.

c.   Skipping claims procedures.

d.   None of these measures will reduce LAE long term.

*Feedback*: *b*. Resisting; researching; negotiating; and, if necessary, litigating inflated settlement demands reduces LAE long term.

## Quality Measures

Three frequently used tools provide quality measures for evaluating a Claims Department's performance: best practices, claims audits, and customer-satisfaction data.

In a Claims Department, the term "best practices" generally refers to a system of identified internal practices that produce superior performance. Best practices are usually shared with every claims representative. An insurer can identify best practices by studying its own performance or the performance of similar successful insurers.

Claims Department best practices are often based on legal requirements specified by regulators, legislators, and courts. For example, a Claims Department may have a best practice stating that claims will be acknowledged within twenty-four hours of receipt. This time frame may have been selected because of a regulation, law, or court decision.

Insurers use claims audits to ensure compliance with best practices and to gather statistical information on claims. A claims audit is performed by evaluating information in a number of open and closed claims files. Claims audits can be performed by the claims staff who work on the files (called a self-audit), or they can be performed by claims representatives from other offices or by a team from the home office. Claims audits usually evaluate both quantitative and qualitative factors. See the exhibit "Quantitative and Qualitative Audit Factors."

The quality of a Claims Department's performance is also measured by customer satisfaction. Claims supervisors and managers monitor correspondence they receive about the performance of individual claims representatives. While compliments are usually acknowledged, supervisors or managers must respond to complaints. Claims Departments have procedures for responding to complaints, which can come directly from insureds, claimants, or vendors or be submitted on their behalf by a state insurance department.

No matter the source, complaints must be investigated by management and responded to in a timely manner. Complaints, such as not receiving a return phone call, may indicate legitimate service issues. Other complaints may simply indicate dissatisfaction with an otherwise valid claim settlement. Review of complaints received in a claims office can show whether problems exist with a particular claims representative, supervisor, or manager.

## Quantitative and Qualitative Audit Factors

| Quantitative | Qualitative |
| --- | --- |
| Timeliness of reports | Realistic reserving |
| Timeliness of reserving | Accurate evaluation of insured's liability |
| Timeliness of payments | Follow-up on subrogation opportunity |
| Number of files opened each month | Litigation cost management |
| Number of files closed each month | Proper releases taken |
| Number of files reopened each month | Correct coverage evaluation |
| Percentage of recovery from subrogation | Good negotiation skills |
| Average claim settlement value by claims type | Thorough investigations |
| Percentage of claims entering litigation | |
| Percentage of cases going to trial | |
| Accuracy of data entry | |

[DA02267]

# IMPORTANCE OF ETHICS AND PROFESSIONALISM FOR CLAIMS REPRESENTATIVES

How does a claims representative balance the interests of the insurer, the insured, and the claimant? While giving equitable treatment to a variety of parties can be challenging, claims representatives can achieve this goal (and fulfill the insurer's promise) through ethical and professional behavior.

Ethics (a set of principles and values) and professionalism (the behavior or qualities that characterize a profession) are the foundation of good-faith claims handling. Good-faith claims handling is evident when claims representatives make an honest effort to determine whether and to what extent a claim is covered.

## Ethics

**Ethics**

The study of what constitutes good and bad behavior, dealing with moral duty and obligation.

**Ethics** is particularly important in good-faith claims handling because claims representatives face numerous ethical dilemmas trying to balance the interests of insureds and claimants, who are their customers, and the interests of insurers, who are their employers.

Ethics is the set of principles and values that determines the better course of action, given the choice of two or more legal courses of action. In today's business environment, being ethical is often equated with merely obeying the law; however, ethical behavior goes beyond merely obeying the law. Legality involves making a choice between what is lawful and what is unlawful. Ethics involves making a choice between two or more acceptable courses of action. For example, it is not illegal for one person to remain silent when someone else—a competitor, for example—is falsely accused of improper behavior. However, not speaking up could be considered unethical, particularly if the accusation causes the competitor harm and the party who remains silent thereby benefits.

## Professionalism

Professionalism involves the behavior and qualities necessary to properly implement an ethical decision. In the example of the falsely accused competitor, professionalism requires the nonaccused party to speak up in a timely, objective manner. Professionals should also act knowledgeably, courteously, and empathetically.

## Role of Ethics and Professionalism in Good Faith

Ethics and professionalism are of utmost importance to insurers and claims representatives when they are establishing good faith. These are three ways good faith is established:

- By satisfying contractual duties and other promises
- By maintaining insurers' credibility
- By complying with legal duty

First, insurers and claims representatives are bound by the insurance contract to act in good faith, and to do so, they must act ethically and professionally. They must keep the promises specified in insurance policies, as well as those created by law. In insurance transactions, the insured pays a premium for the insurer's promise to handle claims in good faith. The insurance policy states the terms of that promise. In fulfilling the promises insurers make in their policies, claims representatives encounter and attempt to satisfy a variety of parties, including insureds, claimants, producers, service providers, regulators, and the general public. When the needs of these parties conflict, claims representatives may be faced with dilemmas that require their understanding of and ability to apply ethical and professional principles.

In addition to the promises made in the insurance policy, claims representatives make many other promises to insureds, claimants, vendors, and their employers. Claims representatives must keep these promises if they want to behave ethically and professionally and comply with good-faith claims handling practices. For example, a claims representative may promise to contact an insured, a claimant, or a vendor within a specified time. Promises to employers may include a promise to follow an employer's code of business conduct, complete a course of continuing education, maintain appropriate licensing, or conform to dress codes.

Another reason ethics and professionalism are important to complying with good-faith claims handling practices is that claims representatives' behavior can affect public trust in and the credibility of insurers. Unethical or unprofessional conduct can affect the insurer adversely. Although claims representatives handle thousands of claims ethically, professionally, and without complaint on a daily basis, one incident that violates the public's expectations of ethical or professional conduct may receive wide publicity and can damage the insurer's credibility and the public's trust. News about collusion between insurers and brokers to fix prices, inappropriate claim denials during catastrophes, and insurance executives' mishandling of corporate funds contributes to a negative public image of the insurance business. Consequently, most insurers recognize that abiding by ethical and professional standards of conduct demonstrates good faith and is essential to improving their public image.

A third reason that ethics and professionalism are important to complying with good-faith claims handling practices is that consumer regulations create legal duties for insurers. Claims representatives have an ethical and professional responsibility to comply with these regulations to ensure that consumers are treated fairly through prompt, honest, and responsive claims handling. Some consumer regulations may also define the minimum expected ethical and professional standards for insurers and claims representatives. In addition, many insurers have good-faith claims handling guidelines in place that exceed these minimum standards, and such guidelines may also describe the insurer's philosophy regarding ethical and professional conduct. Both regulatory requirements and insurers' guidelines can provide guidance to claims representatives regarding ethical and professional claims handling conduct.

Ethical and professional conduct that exemplifies good faith benefits claims representatives, insurers, consumers, and the general public. For claims representatives, ethical and professional conduct can be the foundation of successful, satisfying careers. For insurers, ethical and professional conduct can help retain customers and attract investors. Consumers who believe they have been treated fairly and in good faith are more likely to renew their policies with the same insurer, thus reducing insurers' acquisition costs and improving financial performance. When insurers' financial performance improves, insurers can more easily attract investors.

Ethical and professional conduct that exemplifies good faith can benefit consumers by encouraging fair treatment and prompt payment. Insureds and, by extension, society can reap the benefits of insurance—peace of mind, support for credit, efficient use of resources, and reduction of social burdens—only if the business of insurance is conducted ethically, professionally, and in good faith.

# ETHICAL AND PROFESSIONAL CONCERNS FOR CLAIMS REPRESENTATIVES

Claims representatives may face multiple ethical and professional concerns, which often present various choices, sometimes with no clear distinction among possible correct courses of action.

Ethical and professional concerns can arise from these aspects of a claims representative's activities:

- Conflicts of interest
- Claims handling competency and continuing education
- Licensing
- Customer service
- Communication with represented claimants
- Billing practices
- Privacy
- Fraud detection

## Conflicts of Interest

Ethical concerns often arise from potential **conflicts of interest**. A conflict of interest can occur many ways during claims handling, such as when employees have the opportunity to purchase salvage, when vendors offer claims representatives incentives for referring business to them, when the insurer provides multiple coverages for one insured that are triggered by the same occurrence (overlapping coverages), or when the insurer provides coverages for multiple insureds involved in the same claim (overlapping insureds).

**Conflict of interest**
A situation that occurs when a decision maker's personal interests interfere to the extent that he or she makes decisions that adversely affect customers or employers.

### Salvage

A conflict of interest can occur when a stolen item is recovered and sold as salvage. For example, a one-carat diamond recovered from a theft claim that sells for $5,000 in a retail store might have a salvage value of $600. A claims representative may be tempted to purchase salvage for a slightly higher amount than the highest bid from an outside salvage buyer. This presents a conflict of interest because the claims representative has an advantage over other potential buyers by virtue of knowing the salvage bids and being able to place a slightly higher bid to obtain the item. Because of this potential conflict of interest, claims representatives should not bid on salvage, and most insurers have specific guidelines that prohibit claims representatives from purchasing salvage.

## Vendor Incentives

Claims representatives often employ vendors or refer insureds to vendors that can help them replace or repair lost or damaged property. A conflict of interest can arise when vendors offer gifts (such as vacations or hard-to-get event tickets), favors, gratuities, or other incentives to claims representatives in an effort to get more business. As a result, many insurers have guidelines that either prohibit the acceptance of incentives or set dollar limits on approved incentives.

## Overlapping Coverages or Insureds

Another conflict of interest can arise from overlapping coverages or overlapping insureds. This situation occurs when the insurer provides multiple coverages for one insured that are triggered by the same occurrence or when the insurer covers multiple insureds involved in the same claim. A claims representative faced with decisions involving multiple coverages or insureds may have conflicting responsibilities—for example, deciding how to allocate liability among parties. To avoid this conflict of interest, some insurers have guidelines that require the claim to be bifurcated, with a different claims representative handling each part independently. However, some insurers have gone to a team environment for claims handling, the implementation of which should only be done with advice of legal counsel because of the conflicts of interest issues that could arise. See the exhibit "How Claims Representatives Should Handle Overlapping Conflicts of Interest."

---

### How Claims Representatives Should Handle Overlapping Conflicts of Interest

Example of overlapping coverages—An insured individual is injured in an auto collision with an uninsured motorist who is responsible for the accident. The insured has personal injury protection (PIP) coverage and uninsured motorists (UM) coverage on his auto policy. The claims representative's responsibilities in handling the PIP claim can conflict with those in handling the UM claim because UM settlements are often based on the amount of medical expenses paid under PIP. As a result, the PIP and UM claims may need to be handled by different claims representatives who can make coverage determinations independently of one another.

Example of overlapping insureds—Two insureds, Lucas and Maria, have auto liability coverage from the same insurer and get into an accident with each other. Each alleges the other is responsible. The claims against Lucas and Maria should be handled by different claims representatives who can make liability determinations independently of one another.

---

[DA12782]

# Claims Handling Competency and Continuing Education

Claims representatives who lack competency can commit ethical improprieties by paying claims that are not covered, overpaying claims because of poor investigation or negotiation, and denying claims that should be covered.

Claims representatives should be aware of the five factors that can affect their claims handling competency. See the exhibit "Five Factors That Can Affect Claims Handling Competency."

Claims representatives faced with conflicting demands on their time may be reluctant to take the time necessary to pursue continuing education, but continuing education is important to maintain competency. Many states even require continuing education for claims representatives, and some insurers have additional requirements. Claims can have profound effects on individuals and organizations, and it is an ethical responsibility for claims representatives to obtain continuing education to keep their knowledge and skills current.

# Licensing

State licensure laws vary regarding who is required to be licensed and the procedures and requirements for licensing. Some states require licenses only for independent adjusters and public adjusters. Other states require staff claims representatives, vehicle damage appraisers, and property appraisers to have licenses. Licensing laws may require claims representatives to pass an examination, pay fees, and provide evidence of continuing education. States often grant temporary licenses to out-of-state claims representatives for catastrophe claims handling.

State laws relating to licensing of inside claims representatives can be ambiguous. Licensure-related ethical concerns can arise when a manager or supervisor asks a claims representative to assume claims handling responsibilities in a territory in which the claims representative is not licensed. A claims manager may believe the claims representative can legally take on the assignment, while the claims representative may have ethical concerns. As a result, the claims representative may want to consult with professional claims associations, published guidelines from regulators, or an attorney to address any concerns.

## *Apply Your Knowledge*

You are a claims representative on the phone with Sandra, an insured who has just filed a claim. Sandra has been in an auto accident with another driver, and she gives you insurance information for herself and the other driver. It turns out both drivers have auto policies with your company, and each has

## Five Factors That Can Affect Claims Handling Competency

| Factor | Effect on Claims Handling Competency |
|---|---|
| Changes in the claims environment | Consumer, social, and political forces influence insurance coverage, legal liability, damages, and technology. These are examples:<br><br>• Insurers may broaden a coverage provided by a policy.<br><br>• New court interpretations of policy provisions and evolving liability standards can affect claims handling results.<br><br>• Changes in property damage evaluation can result from policy revisions, new laws, changing technology, and changes in the auto repair field as a result of changes made by auto manufacturers.<br><br>Failure to be alert to changes can lead to errors in evaluating coverage and damages and settling claims. |
| Changes in job responsibilities | Claims representatives' responsibilities can change when they are promoted or reassigned or take a job with a new employer. Some employers offer little formal training to experienced claims representatives. To ensure competency, claims representatives should work with their managers to identify areas where additional training is necessary. |
| Attrition of knowledge over time | There is a tendency for people to lose knowledge over time, especially knowledge that may be fundamental but is not used on a daily basis. For example, claims representatives who rarely encounter a particular type of claim, such as a fatality, may not remember knowledge that was learned some time ago. Continuing education can reinforce the basics of claims work, refresh knowledge, and enhance skills already mastered. Claims representatives should also know how to locate resources, such as statutes and procedures, rather than relying on memory. |
| Limited insurer resources | Insurers vary in the amount of training offered as well as their expectations of claims representatives. It is important for claims representatives to be aware of the resources available through their insurer, but not to rely on them entirely for their training and continuing insurance education. |
| Rewards and promotions | Although claims representatives may aspire to receive rewards, such as bonuses or promotions, it is important that they recognize the intrinsic value of competent claims handling apart from financial and advancement opportunities. Ideally, claims representatives who perform their work at a high level of ethical competency will be rewarded by the management of their organizations. However, even in less than ideal employment circumstances, claims representatives have an ethical obligation to perform their work competently. |

[DA07460]

filed a claim stating the other driver was at fault. Which one of the following best describes how you should handle this situation?

a. Wait for the second driver to call you before doing anything

b. Call the second driver and handle both drivers' claims yourself

c. Make sure both drivers' claims are handled by different claims representatives, who can make liability determinations independently of one another

d. Determine that the second driver is liable for the accident

*Feedback: c.* Both drivers' claims should be handled by different claims representatives, who can make liability determinations independently of one another and avoid conflicts of interest.

## Customer Service

Claims representatives can also encounter ethical concerns regarding customer service. Customers have high expectations about the quality and timeliness of claims service, and these expectations can create ethical and professional issues.

Because of caseloads and competing demands, claims representatives may be unable to provide the same level of service to all customers. For example, if asked to make a major insured's claim a priority, the claims representative may have to set aside the claim of a smaller insured. Claims representatives should try to treat all insureds equally, yet achieve a balance between customer demands and sound business practices, without compromising good-faith claims handling practices.

## Communication With Represented Claimants

Another area of ethical concern is when a claims representative communicates with a claimant who is represented by an attorney without the attorney's consent. Some states have direct prohibitions against such contacts to avoid the unlicensed practice of law by claims representatives and the potential for conflicts of interest. Some states without such regulations have a rule that restricts an attorney from contacting an adverse party without the consent of that party's counsel; often, that rule is also applied to claims professionals by analogy. Still other states consider the prohibitions to be justified as a custom of the industry.

Claims representatives sometimes face ethical concerns about avoiding such inappropriate communications when attempting to acquire information necessary to provide a required benefit, such as an address change for workers compensation benefits or first-party medical payments. Some insurers have customer service representatives, other than the claims representative, who can assist claimants with basic inquiries like this and, thus, help avoid questionable discussions. Claims representatives should consult with their managers or attorneys for guidance on how to handle these types of communications.

## Billing Practices

Ethical concerns can arise for claims representatives when authorizing and allocating bills from service providers and experts, such as attorneys, medical providers, expert witnesses, and investigators. Claims representatives have an ethical duty to make sure service providers and experts follow insurer billing guidelines and understand the scope of their assigned duties so bills are not inappropriate or excessive. When a provider, such as an attorney, submits a bill for work on multiple claims, the claims representative has an ethical responsibility to ensure the charges are allocated correctly to each claim and insured.

## Privacy

Matters of privacy can raise ethical concerns. Claims representatives have access to and acquire personal, medical, and financial information about others in the course of handling claims. The information may come from the insured, claimant, or other sources.

Information gathered by claims representatives may be protected by privacy laws or may be of such a sensitive nature that its disclosure would be harmful. In addition, claims representatives must be aware that some individuals may be concerned about information that may not seem personal or confidential to others. For example, an insured may not want a relative to know the value of her home, business, or other belongings. Even accidental or unintentional disclosure can be harmful. As a result, claims representatives must acquire only the information needed to investigate and settle a claim, and should not misuse acquired information or make it available to anyone who does not need it.

### Apply Your Knowledge

George, a claims representative, receives a medical report on a workers compensation claimant that indicates the claimant has a staph infection. George knows the claimant has returned to work in a role in which he comes in contact with the public. George consults the nurse case manager on his team, who confirms this is a contagious infection. What are the ethical concerns that George confronts? Select all that apply.

a.   The privacy of the claimant

b.   The health of the public

c.   The potential liability of the employer

d.   The effect on the claim if the claimant cannot work

*Feedback: a., b., c., and d.* All of these are ethical concerns that George confronts. There are laws in addition to ethical guidelines that govern the privacy of medical information. However, there are other ethical concerns such as the effect on the public and the insured.

# Fraud Detection

Fraud is illegal, and claims representatives often assume there are no ethical concerns involved in their work that deal with fraud. However, the investigation and management of potential fraud issues can lead to significant ethical concerns. See the exhibit "Examples of Ethical Dilemmas Involving Fraud."

---

### Examples of Ethical Dilemmas Involving Fraud

**Example 1**

A claims representative suspects that an insured has committed fraud in submitting a claim for stolen property by including items that were not stolen. The claims representative believes that the insurer can deny the claim because of the fraud but does not have sufficient evidence to meet the legal standards to prove fraud. The claims representative considers offering less than a fair amount to settle the claim in hopes that the insured will accept the settlement. This course of action would reduce the insurer's loss from a fraudulent claim, close the claim, and avoid costs associated with trying to prove fraud. However, despite the claims representative's suspicions, the insured may not be guilty of fraud and may be entitled to the full amount of the claim.

**Example 2**

A claims representative is handling a claim for XYZ Company, which has a policy written through a profitable and highly respected insurance agency. The agent, who is the claims representative's brother-in-law and who owns the agency, makes it clear to the claims representative that XYZ Company should be given special treatment because it is an important customer. The claims representative's estimate of damages shows that the policy does not cover about 5 percent of the damage, or about $2,000. The claims representative gives the agent this information, and the agent indicates that he will take care of it.

Later, the insured submits a damage estimate from another source that is $2,000 higher than the previous one. If the claims representative accepts the insured's damage estimate, the insured is compensated fully for the loss; the brother-in-law is happy and family harmony is maintained; and the claims representative can close the claim file with adequate documentation to support the payment. However, the ethical dilemma is that the latter estimate may be inflated (fraudulent) in order to cover the entire amount of damages. The claims representative must determine the appropriate course of action based on ethical and professional standards.

---

[DA04006]

# CODES OF ETHICS AND QUALITY CLAIMS PRACTICES

Claims representatives are required to handle claims in good faith, and insurers and claims management play a critical role in their success. Clearly defined best practices and timely and relevant information about claims regulations provide claims representatives with a road map for professional behavior.

Good-faith claims handling is consistently handling claims according to high ethical and professional standards. Three pillars can establish a framework to achieve consistent good-faith claims handling:

- Codes of ethics
- Quality claims practices
- Compliance with laws and regulations

## Codes of Ethics

It is important that insurers and claims representatives have well-defined codes of ethics that form the guidelines of good-faith claims handling. A focus on handling claims ethically, rather than a defensive focus of avoiding bad faith, is the best protection for individual claims representatives and their employers from allegations of bad faith.

Almost all insurers have published codes of ethics for their companies. Some larger insurers have ethics officers who implement codes of ethics and advise management and employees on ethical matters. Both the Society of Registered Professional Adjusters and the National Association of Public Insurance Adjusters have codes of conduct to which their members must adhere.

Individual claims representatives should have personal codes of ethics, beyond those established by their employers. The Institutes provide a comprehensive code of ethics for all insurance professionals. Adhering to both the spirit and the letter of a personal code of ethics offers the best protection for individual claims representatives, as well as their employers, from regulatory penalties or bad-faith lawsuits. See the exhibit "Code of Professional Ethics of The Institutes—Ethical Guidelines for Insurance Professionals."

## Quality Claims Practices

The insurance product is unique. Instead of providing an immediate, tangible good or service, insurers provide a promise. Individuals and organizations pay premiums, usually for many years, in expectation that insurers will fulfill the promise in the event of a loss. The fundamental basis for good-faith claims handling is to meet the promise the insurer has made to the insured. The claims representative also has an ethical responsibility to the insurer not to pay fraudulent or unreasonable claims or to overpay legitimate claims. The

## Code of Professional Ethics of The Institutes—Ethical Guidelines for Insurance Professionals

| Canon 1 | Insurance professionals should endeavor at all times to place the public interest above their own. |
| --- | --- |
| Canon 2 | Insurance professionals should seek continually to maintain and improve their professional knowledge, skills, and competence. |
| Canon 3 | Insurance professionals should obey all laws and regulations, and should avoid any conduct or activity that would cause unjust harm to others. |
| Canon 4 | Insurance professionals should be diligent in the performance of their occupational duties and should continually strive to improve the functioning of the insurance mechanism. |
| Canon 5 | Insurance professionals should aspire to raise the professional and ethical standards in the insurance business. |
| Canon 6 | Insurance professionals should strive to establish and maintain dignified and honorable relationships with those whom they serve, with fellow insurance practitioners, and with members of other professions. |
| Canon 7 | Insurance professionals should assist in improving the public understanding of insurance and risk management. |

[DA07486]

best way for the claims representative to balance duty to the insured and the insurer is to perform a fair, unbiased, and thorough claim investigation.

Most insurers have best practices that outline the duties of claims representatives and time frames for completion of claim activities. Performing these practices conscientiously within the framework of an ethical code provides protection against allegations of bad faith.

A combination of Canons 1 and 4 of the Ethical Guidelines describes how claims representatives should carry out the best practices of claims handling. It is important for claims representatives, who often face time constraints in their work, to continuously keep in mind the perspective of insureds and claimants. A family who has just lost a home and all personal possessions in a fire is in dire need of prompt fulfillment of the insurer's promise to pay for a covered loss. Delays and inaction on the part of the claims representative can cause significant additional distress.

Unintentional action or inaction that does not comply with best practices for claims handling can give rise to allegations of bad faith. Conversely, consistent and ethical application of best practices will provide quality and good-faith claims handling and make bad-faith allegations unlikely to occur.

## Compliance With Laws and Regulations

As stated in Canon 3 of the Ethical Guidelines, ethical conduct involves obeying all laws and regulations. Because insurance is essential to the functioning of modern society and provides critical restoration to consumers after often devastating loss, there are laws that regulate claim activities.

### Unfair Claim Settlement Practices Laws

Most states have enacted a version of the National Association of Insurance Commissioners (NAIC) Model Unfair Claim Settlement Practices Act. Most state versions of this act extend authority to the state insurance commissioner to investigate potential violations of the act and to impose penalties and sanctions for violations. Financial penalties vary by state and typically range from $1,000 to $250,000. See the exhibit "Provisions of Typical Unfair Claim Settlement Practices Laws."

In addition to unfair claim settlement practices laws, there are other federal and state laws that relate to claims handling. Some of these laws contain the possibility of fines or penalties, while others form the basis for bad-faith lawsuits.

### Unauthorized Practice of Law

Popular recent allegations by plaintiff attorneys concern the unauthorized practice of law by claims representatives. Although states have different definitions of the unauthorized practice of law, the area that usually affects claims representatives arises from the direction of legal strategies, either directly through instructions or indirectly through billing guidelines. Another area that can affect claims representatives is related to settlements negotiated with unrepresented claimants.

There have been many instances in which courts have found that the practices of claims representatives constituted the unauthorized practice of law. In these cases, the court found that the insurers breached the implied covenant of good faith and fair dealing. Some courts have also found that failure of an insurer to follow the advice of the insurer's defense counsel is evidence of bad faith. Conversely, there are also cases that find that reliance on the advice of counsel is not a defense for bad faith and that such reliance must be reasonable under the circumstances.

### License and Continuing Education Requirements

Many states require that claims representatives who are employed by an insurer or a third-arty administrator (TPA) be licensed. Most states require that independent and public adjusters be licensed. Failure to meet licensing requirements can result in penalties for employers as well as for individual adjusters.

**Provisions of Typical Unfair Claim Settlement Practices Laws**

These are examples of prohibited claims practices:

- Misrepresenting facts or policy provisions to insureds or claimants

- Failing to promptly acknowledge communications related to claims

- Failing to affirm or deny coverage within a reasonable time (states may specify the time period)

- Failing to provide a reasonable explanation for claims denials or compromise settlement offers

- Failing to provide necessary claims forms promptly

- Not attempting a prompt, fair, and equitable settlement of claims in good faith when liability is reasonably clear

- Compelling insureds or beneficiaries to file suit to recover amounts due under policies by offering settlements that are significantly less than the awards recovered through lawsuits

- Failing to conduct a reasonable investigation before denying a claim

- Settling or attempting to settle a claim for less than a reasonable person would believe the insured or beneficiary was entitled with reference to the advertising materials accompanying an insurance policy

- Settling or attempting to settle a claim based on an application that was altered without the knowledge or consent of the insured

- Making claim payment without indicating the coverage under which the payment is made

- Unreasonably delaying the investigation of a claim or payment of claims by requiring duplicate information or verification

[DA07487]

Those states that require licensing of claims representatives who are employed by an insurer or a claims administrator also typically require continuing education credits to maintain adjuster licenses.

Additionally, states that require adjuster licensing typically require all adjusters to adhere to the state's claims practices laws and to take continuing education courses regularly on ethics. Failure to follow state laws regarding claims handling practices can result in loss of license and other actions against individual claims adjusters as well as their employers.

## Federal Laws

Various federal laws apply directly to claims handling, and many others could be construed to apply to the professional activities of claims representatives.

Federal laws, such as the Gramm-Leach-Bliley Act and the Health Insurance Portability and Accountability Act (HIPAA), in addition to state laws and the common law, impose requirements regarding the privacy of medical, financial, and other personal information.

A federal law that has an impact on certain claim settlements is the Medicare, Medicaid, and SCHIP Extension Act of 2007 (MMSEA). This act amends the Medicare Secondary Payer provisions of the Social Security Act and requires that Medicare's interests be protected in injury settlements involving recipients or potential recipients of Medicare or Medicaid benefits. Potential fines against insurers who do not follow the guidelines in these settlements can be significant (for example, double the amount of the settlement). Failing to follow federal guidelines could have an adverse financial impact on certain insureds in addition to insurers.

Other federal laws can be involved in claims handling due to offsets to Social Security for certain types of benefits, requirements to pay court-ordered child support when paying certain benefits or settlements, and laws regarding the recording of conversations.

There have also been some recent attempts to bring cases against insurers for certain claims practices under the Racketeer Influenced and Corrupt Organization (RICO) Act. These types of cases indicate the aggressiveness of plaintiff attorneys in pursuing allegations of bad-faith claims handling.

---

## Apply Your Knowledge

An insured sustained roof damage from a windstorm, and this damage prevented the insured from occupying the dwelling during repairs. The insured's policy covers the expense for the insured to stay in a temporary lodging while the damage is repaired. The insured rented an apartment and submitted a receipt to the claims representative. However, after repeatedly mailing, faxing, and emailing copies of the receipt, the insured has not been reimbursed. Indicate whether the claims representative has breached a professional standard and, if so, which one(s). Check all that apply.

a. No standard breached

b. Canon of Ethical Guidelines

c. Best practice

d. Unfair claim settlement practices law

*Feedback: b, c, and d.* The claims representative has breached Canons 1, 3, and 4; has likely breached a claims best practice; and has likely breached an unfair claim settlement practices law.

---

# CASE STUDY: ETHICAL AND PROFESSIONAL DILEMMAS OF CLAIM REPRESENTATIVES

In the "real world" of everyday insurance operation, claim representatives are often faced with ethical dilemmas. This case study enables you to sharpen your ability to recognize these dilemmas and encourage you to think about how they can be resolved or avoided.

Identify the ethical dilemmas Ellen faces.

Ellen has worked for Radley Insurance as a claim representative for ten years. She began her employment as soon as she finished college, where she majored in business administration. When she started her employment with Radley, she attended a six-week intensive training course to learn insurance coverages, laws that affect claim handling, Radley's claim procedures, and interpersonal and work skills that would help her become a successful claim representative. Since that time, Ellen has attended three or four local claim association meetings and reads about a dozen articles from a claim magazine per year. Ellen has asked to attend many claims seminars over the past ten years but her supervisor, Grace, has never approved the requests. Ellen believes Grace has not approved the requests as a means of keeping Ellen from leaving the unit. Ellen is afraid to voice her concerns to the claim manager.

Ellen's claim-handling territory currently includes two regions without adjuster licensing laws and two regions that recently began to require adjuster licensing. The new licensing law provides that any claim representative holding the Associate in Claims (AIC) designation from The Institutes is "grandfathered" and does not need to complete a prescribed educational course before being licensed. Ellen has completed the paperwork necessary to get her license and has given it to Grace for filing with the states. She continues to handle claims in the states requiring licenses. Grace has not filed the licensing application because Ellen's assigned territory has changed five times in her ten years with Radley. Grace thinks it might change again in a few months, so she does not want to spend company funds to get Ellen's license.

Over the last four years, Ellen has worked closely with a building repair contractor in more than a dozen serious fire and wind losses and many more minor losses. Ellen refers insureds to the contractor whenever she can because she knows the contractor provides all the paperwork she needs to document her claim files. The contractor appreciates Ellen's referrals and frequently sends her expensive chocolates. Lately, he has been sending her flowers. Ellen has decided that she would like to get to know the contractor on a personal basis outside work and has decided to invite him to dinner some evening next week.

Radley Insurance has a Code of Business Conduct that prohibits accepting anything of value—gifts, gratuities, incentives, or other benefits—from vendors. However, the claim department routinely ignores this prohibition, especially around the holidays when many vendors send candy and fruit baskets to the department. The underwriting and accounting departments receive similar gifts; only the accounting department returns them to the vendors.

In a recent claim, Ellen found herself in an awkward situation with two insureds and their agents. Both insureds were involved in the same multi-vehicle accident, and Ellen believes that neither was at fault. Both had collision coverage with $1,000 deductibles. Ellen discovered in the claim investigation that the responsible driver had minimum property damage liability limits that had already been exhausted by other claims arising from the same accident. She was successful in recovering 30 percent of the damages that Radley paid to the two insureds directly from the at-fault driver. Radley's procedures state that any recovery should be credited to the insured's deductible first; after the insured's deductible has been returned, any excess recovery credits Radley's loss payments. However, the agents for these two insureds were good friends of Ellen's, and she knew that these losses would reduce their loss contingent commissions. She therefore decided to credit the recoveries to Radley's loss payments, because the insureds were not expecting any recovery.

## Tools for Analysis

Although choices between two right courses of action can be difficult, claim representatives can use frameworks for resolving ethical dilemmas.

Claim representatives can answer a series of questions about the ethical dilemma and possible solutions, such as these:

- Who are the stakeholders, and what are their rights?
- Is the information about the dilemma reliable and accurate?
- Who should be involved in making the decision?
- How would I feel if my mother (or children) knew of my decision?
- What would a person whom I respect do in this situation?
- Am I using this decision for my own personal gain?

Claim representatives can evaluate the types of effects that decisions can have:

- The maximizing effect provides the greatest benefit to the greatest number of people.
- The normalizing effect focuses on determining the most common, acceptable standard of behavior.
- The empathizing effect seeks to treat someone in the same way one wants to be treated in the same situation.

Ellen faces these ethical dilemmas:

- Need for education versus fear of supervisor
- Need for adjusting license versus belief that she has her license

- Acceptance of gifts from vendor versus need to maintain good relationship with vendor
- Desire for friendship with vendor versus possible undue influence by vendor
- Violation of Code of Business Conduct versus doing what is generally accepted as a business practice
- Showing preference to agents versus returning deductible to insured

## SUMMARY

Two primary goals of the claims function are keeping the insurer's promise and supporting the insurer's profit goal. Claims personnel help meet these goals by using the claims handling process to promptly, fairly, and equitably pay all legitimate first- and third-party claims and by managing operational and claims handling expenses. Policyholders' satisfaction that the insurer's contractual promises have been upheld promotes goodwill and supports an insurer's profit goals.

Insurers and other insurance organizations have claims departments, which can be structured in various ways. Claims personnel may be staff claims representatives, independent adjusters, employees of TPAs, or producers. Public adjusters can also handle claims by representing the insured's interests to the insurer. Claims Department performance can be measured by a loss ratio and the use of internally identified best practices, claim audits, and customer-satisfaction data.

Ethics and professionalism comply with good faith and are key elements in fulfilling the promises made within an insurance policy. To maintain credibility and public trust and to comply with legal duties, claims representatives should do their best to act ethically, professionally, and in good faith.

Claims representatives can encounter ethical concerns in their professional activities. It is important to be aware of these concerns as they arise and to consistently apply ethical and professional standards to resolve them. Although their employers often have guidelines, claims representatives are personally and professionally responsible for ethical decisions and actions.

Claims representatives should provide consistently ethical, quality claims handling. The framework for establishing and maintaining high ethical and professional standards consists of codes of ethics, quality claims practices, and compliance with laws and regulations.

Claim representatives can frequently encounter ethical dilemmas. Claim representatives who make professional and ethical decisions better represent the insurer, provide better customer service, abide by consumer protection regulations, and may experience greater personal satisfaction.

# 2

# The Claims Handling Process

## Educational Objectives

After learning the content of this assignment, you should be able to:

▷ Evaluate how the claims handling process provides a consistent and effective method for responding to losses.

▷ Illustrate these activities in the claim handling process:

- Acknowledging and assigning the claim

- Identifying the policy

- Contacting the insured or the insured's representative

▷ Describe the following activity in the claim handling process: investigating and documenting the claim.

▷ Evaluate the three bases for legal liability.

▷ Describe the following activities in the claim handling process:

- Determining the cause of loss

- Determining liability

- Determining the loss amount

▷ Evaluate the role of the claims representative in these activities that may be involved in concluding a claim:

- Issuing payments

- Denying a claim

- Alternative dispute resolution

- Litigation

- Closing reports

# The Claims Handling Process

## OVERVIEW OF THE CLAIMS HANDLING PROCESS

To provide consistent and effective claims handling, claims representatives follow a systematic process.

Consistency in the claims process helps ensure that claims are handled in a manner conforming to legal and ethical standards. Although different types of claims may require unique treatment, the same basic activities are performed in every claim, providing a framework for handling all types of property, liability, and workers compensation claims. See the exhibit "Activities in the Claims Handling Process."

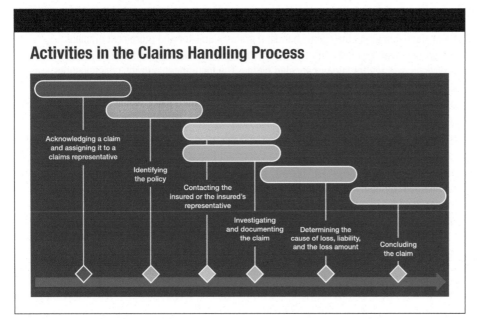

**Activities in the Claims Handling Process**

Acknowledging a claim and assigning it to a claims representative

Identifying the policy

Contacting the insured or the insured's representative

Investigating and documenting the claim

Determining the cause of loss, liability, and the loss amount

Concluding the claim

[DA12595]

While these activities appear to be sequential, they are not always undertaken in an exact order. A claims representative may sometimes perform several activities concurrently, or may repeat some activities as new information is uncovered.

## How a Loss Is Reported

A loss can be reported to the insurer in several ways. Usually losses are reported by the insured, but they can also be reported by a third party (such as an insurance agent) or by notice of a lawsuit.

Losses are often reported using a loss notice form, also called a First Notice of Loss, designed for a particular type of loss, such as auto or general liability. These forms include basic information about the loss, such as the loss date and time, policy number, insured name and address, covered property, loss description, accident location, witness names and addresses, and the names and addresses of any injured persons.

Other methods of reporting losses are by phone or through web-based apps that allow the insured to include photos of damaged property, if applicable. Insurers can use **blockchain** processes that instantaneously refer to multiple sources of verified information. This can minimize the number of insurer-insured interactions that are necessary to settle a claim, streamlining the process to save both time and money for the insurer. See the exhibit "How Blockchain Can Assist in Processing Claims."

**Blockchain**

A distributed digital ledger that facilitates secure transactions without the need for a third party.

---

### How Blockchain Can Assist in Processing Claims

Blockchain can make the claims handling process quicker and more cost efficient through the use of smart contracts. As an example, consider flight insurance that provides coverage for late or canceled flights. The insurance contract, which insures the on-time performance of a flight, is recorded on the blockchain. If the flight is late or canceled, data can be verified digitally by a trusted third party, which automatically triggers a claim payment.

Even when the entire insurance contract isn't recorded on the blockchain, smart contracts can help. For example, a smart contract tied to sensors or telematics in a car involved in an accident can provide the first report of loss to the insurer while simultaneously notifying recommended repair shops and alerting the insured of next steps. As with any new technology or process, care must be given that this process is used in compliance with applicable laws.

[DA12778]

---

Regardless of how a loss is reported, the same basic information is recorded and processed before a claim is settled or denied.

## Claims Handling Process

If the first notice of the loss is a lawsuit, the claims representative must be aware of the deadline for response to the lawsuit, which can vary by state. The claims representative should refer the lawsuit to counsel at the start of the investigation and follow the insurer's procedures to determine whether to issue a **reservation of rights letter**.

**Reservation of rights letter**

An insurer's letter that specifies coverage issues and informs the insured that the insurer is handling a claim with the understanding that the insurer may later deny coverage should the facts warrant it.

Once a loss notice is received and the information is recorded in the insurer's claims information system, the claims handling process begins. Although the sequence of and time spent on the activities in the claims handling process may vary from claim to claim, all of the activities must be performed. For example, even if a loss appears straightforward as reported, an investigation of the loss should still be conducted and documented.

These are the six activities in the claims handling process:

- Acknowledging and assigning the claim—Acknowledging receipt of the claim informs the insured that the claim has been received, and may also provide the name and contact information of the assigned claims representative and the claim number.

- Identifying the policy—At this stage, the claims representative will determine whether the loss is covered by the insured's policy and whether it occurred within the policy's effective period. This can highlight aspects of the claim that may require further investigation.

- Contacting the insured or the insured's representative—The claims representative's first contact with the insured or the party representing the insured, such as a lawyer or public adjuster, allows the representative to make an introduction and explain the claims process. This can reassure the insured that his or her claim is being handled and treated fairly.

- Investigating and documenting the claim—The investigation of a claim should begin as soon as possible to ensure that any information that may be available for only a short time, such as on-site evidence at an accident scene, is gathered and taken into consideration. Investigations should be geared toward obtaining information that will help determine the cause of loss, the amount of loss, and liability. The insurer's claims handling guidelines can help the representative determine the types and extent of investigation needed for a satisfactory claim settlement.

- Determining the cause of loss, liability, and the loss amount—After conducting the investigation, the claims representative should use the information gathered to determine the cause of loss, such as a faulty toaster that started a fire; the liability for the loss, such as a store manager who did not assign someone to clean up a spill in an aisle; and the amount of the loss. For a property claim, the claims representative investigates the amount of damage to the property and the cost to repair or replace it, and may also investigate the amount of business income lost. To determine a loss amount in a bodily injury claim, the claims representative investigates the extent of the injury, the residual and lasting effects of the injury, the amount of pain and suffering the individual has endured, and out-of-pocket expenses the claimant has incurred.

- Concluding the claim—If the insurer must pay the claim, the claims representative often must negotiate the amount with the insured or the claimant. Negotiation involves discussing disputed matters and mutually agreeing on a settlement. In some cases, alternative dispute resolution methods may be used to resolve a disagreement and, ultimately, the claim. The insured may file a lawsuit if no agreement on the claim can be reached.

Failure to handle claims consistently can result in serious consequences. The insurer could become responsible for paying claims that are not actually its responsibility under the terms of the policy and/or applicable law, or coverage that is owed may not be provided, which could result in the loss of an account or a bad-faith claim.

### Apply Your Knowledge

Identify which one of the following activities is not part of the claims handling process.

a.  Contact the insured or the insured's representative

b.  Determine the cause of loss, liability, and the loss amount

c.  Refer the lawsuit to counsel

d.  Acknowledge and assign the claim

*Feedback*: c. Although referring a lawsuit to the insurer's counsel is one of the first things a claims representative should do when notified of a lawsuit, it is not part of the claims handling process.

# EARLY STEPS OF THE CLAIMS HANDLING PROCESS

The first few steps of the claims handling process set the tone for an insured's experience with his or her insurer. Initial contacts provide the insurer with important opportunities to make a good impression, which could help retain current customers and earn new business through customer referrals.

After the insurer is notified of a loss, the facts of the claim should be compared with the applicable policy to verify whether the loss may be covered. After the loss has been assigned to a claims representative and the initial reserve has been established, the claims representative will contact the insured or the insured's representative to begin the process of settling the claim.

## Acknowledging and Assigning the Claim

The first activity in the claims handling process is acknowledging receipt of the claim, whether filed online, via a phone call, or through a mobile app, and assigning it to a claims representative. Some insurers acknowledge a claim immediately upon receiving the loss notice, while others acknowledge the claim after it has been assigned to a claims representative. The purpose of the acknowledgment is to advise the insured that the claim has been received, but it may also provide the name and contact information of the assigned claims representative and the claim number.

Most insurers have time requirements for the assignment and acknowledgment of claims. For example, an insurer may require a claim to be assigned within one business day of its report. Some states also have requirements for acknowledgment of certain types of claims, such as workers compensation, and may require copies of claim reports to be filed with the state. See the exhibit "Record-Only Claims."

---

### Record-Only Claims

Many claims are record-only claims, which are typically assigned to claims personnel to monitor for any subsequent activity. For example, an employee may trip at work but not experience any injury. The employer may report this to the insurer as a record-only claim, and then, if the employee later begins to experience pain attributable to the incident, the employer, employee, or physician would notify the insurer. A claims representative could then begin the claims handling process.

---

[DA12777]

## Identifying the Policy

Upon receiving an assignment, a claims representative will identify the policy in force on the date of loss. A basic identification of the policy must take place on all claims before the investigation begins. The representative should determine whether the loss occurred within the policy period, whether coverage exists under the policy for the type of loss reported, and whether the insured followed the policy's terms and conditions. For some types of losses, the claims representative may need to immediately give the insured instructions to prevent any further loss, such as to cover a damaged roof with a tarp.

Review of the policy along with the loss notice may identify areas for investigation, such as whether an injured person qualifies for coverage and whether an exclusion may apply.

Any significant doubt regarding coverage under the policy may require a reservation of rights letter and/or an immediate referral to coverage counsel. A reservation of rights letter may be sent to the insured along with acknowledgment of receipt of the claim.

---

### *Apply Your Knowledge*

Miguel is a claims representative for an insurer. He receives a claim assignment after a tornado, and the claim report states that a tree fell onto an insured's roof. When Miguel contacts the insured after receiving the claim assignment, what instructions is he likely to give to the insured?

*Feedback*: On first contact, Miguel should instruct the insured to try to avoid any more losses to the insured property. He might advise the insured to move belongings out of the affected rooms of the house if they are exposed to the weather and to make sure that any family members move to more secure housing if necessary, such as a hotel.

# Contacting the Insured or the Insured's Representative

The claims representative's initial contact with the insured serves several purposes: not only can it reassure the insured that the claim will be investigated, but it also provides the claims representative with an opportunity to explain the claims process and begin the claim investigation. There are four critical aspects of a claims representative's initial contact with an insured:

- Timing and method of contact
- Preparation and initial contact
- Good faith
- Waiver and estoppel

## Timing and Method of Contact

For some insurers, or in certain claims as specified in the insurer's guidelines, the claims representative's first contact with the insured occurs at the same time as the claim acknowledgment. Generally, the claims representative reviews the initial loss report and the policy and then contacts the insured or a party representing the insured and schedules a time to speak about the loss. This can be a face-to-face meeting, or it can be by telephone or video call. If the loss involves a third-party claimant, the claims representative will also contact the claimant or the party representing him or her and schedule a meeting to discuss the loss.

By using video conferences or phone calls to discuss losses with the insured, rather than working to fit face-to-face meetings into everyone's schedules, a claims representative can condense the timeline for the settlement of claims and make the claims process more efficient in terms of time and cost. Some complex losses, however, may still require face-to-face meetings.

For some claims, the insured is represented by an attorney or a public adjuster, who is hired by the insured in hopes of improving on the settlement offered by an insurer. In these instances, the claims representative should discuss claim-related issues with the public adjuster or attorney until advised otherwise by the insured.

## Preparation and Initial Contact

Before making the initial contact with any of the parties, the claims representative should prepare a list of questions for the insured or claimant, along with information on how the claim will be handled and what actions the insured or claimant will need to complete as part of the claims process.

The first meeting or discussion with the insured sets the tone for the claim. For the insured or the claimant, the loss has most likely created a disruption resulting in strong emotions, such as anger or grief. Those who have never filed an insurance claim may be apprehensive or confused about how the claim will be handled. The claims representative should be aware of these factors and take them into consideration when initially meeting or speaking with the insured or the claimant.

Because claims representatives frequently find that insureds do not fully understand the details of their insurance coverages, they should be prepared to explain the policy terms and their meanings in relation to the loss. The claims representative should explain any possible policy violation, exclusion, or limitation that can affect coverage because withholding that information can be considered a breach of the claims representative's or insurer's duties. The claims representative must be careful to avoid giving the insured or claimant the impression that a claim will be paid when there may be grounds to deny the claim.

Claims representatives must be aware of the legal implications of their words and actions when communicating with insureds. They must be careful not to mislead the insured or the claimant about the potential coverage for the claim or the amount of the claim payment. Once contact is made, the claims representative should take these steps:

- Tell the insured how to protect any damaged property and to document the claim. Be specific about what the insured should do and any deadlines that might apply.
- Describe the inspection, appraisal, and investigation that will be conducted.
- Describe what additional investigation is needed to resolve any potential coverage issues. Give complete and clear instructions if the insured needs to provide any additional information.
- Explain possible policy limitations or exclusions and obtain a nonwaiver agreement when necessary.
- Obtain authorization to receive medical and wage loss information, if necessary.
- Explain how much time processing and concluding the claim is expected to take.
- Provide a blank proof of loss form for property damage and any necessary written instructions so that the insured can document the claim.

In some cases, the claims representative may record an interview with the insured during the initial meeting or discussion.

### Apply Your Knowledge

Denise is a claims adjuster who is preparing to contact an insured for the first time in regard to a property damage claim filed after a fire in the insured's home. What should she be prepared to tell the insured if she is asked when payment for the loss will be received?

*Feedback:* Because this will be Denise's initial contact with the insured, it is unlikely that the claim would be able to be settled, and it may not even be possible yet to determine whether the loss will be covered by the insured's policy. While Denise may be able to offer a generic timeline regarding the processing and conclusion of the insured's claim, she must make it clear that policy limitations or exclusions could apply to the claim, resulting in possible denial of payment.

## Good Faith

Insurance policies are contracts of utmost good faith. When conducting a good-faith investigation, a claims representative must attempt to correctly and promptly resolve coverage issues. Many situations present coverage issues that require investigation to determine whether the claim should be paid or denied, and, until those coverage issues are resolved, the claims representative and insurer must avoid any conduct that would lead insureds or claimants to mistakenly believe that the claim will be paid. If they do not, the insurer could unintentionally waive its right to deny coverage.

While attempting to resolve the coverage issues, claims representatives must focus on the facts of the loss and decide whether those facts support coverage under the insured's policy. Claims representatives must also quantify the loss so that payment is not delayed if coverage is confirmed.

## Waiver and Estoppel

**Waiver**

The intentional relinquishment of a known right.

When discussing a claim with an insured, claims representatives must avoid accidentally granting a **waiver** for a policy condition or exclusion. For example, a claims representative can waive a right contained in a policy condition or exclusion by telling an insured that a loss is covered before checking the policy. By doing this, the claims representative has waived the insurer's right to deny the claim if the facts later prove that there is no coverage.

Another example of an action by a claims representative that could hinder an insurer's ability to rightfully deny a claim is the representative's providing an insured with bad advice. For instance, a claims representative who tells an insured that damaged goods can be discarded before they are inspected cannot later deny the claim on the grounds that the damaged goods were not available for inspection. This is the principle of **estoppel**.

Frequently, the doctrines of waiver and estoppel are so closely related in meaning that courts often fail to distinguish between them and simply hold that a result is based on the doctrine of waiver and estoppel. See the exhibit "Example of Case Involving Both Waiver and Estoppel."

**Estoppel**

A legal principle that prohibits a party from asserting a claim or right that is inconsistent with that party's past statement or conduct on which another party has detrimentally relied.

---

### Example of Case Involving Both Waiver and Estoppel

An insured calls the claim service center of Atwell Insurance and reports that a large tree fell into her yard during a windstorm. The customer service representative who answers the call tells the insured to have a contractor remove the debris and send the bill to the insurer.

Two weeks later, the insurer receives a bill from the contractor for $1,200. The customer service representative is authorized to settle claims only up to $500, so she takes the bill to her supervisor. Her supervisor indicates that the policy does not cover this type of loss unless the tree damages the insured's house, fence, or other covered structure. The supervisor further explains that when a falling tree damages property, a $500 limit on debris removal applies.

The insured's policy does not cover this loss. However, the customer service representative waived this coverage defense by telling the insured to arrange for the debris removal and to send the bill to the insurer without first explaining the coverage under the policy. Because the insured relied on what the customer service representative told her and incurred expenses, Atwell Insurance may be estopped from denying coverage. Even though coverage does not apply to the original loss, Atwell may have to pay the $1,200 bill. The insurer's failure to notify the insured at the beginning of the claim process that coverage did not apply estopped it from later denying coverage.

[DA02308]

---

Claims representatives can avoid waiver and estoppel through the use of **nonwaiver agreements** and reservation of rights letters, which serve these general purposes:

**Nonwaiver agreement**

A signed agreement indicating that during the course of investigation, neither the insurer nor the insured waives rights under the policy.

- To advise the insured that any action taken by the insurer in investigating the cause of loss or in ascertaining the amount of loss is not intended to waive or invalidate any policy conditions
- To clarify that the intent of the agreement or the letter is to permit a claim investigation and that neither the insured nor the insurer will thereby waive any respective rights or obligations

A nonwaiver agreement protects the insurer from estoppel by reserving the right to deny coverage based on information developed during the investigation. The nonwaiver agreement, which must be signed by both parties, is usually used when the claims representative is concerned about investigating a claim before the insured has substantially complied with the policy conditions or when there appears to be a specific coverage problem or defense. Such concerns can be identified from the initial claim report, during initial contact with the insured, or at any point during the claim investigation.

A reservation of rights letter serves the same purpose as a nonwaiver agreement but is in letter form and is a unilateral document; it does not require the insured to sign or agree to the contents of the letter. For example, a claims representative may offer a nonwaiver agreement when the insured reports the theft of an auto but refuses to make a police report about the theft. If the insured refuses to sign the nonwaiver agreement, the claims representative can use a reservation of rights letter to protect the insurer's rights and advise the insured of the potential coverage issue. Each insurer has its own guidelines for usage of nonwaiver agreements and reservation of rights letters.

Nonwaiver agreements and reservation of rights letters are usually sent by certified mail, return receipt requested, so that the insurer has evidence that the insured received it. While they can be used on any type of first-party claim, they can be used only with the insured and are not sent to third-party claimants because in most states third parties have no obligations under the policy.

# INVESTIGATING AND DOCUMENTING THE CLAIM

Claim representatives must conduct thorough claim investigations and clearly document the results in the claim file. The investigation forms the basis for determining whether there is coverage for the loss.

After acknowledging and assigning the claim, identifying the policy, and contacting the insured, the next steps in the claim handling process are to investigate and document the claim. The investigation can take many different forms, and all aspects must be documented to create a complete claim file.

## Investigating the Claim

Claim representatives begin investigating a claim as soon as it is assigned. They can develop an outline or notes to logically organize the investigation and to ensure that information that may be available only for a short time is investigated first, such as an accident scene or damaged property that may be destroyed or discarded. Claim representatives should contact any third-party claimants early in the investigation. This contact can help establish rapport with claimants and, in turn, facilitate the investigation and lead to a timely settlement.

Claim representatives must also know when they have sufficient information on which to base a decision. The focus of investigations should be on obtaining information that will help determine the cause of loss, the amount of loss, and liability. The insurer's claim handling guidelines help claim representatives determine the types and extent of investigation needed for a satisfactory claim resolution. Once sufficient information has been obtained to make a reasoned determination, the claim representative does not need to continue the initial investigation unless the determination is disputed.

This section provides a basic outline for the claim representative to follow when investigating any type of claim. Claim representatives must use good-faith claim handling practices and insurer guidelines to ensure a thorough investigation. Several types of investigations, including these examples, are common to many types of claims:

- Claimant investigation
- Insured/witness investigation
- Accident scene investigation
- Property damage investigation
- Medical investigation
- Prior claim investigation
- Subrogation investigation and recovery

## Claimant Investigation

In a first-party property claim, the claimant is the insured. In an automobile or a liability claim, the claimant may be a third party who was injured in the accident or a third party whose property was damaged. The claimant could also be considered an insured under the policy because of a relationship to the named insured, such as a family member. In a workers compensation claim, the claimant is the injured worker.

Claim representatives conduct a claimant investigation, usually by taking the claimant's statement, to learn the claimant's version of the incident that led to the claim. This information can help the claim representative determine the value of the injury or damage, how it was caused, and who is responsible.

## Insured/Witness Investigation

Claim representatives often take statements (either written or recorded) from the insured and witnesses because they can provide valuable information about the circumstances surrounding the loss. The insured is the party named as the insured in the policy, although other persons may qualify as insureds under a particular policy.

Witnesses have personal, firsthand knowledge of the incident that resulted in the claim. The witness investigation can support or refute an insured's version of an incident, affecting the liability determination. A statement can also serve as a means of challenging the witness's credibility if later testimony differs from the information given in the original statement.

## Accident Scene Investigation

The accident scene offers crucial clues in automobile, third-party liability, and workers compensation claims. By reviewing details such as tire tracks, curves in the road, and objects or conditions that may interfere with a driver's view or that may cause an accident (such as a pothole in the road), the claim representative can determine whether accounts of the accident are plausible or questionable. Claim representatives also consult weather or traffic reports in certain accident-scene investigations to identify external factors that may have contributed to the loss.

In serious accidents, claim representatives may use field investigators or accident reconstruction experts to visit the accident scene, take photographs, and develop a theory of the causes of the accident.

## Property Damage Investigation

An investigation of the property that was damaged in a loss can be useful in various types of claims to confirm the cause of loss and extent of damage. For example, damage to the rear quarter panel and trunk lid on the insured's vehicle can confirm that the vehicle was struck in a rear-end collision as well as the nature of the vehicle damage. For business income claims, a property damage investigation is useful for determining lost profits or loss of business use resulting from covered property damage. The investigation can also help confirm the need to move operations to an alternate site or to temporarily replace damaged equipment with rented equipment so that business operations can continue while repairs are being made.

## Medical Investigation

Claim representatives conduct medical investigations in all bodily injury claims, including workers compensation claims. A medical investigation helps the claim representative determine the costs of the medical treatment, the expected duration of medical treatment and disability, the need for rehabilitation, and the suitability of medical care for the type of injuries the claimant suffered. This information can also be used to evaluate the degree of pain and suffering that resulted from the accident or injury.

In certain types of claims, such as workers compensation and first-party auto injury claims, the claim representative should typically have access to the medical records of the treating physician. In liability claims, the claim representative will require an authorization from the injured party to obtain medical records. If authorization is refused, the claim representative may not be able to obtain these records unless a lawsuit is filed; in such cases, the claim representative will not usually agree to settle the claim until medical records documenting the nature and extent of the injury are received.

## Prior Claim Investigation

Claim representatives conduct prior claim investigations on most incoming claims to avoid paying for property damage or bodily injury that has been paid through prior claims by the same insurer or other insurers. For example, a prior claim investigation may reveal that the claimant has a history of lower-back injuries or that the insured's vehicle had sustained similar damage from a prior accident. By conducting a prior claim investigation, the claim representative ensures that the insurer pays only new claims for which the insurer has legal responsibility.

The prior claim investigation is usually performed by comparing the facts of the current claim with an industry database containing information from many different insurers. Insurers subscribe to these databases and furnish them with claim information. The databases provide a quick way to check for similar prior claims. If the check returns a likely match, the claim representative should investigate the prior claim history in more detail to determine whether the current claim is for the same injury or damage. If this is the case, the claim representative may have a basis for denying the claim or may conduct further investigation.

## Subrogation Investigation and Recovery

During the course of an investigation, the claim representative may discover that the insured was not at fault and that a third party caused the accident. When an insurer pays a claim to an insured for a loss caused by a negligent third party, the insurer can recover that payment amount from the negligent third party through the right of **subrogation**. Subrogation rights are established by insurance policies and by law. When claim representatives investigate any loss, they must be alert to any subrogation possibilities. These examples describe losses for which a claim representative should investigate subrogation possibilities:

**Subrogation**

The process by which an insurer can, after it has paid a loss under the policy, recover the amount paid from any party (other than the insured) who caused the loss or is otherwise legally liable for the loss.

- Workers compensation losses caused by the negligent operation of an automobile or a piece of construction equipment
- Auto claims in which the road was under construction or visibility was restricted because of the property of a third party, such as a sign
- Property damage claims resulting from fire, explosion, or water losses caused by the negligence of tenants or by construction workers at a building site
- Liability claims in which injury was caused by defectively manufactured or poorly designed products from a third party

The subrogation clauses in most insurance policies require the insured to cooperate with the insurer by assigning the rights of subrogation to the insurer through a subrogation agreement. The subrogation agreement could be included in another form, such as a proof of loss form, that the insured completes for a property damage claim. Most subrogation agreements require the insured to give testimony and appear in court, when necessary, so that the insurer can establish the legal basis to recover from the negligent third party. If an insured breaches the subrogation agreement, the insurer has the right to collect from the insured the amount that could have been recovered from the responsible third party.

Claim representatives must consider the costs required to pursue subrogation, as well as the likelihood of success, and must be alert for any contract that may rescind the right of subrogation (such as a lease agreement). Subrogation can be costly to pursue if litigation is required, and the insurer may in some cases decide that pursuing subrogation is not cost-effective.

When the subrogation action is against a negligent third party who is responsible for a loss, the insurer can present a subrogation claim for payment to the third party's liability insurer. Usually, the liability insurer pays the entire loss or offers a compromise settlement on the claim, depending on the assessment of liability. When the two insurers cannot agree on the liability, they can agree to arbitrate the dispute, often through intercompany arbitration.

## Documenting the Claim

Because they simultaneously handle many claims, claim representatives must have a system for working on and reviewing each claim. While the term for this system can vary (some call it a diary system, a suspense system, or a pending system), the purpose is the same: the system allows the claim representative to work on a claim one day and then diary or calendar it for review. For example, the claim representative may send a letter to the insured requesting a repair estimate and diary that file for review on a date two weeks in the future. During that time, the claim representative would expect to receive the requested estimate. If the estimate has not been received, the review prompts the claim representative to follow up.

As claim representatives perform activities in their investigation, they must document the claim files using both file status notes and reports.

### File Status Notes

File status notes (or an activity log) must accurately reflect and document investigations, evaluations of claims, decisions to decline coverage, and decisions to settle claims. Because lawyers and state regulators can obtain copies of claim files, the file status notes and other file documentation must reflect these elements:

- Clear, concise, and accurate information
- Timely claim handling
- A fair and balanced investigation considering the insured's and the insurer's interests

- Objective comments about the insurer, insured, or other parties associated with the claim
- A thorough good-faith investigation

Clear, concise, and accurate file status notes are essential because a claim file must speak for itself. The file status notes should present a chronological account of the claim representative's activities and can include the claim manager's activities relating to the claim. Ideally, an entry should exist for anyone who works on the file. Additionally, the file status notes should contain short summaries of reports and information received from outside sources.

File status notes should be objective; they should not leave the reader with the impression that the claim representative is taking sides, such as in this statement: "The claimant obviously wasn't paying attention." File notes should not express prejudice of any sort; any remarks about race, religion, or gender should be avoided. Humor is also out of place in file notes. A note that seems innocuous when written can be devastating when read to a jury, and claim representatives should document their notes as if they are potentially discoverable.

Some file status notes can be lengthy because they continue for as long as the claim remains open, which can be years in some cases. They can also be detailed, outlining why reserves are set at a particular dollar amount or how settlement figures are determined. File status notes should not be cryptic or written in personal shorthand because the claim representative who writes them may not be available to interpret them later. Claim representatives should determine from their company guidelines whether there are abbreviations for terms that are acceptable, such as "PR" for police report or "s/s" for stop sign.

## File Reports

In addition to using file status notes, claim representatives document claim activity using reports to various parties. One such report is an internal report. Claim representatives prepare and distribute internal reports to parties within the insurance organization who have an interest in large losses or losses of a specific nature, such as death, disfigurement, or dismemberment. Most insurers have guidelines outlining when and under what circumstances internal reports (such as file status reports and large loss reports) should be prepared. For example, large loss reports may be required for claims with reserves that exceed $500,000. These large loss reports summarize all the file status information for management and are updated as additional information is received or on a timetable set by the insurer.

In addition to the large loss report, claim representatives write three other internal reports while a claim is open: preliminary, status (or interim), and summarized (or captioned) reports. These reports may have attachments, such as estimates, police reports, diagrams, photos, statements, and correspondence. If the claim is handled by in-house claim representatives, attachments may already be included as images in the electronic claim file or included in the paper claim file. Often, these reports are typed directly into a claim entry system (the electronic claim file) using an electronic form; distributed electronically to claim supervisors, managers, or underwriters; and then printed for any necessary outside distribution (such as for attorneys).

Insurers also document claim activity using external reports containing information collected by claim representatives. External claim reports inform interested parties about the claim and inform the public of the insurer's financial standing. These reports are prepared for producers; some states' advisory organizations; and others who have an interest in the claim, such as reinsurers or excess insurers. Because insurers often write business through producers, losses are reported to the producer who sold the insurance. These reports provide details about the losses, such as the amount paid and the amount in outstanding reserve.

# BASES FOR LEGAL LIABILITY

Although a lawyer and a claims representative each have distinct roles to play in good-faith claims handling, a claims professional needs to become comfortable with the concepts and terminology of criminal law, civil law, and the bases of legal liability.

To handle a claim with good faith, a claims representative must investigate and determine the cause of the loss, liability for the loss, and the amount of damages that result from the loss. The claims representative must have a thorough understanding of the concept of legal liability to decide which general investigative tools to use and which aspects of the claim to investigate.

## Bases for Legal Liability

**Legal liability**

The legally enforceable obligation of a person or an organization to pay a sum of money (called damages) to another person or organization.

**Legal liability** is different from criminal liability. Criminal liability arises from wrongful acts that society deems so harmful that the government takes responsibility for prosecution and punishment. Criminal laws are always statutory. In contrast, civil law is based on the rights and responsibilities of citizens with respect to one another; it applies to legal matters not governed by criminal laws.

National, state, and local legislatures enact laws (statutes) to deal with perceived problems. Laws made by local governments are often called ordinances. Collectively, these formal enactments of federal, state, or local legislative bodies are referred to as **statutory law**. See the exhibit "Legal Basis of a Liability Claim."

**Statutory law**

The formal laws, or statutes, enacted by federal, state, or local legislative bodies.

Civil laws include common law, or case law, and administrative laws and regulations, as well as some statutory laws. Civil law governs liability for civil wrongs against people, entities, or property (torts), which include negligent acts, intentional acts, and strict liability. It also governs liability for breach

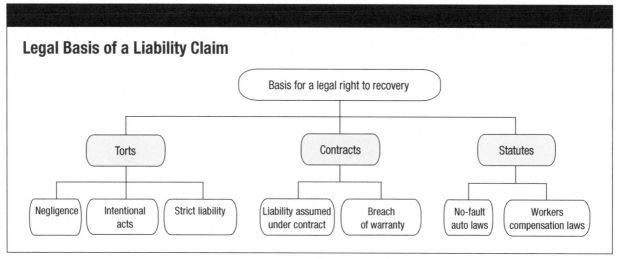

**Legal Basis of a Liability Claim**

[DA02435]

of contract. Contract law, a branch of civil law, deals with the creation and enforcement of contracts and with the settlement of contract disputes.

In contrast to statutory law, common law has evolved in the courts. Common law, or case law, is a body of principles and rules established over time by courts on a case-by-case basis. Each decision became a precedent for similar cases in the future. Gradually, certain principles evolved as judges applied them consistently to all the cases they heard. These principles became known as the common law, or case law. When neither constitutional nor statutory law applies, judges still rely on precedents of previous cases in reaching their decisions.

The two major categories of U.S. law are not mutually exclusive, and a particular act can often have both criminal and civil law consequences. For example, Fatima's car is struck by another vehicle, and Fatima is injured and requires extensive medical care. As a salesperson, Fatima loses existing and potential customers by being out of work for two weeks. Following the accident investigation, the other driver is charged and convicted of driving while intoxicated, a criminal offense. However, Fatima may bring a civil suit against the other driver for her lost business opportunities.

## Liability Based on Tort

A tort is a wrongful act or omission, other than a crime or a breach of contract, committed by one party against another that causes harm and may lead to a civil lawsuit for damages. A person or an organization that commits a tort is called a tortfeasor. Tort law generally applies to civil actions for which damages may be awarded to the harmed person. The three types of torts are negligence, strict liability, and intentional acts.

# Negligence

**Negligence**

The failure to exercise the degree of care that a reasonable person in a similar situation would exercise to avoid harming others.

**Negligence** is the most common type of tort that claims representatives encounter. One individual may invade a legally protected right of another by committing an unintentional act through carelessness, neglect, or indifference. A person who fails to exercise reasonable care is held responsible by law for any injury, loss, or damage that results from that failure. For example, Josh was daydreaming while driving and failed to stop at a stop sign, hitting Emily's car. Josh did not intentionally hit Emily's car, but he was careless and therefore negligent. Josh is responsible for the damage to Emily's car and for any bodily injury Emily suffered in the accident.

Liability based on negligence must establish four elements:

- One party's legal duty to use due care, owed to another party—If there is no legal duty to use due care, there is no negligence. For example, if a car thief is injured because the brakes fail on the car he stole, the car owner is not considered negligent and is not liable for the injury.

- A breach of the duty of care—Such a breach is a failure to conform to the standard of care required in the situation, creating an unreasonable risk of harm. To determine the degree of care that should be exercised, courts apply a reasonable person standard: what a reasonable person, under similar circumstances, would do. For example, a motorist who fails to stop at a stop sign is not behaving reasonably. The motorist is negligent and can be held liable for any damages incurred if an accident results.

- Proximate cause—That is, a causal connection between the negligent act and the harm or injury. The injury or damage must be a direct result of the failure to meet the duty owed. For example, Bill has a duty to keep his sidewalk clear of snow. He breaches that duty by not clearing the snow. While walking on Bill's sidewalk, Susan slips, falls, and breaks her arm. Bill's failure to clear the sidewalk is the proximate cause of Susan's injuries.

- Actual injury or damage—If there is no injury or damage, then no liability for negligence exists. For example, while Peter is driving in congested traffic, his car hits the back of Bob's car. When Bob looks at his bumper, he does not see any damage; even though Peter caused an accident, no damage to Bob's car resulted from it.

In some claims, not all the elements of negligence are present. All four elements of negligence must be present for a liability claim to be viable based on negligence. See the exhibit "Elements of Negligence."

Legal principles that affect liability based on negligence include vicarious liability, contributory negligence, and comparative negligence. Vicarious liability is the legal responsibility that arises when one party is held liable for another party's actions. The liability transfers to this party because of some relationship between that party and the party who is actually responsible. The most common vicarious relationship is that between an employer and an employee. Employers are held vicariously liable for the acts of their employees. For

---

### Elements of Negligence

An easy way to remember the elements of negligence is this:

- Duty owed
- Duty breached
- Proximate cause
- Damages

[DA08598]

example, Sheila is a hair stylist at Sally's Salon. Sheila colors Jane's hair, and it turns green. Sally's Salon is liable for Sheila's negligence in turning Jane's hair green.

The concepts of contributory negligence and comparative negligence may apply if a harmed party is partly responsible for the loss. These concepts are used as defenses in negligence cases; the person being sued can raise them to eliminate or reduce the damages that may be imposed, or even to have the case dismissed. In a state that follows **contributory negligence** principles, a person who has been harmed cannot recover damages if his or her negligence contributed in any way to the harm. Even if the harmed party is only 1 percent at fault for an accident and the other party is 99 percent at fault, the harmed party cannot collect anything from the other party. Most states have deemed this all-or-nothing approach unfair and have modified the concept of contributory negligence into one of comparative negligence.

In a state that follows **comparative negligence** principles, both parties to a loss share the financial burden of the bodily injury or property damage according to their respective degrees of fault. A harmed party who is partially at fault can recover from another negligent party but only to the degree to which the other party contributed to the loss.

Comparative negligence laws vary by state:

- The pure comparative negligence rule—A plaintiff who is 99 percent at fault can still recover 1 percent of the claimed damages.
- The 50 percent rule—A plaintiff can recover reduced damages up to and including the point at which the plaintiff's negligence constitutes not more than 50 percent of the total in a case involving two parties.
- The 49 percent rule—A plaintiff can recover reduced damages so long as the plaintiff's negligence is less than the other party's negligence.
- The slight versus gross rule—A rule of comparative negligence that permits the plaintiff to recover only when the plaintiff's negligence is slight in comparison with the gross negligence of the other party. Under this rule, a court reduces the plaintiff's damages by an amount proportional to his or her contribution.

**Contributory negligence**

A common-law principle that prevents a person who has been harmed from recovering damages if that person's own negligence contributed in any way to the harm.

**Comparative negligence**

A common-law principle that requires both parties to a loss to share the financial burden of the bodily injury or property damage according to their respective degrees of fault.

## Strict Liability

Claims representatives should also be familiar with strict liability torts. Strict liability, or absolute liability, arises from inherently dangerous activities resulting in harm to another, regardless of the degree of care taken. For example, because explosives are inherently dangerous, blasting operations create liability for bodily injury or property damage, even if the explosives are handled carefully. Another activity that may result in strict liability is keeping dangerous animals. Allegations of strict liability also occur in many products liability claims. A harmed party can allege that a product was dangerous when the manufacturer, distributor, or retailer sold it. If the allegation proves to be true, the court may impose strict liability against the manufacturer, distributor, or retailer for any resulting harm.

Workers compensation laws create another type of liability without fault, similar to strict liability. An employer is liable for employee injuries sustained in the course of employment, regardless of whether the employer's negligence caused the injuries.

## Intentional Torts

Another type of tort that claims representatives encounter is an intentional tort. An intentional tort is a tort committed with intent to cause harm or with intent to do the act that causes harm. The tortfeasor may or may not have intended the consequences that resulted from the act. Examples of intentional torts include assault, battery, libel, slander, invasion of privacy, and trespass. Generally, insurance does not cover acts performed with the intent to cause harm because such a policy could encourage people to cause intentional harm with the expectation that insurance would cover it. However, claims alleging intentional injury may also include allegations of negligence. In such cases, claims representatives must conduct good-faith investigations to establish whether an act was intentional or negligent before making a coverage determination.

## Liability Based on Contract

The other basis for legal liability under civil law is contractual liability. Contractual liability is liability imposed on a party by the terms of a contract. It arises when someone's rights under the terms of a contract are violated. Contractual liability may be based on a written contract or an implied contract. Parties may be legally liable because of their failure to perform as agreed in the contract. For example, if a contractor is hired to construct a building and fails to build it or builds it improperly, the contractor is liable to the owner for damages associated with the failure to build the building. Even though the contractor is liable, insurance generally does not cover damages from this breach of contract. However, insurance may apply to claims involving two types of contractual obligations: assumptions of liability stated in the contract and warranties stated in the contract.

Liability assumed by contract arises when, as a condition of a contract, a party agrees to assume financial responsibility for liabilities imposed by law on another party. The responsibilities assumed vary by contract and range from assuming all liability to assuming liability only for the negligence of one's own employees. For example, a landowner may hire a contractor to do specified work on a property. The owner may insist that the contractor assume all liability for the work. The contractor may agree to those terms and assume any liability imposed on the owner, whether the loss is caused by negligence of the contractor's employees, the owner's employees, or the owner.

Claims representatives often handle products liability claims that involve warranties. A warranty is a contractual promise that accompanies the sale of a product; express warranties are promises made orally or in writing by the manufacturer or retailer. For example, a manufacturer of infant pajamas may guarantee that the fabric will not burn. An implied warranty is not specifically expressed, but a purchaser could reasonably infer that the warranty exists.

Whether legal liability is based on tort or contract, understanding the concept allows the claims representative to conduct a thorough, good-faith investigation of a claim. Knowing the legal bases for a claim will help the claims representative make these determinations:

- Whether the claim being presented is valid
- What investigation should be conducted
- Who is ultimately responsible for the claim

## Liability Based on Statute

Statutory liability is legal liability imposed by a specific statute or law. Although common law may cover a particular situation, statutory law may extend, restrict, or clarify the rights of injured parties in that situation or similar ones. One reason for such legislation is to ensure adequate compensation for injuries without lengthy disputes over who is at fault. Examples of this kind of statutory liability involve no-fault auto laws and workers compensation laws. In these legal areas, a specific statute (rather than the common-law principles of torts) gives one party the right of recovery from another or restricts that right of recovery.

In an effort to reduce the number of lawsuits resulting from auto accidents, some states have enacted "no-fault" laws. These laws recognize the inevitability of auto accidents and restrict or eliminate the right to sue the other party in an accident, except in the more serious cases defined by the law. Victims with less serious injuries collect their out-of-pocket expenses from their own insurers without the need for expensive legal proceedings.

A similar concept of liability without regard to fault applies to workplace injuries. Each of the fifty states has a workers compensation statute that eliminates an employee's right to sue the employer for most work-related injuries and also imposes on the employer automatic (strict) liability to pay specified benefits.

In place of the right to sue for negligence, workers compensation laws create a system in which injured employees receive benefits specified in these laws. As long as the injury is work related, the employer pays the specified benefits regardless of who is at fault.

# DETERMINING THE CAUSE OF LOSS, LIABILITY, AND THE LOSS AMOUNT

Claim representatives use the information gained during their investigation to determine the cause of loss, liability, and the loss amount.

The activities required for investigating and determining the cause of loss, liability, and damages depend on the type of claim. The claim representative analyzes the information from the investigation to determine the cause of loss. He or she then evaluates the cause of loss and other claim facts against the policy to determine whether the loss is covered under the policy. The claim representative then determines the amount of the loss and compares this amount to the policy limits. See the exhibit "Activities in the Claim Handling Process."

## Determining the Cause of Loss

As part of the claim investigation, the claim representative should determine the cause of loss. If there are several causes of loss, the claim representative should identify all of them and determine their relative importance in causing the loss and the responsible party or event.

The claim representative should be aware that if the investigation uncovers a cause of loss that is not claimed by the insured or the injured party, the insurer is responsible for determining whether the cause of loss discovered through the insurer's investigation is a covered cause of loss. For example, an insured may claim flood damage to a home covered by a homeowners policy that excludes flood damage. If the claim representative discovers that the water damage resulted from rain entering through the wind-damaged roof, not flood, the claim representative must determine coverage based on the cause of loss revealed by the investigation, namely the wind-damaged roof.

The type and cause of loss are key issues for the investigation and coverage determination. The claim representative must be certain that all of the relevant facts that can possibly be obtained are included in the results of the investigation.

## Determining Liability

After the cause of loss has been determined, the claim representative must determine who is liable for the loss. If the insured is liable, the claim representative must then determine whether coverage exists for that liability under

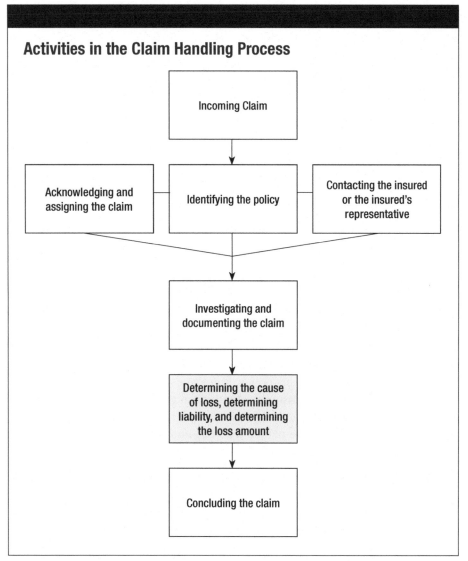

**Activities in the Claim Handling Process**

Incoming Claim

Acknowledging and assigning the claim — Identifying the policy — Contacting the insured or the insured's representative

Investigating and documenting the claim

Determining the cause of loss, determining liability, and determining the loss amount

Concluding the claim

[DA02305_5]

the policy. In a first-party claim, the claim representative would have to determine whether the policy provides coverage for the loss.

Coverage analysis is the process of examining a policy by reviewing all its component parts and applying them to the facts of a claim. A claim representative begins the process of coverage determination by carefully reading the policy form and all endorsements.

A systematic framework for coverage analysis can guide the claim representative in determining coverage. This process ensures that all of the component parts are reviewed. These questions outline the framework for coverage analysis:

- Is the person involved covered?
- Did the loss occur during the policy period?
- Is the cause of loss covered?
- Is the damaged property covered?
- Is the type of loss covered?
- Is the location of loss covered?
- Do any exclusions, exceptions, or endorsements apply?
- Does other insurance apply?

These questions do not need to be answered sequentially, but claim representatives should address all of them when they are determining coverage for a loss.

## Is the Person Involved Covered?

Some policies cover only insureds named or listed in the policy. However, most policies define "insured" to cover additional persons. For example, family members of the named insured who reside in the home may be covered under the named insured's homeowners policy. Employees of the named insured may be covered under the named insured's commercial general liability policy. A person who was granted permission by the named insured to use a covered auto may be covered under the named insured's auto policy.

Some claims, such as those involving contractors and subcontractors, may involve complex analysis regarding who is an insured under the policy. Claim representatives should attempt to obtain copies of all relevant contracts, agreements, and other documents during the investigation to assist in determining whether a person or party qualifies as an insured under the policy.

## Did the Loss Occur During the Policy Period?

Most policies are written to cover only losses that occur during a specific policy period. The policy period typically begins and ends at one minute after midnight (for example, from 12:01 a.m. on January 25, 20X1, to 12:01 a.m. on January 25, 20X2).

The date and time of loss occurrence usually determines whether the loss occurred during the policy period. However, the date of loss is not always straightforward. Occupational disease claims in workers compensation, for example, may not have a definite date of occurrence. Environmental damage may not have a readily definable date on which it began.

Although most policies are occurrence forms that cover any occurrence during the policy period, some policies are claims-made forms that cover claims that are made during the policy period for losses that may have occurred before the policy period. Claims-made forms are usually used for environmental, medical malpractice, or directors and officers policies. Claim representatives must understand whether the policy is an occurrence or a claims-made form and the dates of the policy period.

## Is the Cause of Loss Covered?

To answer this question, claim representatives should have thoroughly investigated all of the facts concerning the loss and should apply them to the language in all of the policy provisions. Exclusions must be read very carefully to find the exceptions that are contained in many policy exclusions. Policy definitions must also be analyzed.

For example, fire may appear to be a straightforward cause of loss with a clear definition. However, does "fire" cover smoke or excessive heat if there is no actual flame? Does the policy cover "friendly fire," which is contained in a device such as a stove? Is damage caused by firefighters who extinguish a fire covered?

## Is the Damaged Property Covered?

The claim representative must also determine whether property damaged in the loss is covered. For example, if a claim investigation reveals that an auto involved in an accident does not appear in the declarations or fall within the definition of "your covered auto," coverage may not exist for the vehicle. In another example, roofing material is stolen from the garage of a home and reported under the homeowners policy. If the named insured purchased the material to repair the roof of the home, there would be coverage. However, if the named insured is a roofing contractor and planned to use the material in his business, there would not be coverage under the homeowners policy.

## Is the Type of Loss Covered?

A loss can be classified as a **direct loss** or an **indirect loss**. A crushed car fender is a direct loss. Indirect losses reduce future income, increase future expenses, or both. For example, if fire destroys an insured's home, the cost of rebuilding the home is a direct loss. The rental cost for temporary living quarters for the insured while the home is being rebuilt is an indirect loss. The loss of earnings and the extra expenses incurred over a period of time after a fire damages a business are also indirect losses.

Many property policies cover direct losses only. Other policies cover some types of indirect losses, such as the coverage under homeowners policies for certain increases in living expenses after a covered loss renders the home untenable.

Direct loss
A reduction in the value of property that results directly and often immediately from damage to that property.

Indirect loss
A loss that arises as a result of damage to property, other than the direct loss to the property.

## Is the Location of the Loss Covered?

The location where the loss occurred must be within the policy's territorial limits. For example, most personal auto policies define the policy territory as the United States and its territories or possessions, Puerto Rico, and Canada. Therefore, an auto accident in Mexico would not be covered. A homeowners policy typically provides coverage for a dwelling only at the location listed in the declarations. However, personal property covered under a homeowners policy is typically covered anywhere in the world.

## Do Any Exclusions, Exceptions, or Endorsements Apply?

Some losses may be excluded under the policy. For example, homeowners polices usually exclude losses caused by insects or animals, such as termite damage.

When claim circumstances fall within a specific exclusion, coverage does not apply. An exclusion will bar coverage even if all other coverage requirements are met. For example, suppose that an insured uses his car as a taxi and is involved in an accident. The loss appears to be covered because all of the other coverage criteria are met—the insured, property, type of loss, cause of loss, and date and location of loss are all covered. However, there is an exclusion for any loss that occurs while the car is used as a public or livery conveyance. Therefore, there would be no coverage for the loss.

However, exclusions can contain exceptions. For example, an auto policy excludes liability coverage for damage to property used by the insured, with an exception for property damage to a residence used by the insured. Claim representatives who carefully read the policy can avoid incorrectly denying coverage based on an exclusion when an exception applies.

Endorsements to a policy can grant coverage that is otherwise excluded, exclude coverage that is otherwise provided, add or delete insureds, and otherwise modify the policy. For example, an insured who has a particular breed of dog may have an endorsement added to the homeowners policy that excludes coverage for any loss caused by the dog. Claim representatives must review endorsements to determine whether and how they apply to coverage for a loss.

## Does Other Insurance Apply?

The claim representative should determine during the investigation whether other insurance applies to the loss. For example, an insured could have two residences insured under separate homeowners policies. While traveling between the two residences, the insured could be involved in an accident in which suitcases containing clothing and other personal articles are damaged. Coverage exists under both homeowners policies for the personal property damage.

Policies usually contain conditions that describe how the policy will apply in the event that there is coverage under one or more additional policies. Some policies provide primary coverage, some provide excess coverage, while others provide **pro rata contribution** in the event of one or more additional policies.

## Determining the Loss Amount

Claim representatives should determine both the type and amount of any damages that are claimed as a result of a loss. They should then determine whether these types and amounts are covered under the policy.

For property damage claims, the amount of loss payable is usually limited to physical damage to, destruction of, or loss of use of tangible property. The amount is usually based on the cost to repair or replace the damaged property with that of like kind and quality. Claims for indirect loss, such as loss of business income, can be payable if indirect loss coverage is included or has been added to the policy.

Most property insurance policies limit recovery to the amount of a person's **insurable interest** in the damaged or destroyed property. However, insurable interest alone does not guarantee coverage. For example, an individual may have an insurable interest in a building but not be considered an insured under the policy because the person's name is not listed in the declarations or on an endorsement.

For liability claims, damages for which the insured may be liable include compensatory and punitive damages. **Compensatory damages** include **special damages** and **general damages**. **Punitive damages** punish a wrongdoer for a reckless, malicious, or deceitful act with the purpose of deterring similar conduct. See the exhibit "Damages."

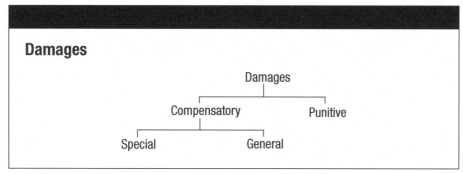

**Damages**

[DA03111]

Some policies do not define or list the types of damages payable under the policy. However, the term "damages" generally refers only to compensatory damages. In some states, the insurer is not permitted to pay for punitive damages because such payment by an insurer would not punish or deter the insured. Even if insurers are not prohibited by law from providing coverage for punitive damages, most policies expressly exclude them.

**Pro rata contribution**

An approach to other insurance by which the insurers contribute to the loss payment in the proportion to which they contribute to the total amount of coverage purchased (their limits of liability).

**Insurable interest**

An interest in the subject of an insurance policy that is not unduly remote and that would cause the interested party to suffer financial loss if an insured event occurred.

**Compensatory damages**

A payment awarded by a court to reimburse a victim for actual harm.

**Special damages**

A form of compensatory damages that awards a sum of money for specific, identifiable expenses associated with the injured person's loss, such as medical expenses or lost wages.

**General damages**

A monetary award to compensate a victim for losses, such as pain and suffering, that does not involve specific, measurable expenses.

**Punitive damages (exemplary damages)**

A payment awarded by a court to punish a defendant for a reckless, malicious, or deceitful act to deter similar conduct; the award need not bear any relation to a party's actual damages.

In addition to ensuring that the types of loss and damage are covered, claim representatives must verify that the amount of actual or anticipated damages is within the policy limits. In addition to limits of liability in a property policy, there may also be sublimits for certain types of property or expenses. For example, homeowners policies usually contain a limit for the dwelling and another limit for personal property, with sublimits for various types of personal property such as jewelry or money. There are also deductibles and conditions that describe how damaged or destroyed property should be valued, such as actual cash value or replacement cost. There may also be **coinsurance clauses**, and, if so, the total value of the property must be determined and compared to the insured value.

**Coinsurance clause**

A clause that requires the insured to carry insurance equal to at least a specified percentage of the insured property's value.

Some policies contain both occurrence and aggregate limits. For example, most commercial general liability policies have a policy limit that applies to each occurrence and another limit that applies to all losses within the policy period. The claim representative must determine the available aggregate limit as well as the occurrence limit for losses under these types of policies.

Some insureds have a self-insured retention (SIR) in which the insured is responsible for paying losses up to the SIR level. Once the SIR has been exceeded, the insurer is responsible for payment. This information should be contained in the policy and/or in the insurer's system.

The claim representative must verify all the policy limits applicable to a loss before making any payments to ensure that the payment falls within the available limits of coverage. The claim representative should also notify the insured if it appears that a loss will exceed policy limits. The claim representative may also need to notify a reinsurer for the insurer or an excess insurer for the insured when a loss is likely to exceed policy limits.

## CLAIMS HANDLING PROCESS: CONCLUDING THE CLAIM

While there are many simple claims for which the claims representative will face an easy yes or no decision regarding payment or denial, concluding the claim can be complicated by negotiations. A savvy rep will know insurer guidelines as well as state and federal laws governing payments, denials, and dispute resolution. A claims representative who fully understands the process of concluding a claim is in a better position to ensure that claims are handled fairly, efficiently, and legally.

Once the investigation is completed and all documentation is received, the claims representative must decide whether to pay the claim or deny it. If the claim is to be paid, the claims representative often must negotiate the amount with the insured or the claimant. Negotiation involves discussing disputed matters and mutually agreeing on a settlement. In some cases, alternative dispute resolution methods may be used to resolve a disagreement and, ulti-mately, the claim.

When an agreement on the settlement amount is reached, the claims repre-sentative secures the necessary final documents so that payment can be made. If the claim is denied, the insured or claimant may accept the denial or choose to file a lawsuit to challenge the denial. Litigation may also be started if no agreement on the claim can be reached.

## Payments

When a covered claim is concluded through negotiation or other means, the claims representative or claims personnel must issue a claim payment. Claim payments can be made by check, draft, or electronic transfer of funds.

A check creates a demand for payment on the insurer's bank account and can be presented for payment without further insurer authorization. A draft is similar to a check; however, when the claimant presents the draft to the insurer's bank (often through the claimant's bank transaction), the bank must verify that the insurer has authorized payment before disbursing any funds. Because of this required authorization, a claimant cannot present a draft at a bank for immediate payment. This delay in disbursing funds allows the insurer to confirm that the payment is proper. Funds can also be electronically trans-ferred into an account of the insured's choosing.

When issuing claim payments, claims personnel must ensure that the proper parties are being paid. Many other parties, such as mortgagees on homes and loss payees on autos and personal property, can have a financial interest in the property. Parties named in the policy have rights, described in the policy, to be included as a payee under certain circumstances, such as for property that has been destroyed. For third-party liability claim payments, the claims representative must determine whether an attorney or a lienholder, such as a medical service provider, should be named as an additional payee on the payment. The claims representative is responsible for including all required payees when issuing a claim payment.

Claims representatives must also check various databases to ensure that the claim payment complies with federal and state laws. The Office of Foreign Asset Control, U.S. Department of the Treasury, requires all claims payors (insurers, self-insureds, and third-party administrators [TPAs]) to check the master list of potential terrorists and drug traffickers before making a claim payment. Claims payors may be prohibited from paying a claim to an individ-ual or entity appearing on this list. Many insurers and TPAs have contracted with third parties to provide an automated means of performing this check. Failure to comply with this requirement can result in substantial penalties to the payor.

Insurers and other claims payors must also be aware of state child support enforcement initiatives that can affect claim payments. Many states have statutes that require a claims representative to check a database to determine whether a claimant or beneficiary owes unpaid child support. If child support is owed, the claims representative must follow specific procedures when issuing the payment because the unpaid child support has priority. The claim payment goes toward reducing the amount of the child support in arrears rather than to the injured party. For example, Massachusetts law requires that an insurer licensed to do business in Massachusetts check the database before making payment on a claim of $500 or more. Failure to comply can result in financial consequences to the insurer. Many insurers and claims payors have created ways to automate the process.

Claims representatives handling workers compensation claims and third-party bodily injury claims must be aware of the Medicare Secondary Payer Program and how this program can affect claim payments. The Center for Medicare and Medicaid Services (CMS) must approve a proposed settlement in specific situations. The settlement must be approved for claimants who are Medicare beneficiaries or who have reasonable expectations of Medicare enrollment within thirty months of settlement and when the settlement is $250,000 or more. Failure to gain CMS approval can expose the insurer to a bad-faith suit because Medicare goes directly to the claimant for reimbursement. Insurers are integrating this approval process into their claims practices to ensure compliance.

Claims representatives must ensure that all of these checks have been completed before issuing payment. If they are not, the insurer can be subject to fines, penalties, and possibly additional payments to satisfy these parties.

## Claims Denial

A claim may conclude instead with denial. When claims investigations reveal that a policy does not provide coverage for a loss or when an insured fails to meet a policy condition, the claims representative must make a timely claims denial. Insurers often have strict guidelines that claims representatives must follow when denying claims, and some insurers require a claims manager's approval to issue a claims denial.

Before denying a claim, the claims representative must analyze the coverage carefully, investigate the loss thoroughly, and evaluate the claim fairly and objectively. Courts often favor insureds when a claims denial fails to meet these requirements, and the insurer can be assessed penalties in addition to the loss amount.

Once claims management gives authority to deny a claim, the claims representative must prepare a denial letter as soon as possible. Some denial letters are drafted by lawyers to ensure that they comply with the jurisdiction's legal requirements. For example, a denial letter must usually state all the known reasons for the claims denial. Specific policy language should be quoted, and the location of the language in the policy should be cited. The policy provisions should be described in relation to the facts of the loss. Also, an insured who disagrees with the denial should be invited to submit additional information that would give the insurer cause to reevaluate the claim. The denial letter should be signed and sent by the claims representative, even if it is drafted by a lawyer.

Insurers usually send denial letters by certified mail with a return receipt requested to be signed by the addressee. Some insurers also send a copy of the letter by regular mail, marked "personal and confidential," in case the certified mail is not claimed. These procedures help ensure that the denial letter reaches the correct party, and they provide documentation that it was received.

# Alternative Dispute Resolution

If an insurer and an insured or a claimant cannot agree on the claim value or claim coverage, they may resolve the disagreement in court. However, court costs and delays in the court system have encouraged insurers, insureds, and claimants to seek alternative ways of resolving their disputes about claims that are less expensive and time consuming than litigation. Such processes also help relieve the courts of the burden of handling such disputes. **Alternative dispute resolution (ADR)** refers to methods for settling disputes outside the traditional court system. The most common ADR techniques are mediation, arbitration, appraisals, mini-trials, summary jury trials, and pretrial settlement conferences.

**Alternative dispute resolution (ADR)**
Procedures to help settle disputes without litigation, including arbitration, mediation, and negotiation.

## Mediation

**Mediation** is an ADR method by which disputing parties use a neutral outside party to examine the issues and develop a mutually agreeable settlement. The mediator, often a retired judge or an expert in the field under dispute, manages the process. The mediator may be appointed by the court or selected by the parties. Each party presents its case to the mediator, who leads the parties through in-depth settlement discussions. The mediator points out the weaknesses in each argument or in the evidence presented, proposes solutions, and helps the participants reach a mutually agreeable settlement. If mediation does not resolve the dispute, the parties may consider another ADR method or litigation.

**Mediation**
An alternative dispute resolution (ADR) method by which disputing parties use a neutral outside party to examine the issues and develop a mutually agreeable settlement.

## Arbitration

**Arbitration** is an ADR method by which the disputing parties use a neutral outside party to examine the issues and develop a settlement, which can be final and binding. The arbitrator acts as a judge, weighing the facts of the case and making a decision based on the evidence presented. The advantage of arbitration is that someone other than the insurer and the claimant decides the case.

**Arbitration**
An alternative dispute resolution (ADR) method by which disputing parties use a neutral outside party to examine the issues and develop a settlement, which can be final and binding.

The type of arbitration determines whether the decision is binding on the parties. Under binding arbitration, which some states' laws require for arbitrated claims disputes, the parties must accept the arbitrator's decision. Under nonbinding arbitration, neither party is forced to accept the arbitrator's decision. However, the decision provides the "winner" with leverage for future negotiations. This method of alternative dispute resolution is cost-effective for all parties and relieves the courts of the burden of handling such disputes.

When two policies issued by different insurers cover the same loss, arbitration can be used to settle a dispute about which insurer should pay the claim and how much should be paid. Generally, one insurer settles with the insured. The case is then submitted to an arbitration service to determine what each insurer owes. Insurers may use an organization such as Insurance Arbitration Forums, Inc., or the American Arbitration Association. Insurer trade associations also offer arbitration services and other forms of ADR to member companies.

## Appraisals

**Appraisal clause**

A policy provision that prescribes a method for resolving a disputed claim about the value of property or the amount of a property loss.

Property insurance policies include a provision that requires a form of ADR before litigation. This provision, called the **appraisal clause**, is used to settle disputes between insurers and their insureds over the amount owed on a covered loss. It is not used to settle coverage disputes, only the amount of damages. Almost all property insurance policies contain an appraisal provision. For example, the HO-3 provides that the insurer or the insured can demand an appraisal if either disagrees on the loss amount. Each party chooses an appraiser, and the two appraisers choose a third appraiser to act as an umpire. Each party pays its own appraiser, and the two parties share the cost of the umpire. The appraisers can hear evidence that is typically excluded from trial. The two appraisers estimate the property damage separately. If their estimates match, the insurer pays the insured that amount. If the estimates are different, the umpire offers a binding decision on the loss amount.

## Mini-Trials

**Mini-trial**

An alternative dispute resolution method by which a case undergoes an abbreviated version of a trial before a panel or an adviser who poses questions and offers opinions on the outcome of a trial, based on the evidence presented.

**Mini-trials** are another form of ADR. A mini-trial enables parties to test the validity of their positions and continue negotiations. Parties can terminate the process at any time. The parties agree not to disclose in future litigation anything that occurs during the mini-trial, to preserve their rights in litigation if the negotiation fails.

The parties select an impartial adviser, often a retired judge, an executive, or an expert, and decide the role of the adviser, whether that of passive participant, arbitrator, or judge. The adviser has no authority to make a binding decision; however, he or she can pose questions that test the validity of each side's case and offer an opinion based on the evidence.

Before the mini-trial, parties can exchange information about their anticipated testimony and the documents that they plan to introduce as evidence.

Such information may also be given to the adviser. Witnesses and experts may testify during the mini-trial. Lawyers are allotted a limited time to present their cases. The main advantage of mini-trials is that claimants and insurers can learn the likely outcome of their cases without having to contend with delays in the legal system.

## Summary Jury Trial

A **summary jury trial** offers a forum for deciding the merits of cases for court proceedings and may assist in negotiations. A summary jury trial is staged much like a regular jury trial, except that only a few witnesses are used to present the case. Mock jurors are pulled from a pool of persons selected to serve as possible jurors in an actual court case. Evidence and witnesses' testimony may be presented in both oral and written format for the mock jurors. Lawyers summarize information for the sake of brevity. The mock jurors decide the case based on the limited, though representative, presentation of evidence.

A summary jury trial can be concluded in a relatively short time, so legal costs are significantly reduced. Fewer witnesses mean less expense for witness fees. Although lawyers are required, the time required to develop the case and prepare for trial is considerably less. Summary jury trials can produce an effective settlement and control legal expenses.

Summary jury trial
An alternative dispute resolution method by which disputing parties participate in an abbreviated trial, presenting the evidence of a few witnesses to a panel of mock jurors who decide the case.

## Litigation

Even with the variety of ADR methods available, many cases are concluded through litigation. Litigation can occur at almost any point during the life of a claim. It occurs most often when the parties to the claim are unable to reach an agreement by negotiation or ADR, or when a claim is denied. ADR reduces, but does not eliminate, the chance that a claimant will sue and take a case to trial. Accordingly, insurers must be prepared to litigate some claims.

Many insurance policies require insurers to defend their insureds at trial. The HO-3, for example, states that the insurer must "provide a defense at our expense by counsel of our choice, even if the suit is groundless, false, or fraudulent." The duty to defend generally terminates when the amount the insurer has paid in settlements or judgments on the claim equals the insurer's limit of liability.

When litigation cannot be avoided, claims representatives participate in developing a litigation strategy for the insured's defense and for litigation expense control. Claims representatives must carefully select and direct defense lawyers. The lawyer's role is to be the insured's advocate; he or she must address every aspect of the claimant's case, from liability to damages, to mitigate the claim against the insured and to encourage the claimant to settle out of court.

## Closing Reports

When a claim is resolved, the claims representative may complete a closing or final report, which can include the claims representative's recommendations on subrogation, advice to underwriters, and other suggestions. In some instances, these reports are used by subrogation claims representatives to evaluate the likelihood of a successful subrogation action. Claims supervisors and managers may use the reports to audit the claims representative's performance. These reports can also be submitted to reinsurers for reimbursement of loss payment. Claims representatives should be aware of claims that should be referred to reinsurers and must complete reports on those claims based on the insurer's internal guidelines and reinsurance agreements.

# SUMMARY

The claims handling process provides claims representatives with a framework for consistent claims handling after the insurer receives notice of the loss.

The claims process begins with acknowledgment and assignment of a claim. After receiving a claim assignment, a claims representative's initial activity is to identify the policy. After acknowledging and assigning a claim, identifying the policy, and establishing claim or case (loss) reserves, the claims representative contacts the insured or the insured's representative to explain the claims process and begin the claim investigation. A claims representative may use a nonwaiver agreement or reservation of rights letter to advise the insured that any action taken by the insurer in investigating the cause or in ascertaining the amount of loss is not intended to waive or invalidate any policy conditions for either the insurer or the insured.

Claim representatives spend much of their time investigating and documenting claims. They often take statements from insureds, claimants, and witnesses. They can perform accident-scene investigations themselves or hire independent adjusters to complete them. Claim representatives use the results of their investigations to determine the cause of loss, liability, and loss amount.

Claim representatives use file review systems and submit status notes and reports to document the claim file. Timely review of the claim in the file status notes is one means of showing good faith. Internal and external reports communicate the details of the loss and the loss adjustment process to those who need this information.

In preparation for performing a good-faith investigation, the claims representative must understand the concept of legal liability. Legal liability arises from civil law and is based on torts, contracts, and statutes. The three classes of torts applicable to claims representatives are negligence, strict liability, and intentional torts.

After the claim investigation, the claim representative must determine the cause of loss. Once the cause of loss has been determined, the claim representative determines coverage through an analysis of the policy. The types and amounts of damages, along with the coverage available under the policy, should then be determined.

Once the investigation is completed and all documentation is received, the claims representative must decide whether to pay the claim or deny it. If the claim is to be paid, the claims representative often must negotiate the amount with the insured or the claimant. Many disputed claims are concluded by negotiation. Those that are not may be resolved by ADR methods such as mediation, arbitration, appraisal, mini-trial, or summary jury trial. In cases in which all else has failed, litigation is used to resolve the claim.

# Direct Your Learning ▶▶

# Setting Case Reserves and Investigating Claims

## Educational Objectives

After learning the content of this assignment, you should be able to:

▷ Summarize the five methods of setting a case reserve and the causes of reserve errors.

▷ Given a claim, assess the factors affecting the reserve amount using the individual case method.

▷ Evaluate the insurer's duty to investigate in regard to:

- Authority

- Reasonableness

- Good faith

- Promptness

- Privacy issues

▷ Examine the insured's duty to cooperate with the insurer in regard to:

- Compliance with a reasonable request

- Production of documents and evidence

- Examination under oath and other types of statements

- Independent medical examination

- Consequences of noncooperation

▷ Explain when and how each of the following investigative tools is used in a claims investigation:

- Loss notice form

- Policy information

- Statements

**3**

- Diagrams, photos, and videos
- Experts
- Records and reports
- Industry databases
- Social networking sites
- Other investigative tools

▶ Illustrate the critical information in the first notice of loss and how it is reconciled with coverages provided by the policy.

# Setting Case Reserves and Investigating Claims

## ESTABLISHING A CASE RESERVE

Inaccurate case reserving is a leading cause of insurer insolvency. Claims representatives should be familiar with the advantages and dangers of the methods used to establish case loss reserves.

Insurers can establish case reserves using any of several different methods. These are five common methods:

- Individual case method
- Roundtable method
- Average value method
- Formula method
- Expert system method

Reserving errors can occur when any of these methods is used inappropriately, such as when misusing the more subjective individual case method results in the need to repeatedly raise the reserve amount.

### Types of Case Reserving Methods

Although the exact timing may differ among insurers, the setting of an initial reserve(s) usually occurs early in the claims handling process. Claims representatives often establish claim or case (loss) **reserves** in conjunction with identifying the policy. An insurer's claims information system often determines the types of reserves that are established, such as one reserve for property damage and another for bodily injury. Some systems require separate reserves for each claimant in a claim, and some systems require separate expense reserves for the costs of handling the claim. For example, in a claim for an auto accident, an individual reserve may be set for damage to the insured's vehicle, damage to the other party's vehicle, medical expenses for the insured, and the bodily injury of the claimant. Setting accurate reserves is an important part of the claims representative's job. Reserves that are too high or too low can affect the insurer's profitability. Establishing and maintaining adequate reserves is important for the insurer's financial health because reserves affect the insurer's ability to maintain and increase its business. See the exhibit "Common Methods of Setting Case Reserves."

One method of setting claim reserves is the **individual case method**. Claims representatives set an individual or case reserve for each claim or cause of loss,

**Reserve**
The amount the insurer estimates and sets aside to pay on an existing claim that has not been settled.

**Individual case method**
A method of setting reserves based on the claim's circumstances and the claims representative's experience in handling similar claims.

---

**Common Methods of Setting Case Reserves**

1. Individual case method
2. Roundtable method
3. Average value method
4. Formula method
5. Expert system method

The individual case method and the roundtable method rely on the claim representative's judgment. The other methods rely on statistical analysis to set the reserve.

[DA05562]

based on the claims representative's expectation of what the insurer will pay. When the individual case method is used on each claim, the claims representative estimates the case reserve based on the claim's circumstances and his or her experience with similar claims.

Because of the subjective nature of the evaluation and the number of factors a claims representative must consider when using the individual case method for a bodily injury claim, reserves can vary widely by claims representative. See the exhibit "Individual Case Method Considerations."

**Roundtable method**

A method of setting reserves by using the consensus of two or more claims personnel who have independently evaluated the claims file.

Another method of setting claim reserves is the **roundtable method**. Ideally, at the start of this process, claims personnel should not know the reserves the others have set. After an evaluation and a discussion, a consensus reserve figure may be reached, or an average of all the figures may be calculated. Because this method is time-consuming, it is not appropriate for setting initial reserves. However, for serious or prolonged claims, it is a suitable method to review initial reserves.

**Average value method**

A case reserving method that establishes a predetermined dollar amount of reserve for each claim as it is reported.

Claims representatives (or claims-processing computer systems) may also set claim reserves using the **average value method**. This method is useful when there are small variations in loss size for a particular type of claim and when claims can be concluded quickly. The average values are usually based on data from past claims and adjusted to reflect current conditions. For example, auto windshield claims may be initially reserved at $650 based on an insurer's previous loss experience with those claims. That figure may remain the same until the claim has been concluded. For some claims, the initial reserve is based on the average value method, but claims representatives are required to modify the initial reserve within a specified number of days to reflect each claim's circumstances.

**Formula method**

A method of setting claim reserves by using a mathematical formula.

Another method of setting claim reserves is the **formula method**, in which a formula for setting a reserve is determined by the insurer and is automatically created for the claims representative based on the facts of a claim. For example, a formula may be based on the assumption that a certain ratio exists between the medical cost and the indemnity (or wage loss) in a workers compensation claim. Based on an insurer's loss history with many similar

# Individual Case Method Considerations

Considerations a claim representative may use when setting reserves on a bodily injury claim using the individual case method include the following:

1. Claimant profile (factors in calculating economic loss)
   a. Age
   b. Gender
   c. Occupation
   d. Level of education
   e. Dependants, if any, their ages, and to what extent they rely on the claimant financially and for companionship
2. Nature and extent of the injury (factors in calculating general damages)
   a. Whether the injury is permanent
   b. Extent of pain and suffering
   c. Extent of disruption the injury creates in the individual's lifestyle
3. Special damages (factors in calculating special damages)
   a. Anticipated medical bills incurred to date and for future care
   b. Type of medical care that has been or is being provided; whether it includes diagnostic care or treatment
   c. Whether the claimant will lose any wages
4. Claimant representation (factors in determining the likelihood of a lawsuit and predicting general damages that could result)
   a. Whether the claimant is represented by a lawyer
   b. If so, the lawyer's reputation
   c. Typical value of local court verdicts
5. Liability factors (factors in calculating compensatory and/or punitive damages)
   a. Whether the case involves ordinary negligence or gross negligence
   b. Whether the case involves any comparative or contributory negligence
   c. Any legal limits to recovery, such as a cap on certain types of damages
   d. Any other parties' contribution to the loss or responsibility for contributing to the settlement
6. Miscellaneous factors
   a. General economic conditions in the geographic area (factor in calculating economic loss)
   b. Whether the insured's conduct in causing the loss was outrageous (factor in calculating compensatory damages)
   c. Whether drinking or drug use contributed to the loss (factor in calculating liability)
   d. The insured's credibility as a witness (factor in determining likelihood of successful lawsuit)
   e. The claimant's credibility as a witness (factor in determining likelihood of successful lawsuit)

[DA02310]

claims, the indemnity reserve may be set at a certain percentage of the medical reserve. The formula method may also be used to set the additional living expense reserve under a homeowners policy if the home is destroyed by fire; the reserve may be set as a certain percentage of the coverage limit.

**Expert system method**

A method of setting reserves with a software application that estimates losses and loss adjustment expenses.

Claims representatives may also set claim reserves using the **expert system method**. The details of a particular claim are entered into a computer, and the program applies the appropriate rules to estimate the amount of the loss and the loss adjustment expenses. An expert system can provide more-consistent reserves than the individual case method can. While similar in operation to the formula method, the expert system includes more subjective information, such as loss location or the name of the treating physician, in creating the reserve. See the exhibit "IBNR Reserves."

---

### IBNR Reserves

Additionally, insurers are required by law and good accounting practice to establish reserves for losses that have been incurred but not reported (IBNR). Although the name refers only to incurred but not reported losses, unreported losses account for only a portion of the reserve in many cases. Often, the IBNR reserve also includes an amount for reported losses for which the case reserves are judged to be inadequate. A reserve for claims that have been closed and then reopened may also be included in the IBNR reserve.

Claims representatives are rarely involved in setting IBNR reserves. Actuaries analyze the insurer's experience by comparing paid losses with case reserves to determine whether the insurer typically underreserves or overreserves claims. If the insurer typically underreserves claims, the IBNR reserve will be set at an amount to cover the ultimate cost of the claim. IBNR reserves are calculated in aggregate rather than associated with an individual case.

---

[DA12775]

## Causes of Reserve Errors

Reserve adequacy and accuracy are important to an insurer's continued solvency and capacity (ability to write new business). Claims representatives can negatively influence solvency and capacity by undervaluing claim reserves. Although an occasional inadequate or inaccurate reserve may have little or no effect on an insurer, consistently inaccurate or inadequate reserves on thousands of claims can distort the ratemaking process, eventually affecting an insurer's ability to write business competitively and, ultimately, its solvency.

Reserving errors can be caused in several ways. Initial reserves may be inaccurate because of limited information. Thus, many insurers require that initial reserves be reviewed and adjusted for accuracy within a short time frame. In addition, most insurers require reserves to be evaluated whenever a claim file is reviewed. That evaluation ensures that reserves reflect the most current information contained in the claim file.

Reserve inaccuracy can also be the result of the claims representative's poor planning, lack of expertise in estimating claim severity, or unwillingness to reevaluate facts. In these cases, the claims representative may set a modest initial reserve but then raise the reserve by a few thousand dollars to issue payments. Later, the reserve will be increased again when more bills arrive. This process is called stairstepping the reserve.

On a claim that concludes in thirty, sixty, or ninety days, stairstepping has little effect except to reveal the claims representative's poor claims handling practices. But if the claim remains open for several years, as many liability and workers compensation claims do, the insurer's total case reserves will be understated, increasing the risk that future payments will not be fully funded.

This does not mean that claims representatives cannot adjust a reserve up or down during the course of a claim. However, they should make those adjustments because of new information or changes in the circumstances of the claim, not because of poor planning or other poor claims handling practices.

Stairstepping can be avoided if proper claims handling practices and reserving methods are used. For example, the roundtable method or expert system method may result in a realistic reserve that would prevent frequent stairstepping.

Because reserves should reflect the ultimate cost of a claim and not the claim's present value, the reserve should account for the claim's future settlement value. For example, a claim for a catastrophic injury may take years to settle. During that time, inflation may increase the cost of medical care, or new and expensive medical technology may be developed. The reserves for such claims should anticipate those increased costs.

Claims representatives may underestimate the future settlement value of a claim if they are overconfident of their ability to conclude the claim for a lesser amount. Reserves should always be based on the value of a claim, never on the perceived likelihood of successful negotiation and settlement. Analysis of verdicts rendered in similar cases helps show the potential value of a claim and discourages the tendency to base reserves on negotiation expertise.

Some inadvertent errors in setting reserves can be detected using computer software that stores claims information. Some claims-information systems provide a data-entry check. For example, the software might require that the reserve amount be entered twice to allow the user a chance to verify the amount. Additionally, claims managers can review reports of reserves from the preceding day for unusual entries or reserves that exceed authority. For example, a report listing all reserves of $100,000 or more might uncover a $10,000 reserve that was incorrectly entered as $100,000.

As claims representatives investigate and evaluate claims, they should increase or decrease the reserve to reflect new information received. For example, if the estimate for medical bills is $5,000, the claims representative would set up a reserve of $5,000. If further testing reveals a need for more costly treatment and the estimate is revised to be $10,000, the claims representative should change the reserve to reflect this increase in the anticipated medical costs. Likewise, if an estimate is lowered, the reserve should be changed to reflect the decrease. Because such changes are based on changes in the facts of the claim, they are not considered stairstepping.

# RESERVING CASE STUDY

The individual case method of setting claim reserves relies largely on the judgment and experience of the claims representative. Developing expertise in using this method can help a claims representative set reserves that are adequate but not excessive.

## Case Facts

Four months ago, Sara was a passenger in her neighbor's car when the neighbor tried to get through an intersection at a light that had just turned red. Their vehicle was struck by another vehicle driven by someone who was just over the blood alcohol limit for drunk driving. Sara suffered lacerations and broken bones in her arm and leg. She was taken by ambulance to a hospital, where healthcare providers performed a battery of diagnostic tests and treated her injuries.

Sara has incurred $60,000 in medical expenses to date and will need little to no medical care in the future for the injuries she suffered in the accident. Her doctors believe that she will be able to return to work full time as an accountant in two months with no permanent disability and no scarring. She has a bachelor's degree in accounting from a local university, and before the accident, she was earning $85,000 per year.

The local economy has caused many in Sara's profession to be laid off. Her employer at the time of the accident has since informed her that her position is no longer available. Sara, thirty-five, has managed to take care of herself and her five-year-old son since being discharged from the hospital, although she still takes pain medication infrequently. The child's father was killed while serving in the military.

Sara is represented by a competent but inexperienced attorney. The limits of the neighbor's and the drunk driver's personal auto policies are not a concern. The claims representative for the neighbor's insurer set the initial case reserve at $40,000 but realizes, as new medical records and bills have come in, that the reserve needs to be raised. The claims representative's supervisor suggests that the individual case method be used to evaluate Sara's bodily injury claim.

## Case Analysis Tools

When the individual case method is used, the representative evaluates the settlement value based on all the circumstances of the claim and his or her experience with similar cases. Because of the numerous factors that must be analyzed and their subjective nature, the individual case method can yield settlement valuations that vary widely from one representative or attorney to another. However, for serious injuries, the individual case method is still the preferred technique for settlement evaluation.

## Overview of Steps

Considerations a representative may use when setting reserves on a bodily injury claim using the individual case method include these:

- Claimant profile
- Nature and extent of the injury
- Special damages
- Claimant representation
- Liability factors
- Miscellaneous factors

## Claimant Profile

The claimant profile considers factors that are used to calculate economic loss, which include these:

- Age
- Gender
- Occupation
- Level of education
- Dependents, if any; their ages; and to what extent they rely on the claimant financially and for companionship

Sara is thirty-five years old, a good age at which to recover from physical trauma. Because Sara has no permanent disability, her economic loss will be less than it may have been had she been much older. Her gender is likely not a factor in her recovery. Her occupation as an accountant typically does not involve intense physical exertion such as heavy lifting, which will also allow her to get back to work sooner. Her level of education, like her gender, is likely not a factor in her recovery or damages. Sara does have a dependent son who is totally reliant on her financially, a factor that may raise her settlement value.

## Nature and Extent of the Injury

Factors used to calculate general damages that regard the nature and extent of the injury include these:

- Whether the injury was permanent and/or disfiguring
- Extent of pain and suffering
- Extent of disruption to the individual's lifestyle caused by the injury

Sara's injuries were not permanent. She was told by her doctors that she could return to work without disability six months after her accident. However, four months after the accident, her pain is still sometimes severe enough that she must resort to pain medication. Her lifestyle has been disrupted, as she is unable to work and is likely under considerable stress while caring for her injuries and her five-year-old son. The fact that her injuries did not result in permanent disability will be a factor in establishing her claim's settlement value. However, her pain and suffering, as evidenced by her continued use of pain medication and the disruption to her lifestyle, are factors that will increase her claim's settlement value. The fact that Sara's child's father was killed while serving in the military is likely not admissible, but if the jury were to hear it, the value of her general damages claim would likely increase.

## Special Damages

Factors used to calculate special damages include these:

- Medical bills incurred to date and anticipated amounts for future care
- Type of medical care that has been or is being provided and whether this includes diagnostic care or treatment
- Whether the claimant will lose any wages

Sara has incurred $60,000 in medical bills to date, and doctors do not expect her to incur any additional amounts because of her injuries. Also, a substantial portion of the $60,000 incurred was for the diagnostic tests performed at the hospital soon after her accident; those tests will likely not be needed again. Therefore, the $60,000 appears to be a stable ceiling on Sara's medical expenses. This will not lower her settlement value, but it will keep it from rising.

In addition to medical costs, the accident has caused Sara to lose wages. Being unable to work for six months when she would have earned $85,000 per year means that she has a $42,500 claim for lost wages. Further, because her employer did not hold her position open until she could return, she may be able to increase her claim as she searches for work.

In all, Sara's special damages are at least $102,500 ($60,000 + $42,500).

## Claimant Representation

Factors used in determining the likelihood of a lawsuit and predicting the general damages that could result are these:

- Whether the claimant is represented by a lawyer
- If so, the lawyer's reputation
- Typical value of local court verdicts

Sara is represented by an attorney, which can increase the length of time her claim is open—and the longer a claim remains open, the more likely its cost will increase. The lawyer's reputation is that he is competent but inexperienced. Being competent, he should be able to present a good case to a jury or judge. Being inexperienced, he may have difficulty accurately appraising the value of Sara's claim. However, researching the typical values of local court verdicts of similar claims may help Sara's attorney correct that problem. For a variety of reasons, some jurisdictions may have court verdicts that are higher than or lower than average. For the purposes of this case study, assume that the jurisdiction where Sara's case will be tried typically has average court verdicts.

## Liability Factors

Factors used to calculate compensatory and/or punitive damages include these:

- Whether the case involves negligence
- Whether the case involves any comparative negligence
- Any legal limits to recovery amount, such as a cap on certain types of damages
- Any other parties' contributions to the loss or responsibility for contributing to the settlement

Both drunk driving and going through a red light appear negligent; therefore, both drivers could be found liable for Sara's damages. This would increase the value of Sara's claim. Because Sara was not driving and there is no indication that she impeded her neighbor's ability to control the vehicle, it is unlikely that any potential comparative negligence damages would be assessed against her. For the purposes of this case study, assume that the accident did not occur in a state that imposes a legal limit to Sara's recovery. It is possible that the drunk driver has some responsibility for causing the accident, because that driver may have had the last clear chance to avoid hitting the vehicle in which Sara rode and may have been able to do so if he or she had not been drunk. So the drunk driver's insurer will likely contribute to the settlement, which will lower the cost of the settlement for the neighbor's insurer.

## Miscellaneous Factors

The miscellaneous, or catch-all, category of factors used in the individual case method include these:

- General economic conditions in the geographic area (a factor in calculating economic loss)
- Whether the insured's conduct in causing the loss was outrageous (a factor in calculating compensatory damages)
- Whether drinking or drug use contributed to the loss (a factor in calculating liability)
- The insured's credibility as a witness (a factor in determining the likelihood of successful lawsuit)
- The claimant's credibility as a witness (a factor in determining the likelihood of successful lawsuit)

The poor local economy that has caused many in Sara's profession to be laid off will decrease the value of her claim for economic loss. The insureds in this case are the neighbor and the drunk driver, and the jury may consider their actions (running a red light and driving drunk) to be outrageous. That may increase Sara's claim for compensatory damages. Drinking and driving, despite having a green light, can be a factor in calculating liability. Sara's credibility as a witness should be adequate. The fact that her child's father was killed while serving the country, if told to a jury, may make her more sympathetic and credible, so the claims representative should account for this potential development. The drunk driver, because of his inebriation at the time of the accident, may not be perceived to be as credible as the neighbor by a jury if their versions of the facts conflict.

## Setting the Reserve

After analyzing the various factors that apply in the individual case method, the claims representative lists the factors that could increase or decrease Sara's settlement value. See the exhibit "Factors That May Influence the Value of Sara's Claim Settlement."

Aside from potential contribution from the other drivers' insurers, the initial case reserve of $40,000 appears to be inadequate. The low setting may have been a result of the representative's poor planning or lack of expertise in estimating claim severity; it could lead to stairstepping, or incremental increases in the reserve, as more bills arrive.

Analyzing these factors will help the claims representative determine a dollar range for an adequate reserve.

### Factors That May Influence the Value of Sara's Claim Settlement

| Factors that increase the claimant's settlement value | Factors that decrease the claimant's settlement value |
|---|---|
| Dependent son: 5 years old. | Age: 35. |
| Pain and suffering continue 4 months after accident. | Occupation: accountant. |
| Disruption of lifestyle. | Injury not permanent. |
| Lost wages may increase beyond 6 months while claimant searches for work in a down economy. | Future medical bills, if any, expected to be small. |
| Claimant represented by an attorney. | Battery of diagnostic tests will likely not need to be repeated. |
| Attorney has reputation of being competent. | Attorney has reputation of being inexperienced. |
| Neighbor driver ran a red light in a busy intersection. | Drunk driver's insurer may contribute to settlement, reducing the cost of the settlement to the neighbor driver's insurer. |
| Other driver was drunk and may have had the last clear chance to avoid the accident. | General economy is down. |
| Claimant was not driving and can have little to no comparative negligence assigned to her. | |

[DA07296]

# INSURER'S DUTY TO INVESTIGATE

Insurers want to avoid allegations of **breach of contract** and **bad faith**. To help prevent these, claims representatives should know how to conduct appropriate claims investigations.

When an insurer receives a claims notice, a claims representative is assigned to determine whether the claim is a covered loss. While a claims representative can fairly easily understand the terms of a policy, the facts of the claim often can be learned only through an investigation. A claims investigation should be handled with the insured's authority, reasonably, in good faith, promptly, and with an awareness of privacy issues.

**Breach of contract**

The failure, without legal excuse, to fulfill a contractual promise.

**Bad faith**

An insurer's denial of coverage without cause, which can result in extracontractual damages, punitive damages, or both.

## Authority

The terms of a policy often give the insurer the authority to investigate the facts of a claim. Insurance Services Office, Inc. (ISO) uses similar language in several of its policy forms to grant this authority. See the exhibit "Samples of Policy Language Granting Authority to Investigate."

### Samples of Policy Language Granting Authority to Investigate

| Insurance Services Office, Inc. (ISO) Policy | Policy Language |
|---|---|
| Homeowners 3—Special Form (HO 00 03 05 11) and Personal Umbrella<br><br>Personal Liability Policy (DL 24 01 07 14) | "We may investigate and settle any claim or suit that we decide is appropriate." |
| Commercial General Liability Coverage Form (CG 00 02 04 13) | "We may, at our discretion, investigate any 'occurrence' and settle any claim or 'suit' that may result." |
| Business Auto Coverage Form (CA 00 01 10 13) | "We may investigate and settle any claim or 'suit' as we consider appropriate." |

[DA12780]

In the samples provided, the authority to investigate is phrased as a contractual right but not a duty to investigate ("We may investigate ..." or "We may, at our discretion, investigate ..."). However, state law typically imposes such a duty on the insurer, regardless of the terms of the policy. Policies also frequently require an insured to cooperate with the investigation.

## Reasonableness

An insurer must perform a reasonable investigation. If an investigation is not reasonable, denying a claim could result in an insurer being held liable for damages beyond a policy's limits. As an additional challenge for a claims representative, what may be reasonable with one claim may not be reasonable with another claim. However, generally, a claims representative should take these actions:

- Take into account all facts in the insurer's claims file
- Check facts provided by an insured through an independent source prior to rejecting his or her position

A court, for example, would likely find that an insurer failed to perform a reasonable investigation if it denied a claim even though it had paid two similar claims earlier to the same insured under the same policy and coverage.

The reasons the earlier claims were paid should be in the insurer's claims files. A reasonable investigation would include reviewing the earlier claims and determining whether a different reason prevented the current claim from being accepted.

A claims representative should also check the facts stated by an insured before rejecting them. A court would likely find an insurer's investigation unreasonable if it failed to confirm or deny an insured's version of an incident that resulted in injury to a third party. For example, Alex, a third party, may allege that Elijah, an insured, intentionally injured him—which, if true, would likely cause the claim to be denied. However, Elijah may assert that the injuries were accidental, in which case the claim would likely be covered. When two conflicting accounts are presented in this way, a claims representative may need to contact other witnesses as independent sources to confirm or deny the insured's version of the facts.

## Good Faith

**Good faith**, or considering the insured's interests as equal to the insurer's, relies on common sense and good judgment. Good-faith claims handling involves thorough investigation, documentation, evaluation, negotiation, communication, and pursuit of legal advice when appropriate. The insurer's management of the claims process is also important to good-faith claims handling.

Claims representatives should investigate claims thoroughly and make sure they have sufficient evidence of their good-faith efforts before concluding claims. That evidence is helpful in defending bad-faith lawsuits. In addition, claims representatives should seek legal advice when appropriate.

Digital claims files provide a way for claims representatives to have easy access to pertinent information, such as repair estimates, medical bills, photographs, and police reports. When a claims representative receives such information via an app, an email, or a text, it should immediately be included in the claims file. A digital claims process also allows for live updates to the insured about the status of the claim. For this reason, it is important that any information a claims representative enters is accurate. If an insured receives a text message notification that her damaged roof is being inspected by a claims representative on Monday yet does not hear the result of that inspection until Thursday, it leads to a negative customer experience and diminishes the efficiency of the digital process.

In a thorough investigation, the claims representative is on the alert for new information that may change the course of a claim. For example, a homeowner filed a claim for an injury to a visitor who fell on the homeowner's front step. This may appear to be a simple claim. However, a claims representative may discover from the homeowner's statement that the visitor was actually a resident of the household or was on the premises as a business customer. Either situation may exclude coverage under the homeowner's policy. Without

**Good faith**
The manner of handling claims that requires an insurer to give consideration to the insured's interests that is at least equal to the consideration it gives its own interests.

the additional investigation, the claims representative may have paid a claim that was not covered by the policy.

A claims investigation should never be biased, meaning there should be no predisposition to find a particular outcome. Claims representatives should avoid asking misleading questions that slant the answers to a particular outcome, such as "The light was red when you saw it, wasn't it?" In addition, claims representatives should work with service providers that are unbiased and have no conflict of interest. Courts and juries may not look sympathetically on medical providers or repair facilities that always favor insurers. Investigations should seek to discover the facts and consider all aspects of the claims so that decisions are impartial and fair.

## Promptness

An investigation must be timely. An insured who makes a claim expects prompt contact from the claims representative. Most insurers have guidelines requiring the claims representative to contact the insured and/or claimant within a specific period, such as twenty-four hours after submission. Such timely contact benefits the insurer these ways:

- All parties are more likely to remember details of the loss accurately. Memory fades over time; therefore, claims representatives are more likely to get complete, accurate information from insureds and claimants if they contact them quickly.

- Parties are more likely to share information if contacted soon after an incident; prompt contact assures insureds and claimants that their claims are important and makes them less likely to accept the advice of others who may encourage them to retain a lawyer or pursue unnecessary litigation.

By automating parts of the claims process, artificial intelligence and block-chain technology can further reduce response lag times. For example, using an app, a customer can submit a claim without ever speaking to a claims representative. This is particularly relevant in the auto insurance industry and allows for insurers to quickly assist their insureds. Taking things even further, connected cars could use telematics and blockchain technology to trigger first notice of loss reports for accidents without the insured having to contact the insurer at all.

Claims representatives should always remember that unnecessary delays in resolving a claim may cause an insured to incur additional, avoidable damages. An investigation should continue only as long as new, relevant facts develop or become available. Claims representatives should obtain the information and documentation necessary to determine liability and damages and should make decisions once they believe they have sufficient information.

# Privacy Issues

Because claims representatives handle highly sensitive information, they need to be aware of privacy issues. Many privacy issues are regulated by law, and insurers should also adopt privacy best practices to protect themselves and their insureds.

State laws that apply to licensing, unfair trade practices, unfair claim settlement practices, and privacy are in place to protect the public. Federal statutes, also designed to ensure the privacy of confidential information, include the **Health Insurance Portability and Accountability Act (HIPAA)**; the Gramm-Leach-Bliley Act, which requires financial institutions (including insurers) to explain information-sharing practices and protect sensitive data; the **Sarbanes-Oxley Act of 2002**; and the Fair Credit Reporting Act. See the exhibit "GDRP Compliance."

**Health Insurance Portability and Accountability Act (HIPAA)**

Federal legislation establishing standards for health insurance information exchanges and health coverage protection when jobs are lost or changed.

**Sarbanes-Oxley Act of 2002**

A federal statutory law governing corporate directors in the areas of investor protection, internal controls, and penalties, both civil and criminal.

---

### GDRP Compliance

As awareness of cyber risk increases, new regulations have been put into place, such as the European Union's (EU's) General Data Protection Regulation (GDPR), which is intended to give consumers control over their personal data. While this regulation applies to countries in the EU, United States organizations that conduct business with European countries, including insurers, must also comply with it. Unlike many other privacy regulations, the GDPR charges both controllers (entities deciding what to do with personal data) and processors (entities collecting, storing, and/or using the personal data but not deciding how it is used) with protecting data.

Most insurers are controllers that sometimes rely on processors handling insureds' data. Noncompliance with GDPR can have serious results, with high fines for organizations and compensation for victims.

[DA12779]

---

### *Apply Your Knowledge*

Karen has been with the same insurer for her personal auto coverage for twenty years. In that time, she has been at fault in two car accidents that resulted in significant damage to Karen's car. Both times, Karen called to report the claim, and both times her damage was covered by the policy. Karen has been pleased to be with the same insurer for so long and has always paid her premium on time.

Karen is driving home from work when she is in a third accident for which she is at fault. Karen is able to drive her damaged car home and decides to submit a claim through her insurer's new app. She receives an automatic notification that her claim has been received. After getting her car repaired and submitting all the requested documentation, Karen receives notice through the app that her claim has been denied without any further explanation.

Which one of the following is correct regarding how Karen's claim was handled?

a.   The claims handling investigation was not reasonable.

b.   The claims handling experience was not prompt.

c.   The claims handling investigation violated Karen's privacy.

d.   The claims handling was conducted in good faith.

*Feedback: a.* Karen's claim was not handled reasonably because the insurer denied her auto damage claim without citing a reason, even though it had previously paid two similar claims under the same policy and coverage. Karen did receive prompt notification that her claim had been received, but her experience reflects poorly on the insurer's new automated claims process. There is no indication that Karen's privacy or data was compromised; however, her investigation may not have been handled in good faith. Karen could allege bad faith because no reason was given for her claim denial.

# INSURED'S DUTY TO COOPERATE

Many claims representatives will face claims in which an insured does not fully cooperate. To successfully resolve these claims, a representative should understand the insured's contractual duties and be familiar with tools that can help enlist an insured's cooperation.

The terms of most insurance policies make it clear that the insured has a duty to cooperate in the investigation, settlement, and/or defense of a claim under the policy. See the exhibit "Samples of Policy Language Requiring Insured's Cooperation in Investigation."

### Samples of Policy Language Requiring Insured's Cooperation in Investigation

| Insurance Services Office, Inc. Policy | Policy Language |
| --- | --- |
| Personal Auto (PP 00 01 09 18) and Homeowners 3—Special Form (HO 00 03 05 11) | "Cooperate with us in the investigation, settlement or defense of any claim or suit." |
| Commercial General Liability Coverage Form (CG 00 02 04 13) and Business Auto Coverage Form (CA 00 01 10 13) | "Cooperate with us in the investigation or settlement of the claim or defense against the 'suit'." |

[DA12781]

The insured's duty to cooperate involves several key aspects, including compliance with an insurer's reasonable request, production of documents and evidence, examination under oath or other types of statements, participation in an independent medical examination, and acceptance of consequences for noncooperation.

## Compliance With a Reasonable Request

The insured is contractually required to cooperate in a claims investigation and to respond to reasonable requests. Several questions can be used to determine whether a request for information is reasonable:

- Is the information requested relevant to the claim?
- Is the request specific and clear?
- Is the insured given an ample opportunity to comply?
- Is the insured able to provide at least some of the information requested?

In certain claims, such as when an insurer suspects fraud, the insurer may appear to ask for irrelevant information. For example, an insured named Catherine reports that her truck has been stolen and recovered, but indicators suggest she may have committed claims fraud.

The insurer asks Catherine to provide her income tax returns, bank records, and cell phone records, accordingly. Catherine thinks these requests are irrelevant and refuses the insurer's multiple requests for this information. The insurer, in turn, denies the claim, and Catherine sues for breach of contract and bad faith. The insurer, however, will likely win the case once it presents the circumstances: that the request for information was indeed relevant, that Catherine was provided with a reasonable opportunity to respond, and that Catherine did not comply with the request.

## Production of Documents and Evidence

Insurance policies that provide coverage for an insured's property—for example, a homeowners policy—typically allow the insurer to review and copy the insured's books and records.

An insured has a "reasonable amount of time" to comply with the insurer's request for documentation. This standard may depend on the circumstances of the insured after the loss. A fire loss, for instance, may destroy the insured's tax returns that an insurer wants to see.

Some delays are considered unreasonable no matter what the circumstances. For example, an insured could not reasonably ignore an insurer's multiple requests for information only to file suit against the insurer and then provide the requested information during litigation.

While an insurer is entitled access to adequate records to settle a claim, it is not allowed unlimited access to an insured's records. All requests must be reasonable and specific.

# Examination Under Oath and Other Types of Statements

**Examination under oath (EUO)**

A statement given by a person who has sworn to tell the truth before an officer of the court.

Anyone seeking benefits under an insurance policy must be willing to answer the insurer's questions. An **examination under oath (EUO)** is a valuable tool to use when an insured is suspected of submitting a fraudulent claim. During an EUO, the insured or claimant is sworn in under oath to give truthful answers as recorded by a court reporter. An attorney hired by the insurer usually asks questions of the insured, who may or may not be represented by an attorney.

**Deposition**

A pretrial discovery tool involving oral examination of a witness under oath to produce a written verbatim record.

An EUO is similar to a **deposition**. There are, however, two distinct differences between them. First, an EUO may be demanded by an insurer before litigation has begun. Second, an insurer may demand that an EUO be done more than once. (This is rare, generally only occurring if the insured produces information that contradicts the insured's prior position.)

**Proof of loss**

A statement of facts about a loss for which the insured is making a claim.

In property claims, most claims representatives prefer asking the insured to submit a sworn **proof of loss** before asking for an EUO. A proof of loss commits the insured under oath to a specific set of facts, including these:

- Amount of loss
- Records supporting the amount of loss
- Date and cause of loss
- Person asserting a claim under the policy and an interest in the property that was damaged or stolen
- Records of a governmental investigation, such as a police or fire marshal's report

---

### *Apply Your Knowledge*

Gabriela files a claim with her personal auto insurer for damage to her car that occurred when she skidded off a road in a snowstorm and ran into a tree. Maria, a new claims representative, is assigned to the claim. Maria takes Gabriela's statement about the accident and asks her for a repair estimate, a police report, and bank statements for the past five years. Gabriela says she is not sure how quickly she can provide her bank statements and that, furthermore, she does not think Maria should request them. Maria tells Gabriela that she needs to rule out any chance of fraud, so she must have them. Which one of the following statements about Gabriela's duty to cooperate with Maria's request is correct?

a.   If Gabriela does not provide her bank statements to Maria and the insurer denies the claim for that reason, a court will likely rule in the insurer's favor.

b.   Gabriela has a duty to provide any information Maria asks for during the claims handling process.

c.   Maria's request for Gabriela to provide her past five years of bank statements is not reasonable or relevant, and a court will likely rule in Gabriela's favor if the insurer denies the claim.

*Feedback: c.* Maria's request for Gabriela to provide her past five years of bank statements is not reasonable or relevant. Provided that Gabriela submits a repair estimate and police report, and that there are no other fraud indicators, the insurer would not have a case for denying the claim because Gabriela failed to provide her bank statements.

# Independent Medical Examination

Claims representatives rely on medical records to evaluate bodily injury damages. If a medical dispute arises, a claims representative may ask a doctor to perform an **independent medical examination (IME)** to resolve the dispute and determine the amount of damages.

A medical dispute might involve issues such as these:

- Whether the insured will remain totally disabled
- Whether tests that would objectively validate the insured's claims of pain should be performed
- Whether the insured's progress or lack thereof with current treatment should be assessed and whether potential treatment alternatives should be reviewed

Many policies allow an insurer to request that an injured insured submit to an in-person examination. Because such an exam is listed as a policy condition, a claims representative may believe he or she can demand that an insured submit to one. However, because an IME involves in-person physical contact with a doctor chosen by the insurer, an insured may not be required to submit to it. Accordingly, caution should be used in making IME requests.

Additionally, an IME is not required to deny coverage; a doctor's review of the insured's medical records may be sufficient for a denial. A claims representative should be careful to not provide his or her opinion of the insured's medical condition and rely solely on a medical specialist.

**Independent medical examination (IME)**

A direct intervention technique that includes a brief review of the patient's history and treatment and a physical examination of the patient. Insurers use this technique in disputed claims for determining causation, current physical impairment, and the need for present or future treatment.

## Consequences of Noncooperation

An insured that makes a claim typically has firsthand knowledge of that claim. And because knowledge must be shared with the insurer, most policies require the insured to cooperate in the insurer's investigation and defense of the claim. For example, the Insurance Services Office, Inc., Personal Auto Policy states that the insurer does not have a duty to provide coverage if the insured's failure to cooperate in the investigation, settlement, or defense of a claim or suit is prejudicial to the insurer.[1]

When determining whether an insured has forfeited the right to coverage for failure to cooperate, courts often assess whether certain factors, such as these, apply:

- The insured has not cooperated at all or only partially.
- The insurer's investigation and/or defense has been compromised.
- The insurer's requests for cooperation were reasonable.

Let's take a look at how these factors could affect a claim. For example, Brett, an insured, suffered a fire loss at his home, and the fire investigator confirmed arson. The claims representative wants to determine whether Brett was involved in the arson.

In an EUO, the insurer asks Brett to provide his income tax returns to determine whether he had a financial motive to commit arson. Brett refuses to provide these records, a reaction a court will likely find unreasonable. Accordingly, the court will likely determine that the insurer should be allowed to deny coverage.

## GENERAL INVESTIGATIVE TOOLS

Conducting a claims investigation is a lot like solving a mystery. Working with unproven evidence about a loss and around a tight timeline for resolution, claims investigators rely on various tools to make crucial determinations about what actually happened, how the loss occurred, whether the relevant policy applies, and the monetary value of the loss.

Here are some of the tools that help claims investigators make such determinations in virtually any claims investigation:

- Loss notice forms
- Policy information
- Statements
- Diagrams, photos, and videos
- Experts
- Records and reports
- Industry databases

- Social networking sites
- Other investigative tools

## Loss Notice Forms

Generally, losses are reported to insurers on loss notice forms, such as those issued by the Association for Cooperative Operations Research and Development (ACORD). A loss notice form conveys essential information about the insured, the claimant, the type of injury or property damage, and the circumstances of the loss.

But losses aren't always reported on loss notice forms. An insurer may receive loss reports through phone calls, emails, loss notification apps, legal filings, and other means. These methods may not be as comprehensive as a formal loss notice, though, and require the claims representative to gather basic facts just to start the investigation. See the exhibit "The Loss Notice Form and the Investigation Plan."

---

### The Loss Notice Form and the Investigation Plan

- Severity of the accident—Losses that can be immediately recognized as severe (fatal injuries, property losses described as a total loss or severe) indicate the need for a very thorough investigation and usually an investigator to visit and photograph the accident scene.

- Questionable cause of loss—Property loss after a hurricane requires investigation into whether the damage was caused by wind or flood; an unwitnessed slip or fall usually indicates a need for additional investigation.

- Third-party involvement—An auto accident involving a collision with another vehicle or a workplace injury involving a third party usually requires additional investigation.

- Minor losses—Minor auto damage claims, record-only minor workers compensation injuries, and minor property losses may not require additional investigation beyond the policy review. Investigative resources should be allocated where they have the greatest potential to produce results.

---

[DA06800]

## Policy Information

Another useful source of investigative information is the policy itself, which should be explicitly reviewed when examining a claim—even if the claim seems simple and routine. If the handling of a claim is challenged in court, a claims representative's admission that he or she relied on memory to determine policy coverage or exclusions could seriously harm an insurer's defense. Plus, reviewing the policy may reveal endorsements that change the coverage—for example, by adding or deleting locations or changing limits.

A preliminary review of the policy should focus on these questions:

* Who is covered?
* What is covered?
* When is coverage in effect?
* What causes of loss are covered?
* What is excluded?

After gathering information about the loss from the first report and coverage information from the policy review, the claims representative can either conclude the investigation (for minor claims) or continue it, using one or more additional investigative tools. See the exhibit "The Importance of Policy Reviews in Claims Investigations: An Example."

---

### The Importance of Policy Reviews in Claims Investigations: An Example

This example illustrates how a review of the policy and underwriting file can provide information that is not initially significant but becomes important later in the investigation.

ABC Insurance Company issues a property policy to Acme Warehouse. Several months after the policy takes force, Acme Warehouse burns to the ground. The claims representative reviews the policy and learns that in its policy application, Acme stated that it stores only household goods. Several weeks later, the fire investigation indicates that the fire and extensive damage to the building resulted from the storage of a large amount of highly combustible and unstable chemicals used in a special manufacturing process. The claims representative realizes, based on the application, that more investigation into the loss and the policy is needed because of a potential increase in hazard from the storage of the chemical. While the nature of the insured's business initially did not seem to be an issue, it later became important in determining coverage.

---

[DA06801]

## Statements

Depending on the type of loss, statements from the insured, the claimant, witnesses, and other interested parties, such as an injured worker's supervisor, may prove valuable. Statements are best taken shortly after the loss occurs so that time does not diminish the person's memory of the event.

## Diagrams, Photos, and Videos

Diagrams, photos, and videos can illustrate what the loss scene looked like, how an accident happened, and the extent of the property damage and bodily injuries. These visual exhibits may be gathered by the claims representative, a field adjuster, or an investigator. In cases where the site of a loss is inaccessible or hazardous, they may instead be recorded by aerial drones or remotely controlled robotic sensors.

## Experts

During the claims investigation, an expert may be needed to evaluate the cause or value of a loss, investigate the possibility of fraud committed by an insured or a third-party claimant, or provide legal advice. Many insurers employ a panel of experts who are impartial, respected in their fields, and credible. Accordingly, when needs arise for field experts, the claims representative can select a panel member who best fits the investigation's needs.

## Records and Reports

Records and reports can verify the facts of an accident or the nature and extent of damage or injury, as well as reveal new information. Certain records and reports are common. For example, police and fire reports can be found in both property and liability claims, including some workers compensation claims. Workers compensation claims and liability claims that deal with bodily injury can include medical reports and records, as well as reports that verify income.

Other types of records and reports are exclusive to one type of claim. For example, motor vehicle title and registration records are used to verify the existence and ownership of vehicles in auto claims. In large property claims, claims representatives may request income tax records, inventory records, and bank records from the insured to verify the value of inventory involved in a claim.

## Industry Databases

Determining whether a claim is fraudulent may be difficult when relying only on the facts associated with the claim itself. For example, a claims representative may not realize that someone filing a claim for damages from a seemingly legitimate car accident has filed suspiciously similar claims in the past. An industry database, however, could reveal such patterns, putting the investigation in a different context.

Industry databases, such as ISO ClaimSearch, pool claims information from insurers, third-party administrators (TPAs), and industry organizations. Claims representatives can search a database to detect fraud or find data on property, liability, auto, and workers compensation claims.

## Social Networking Sites

Social networking sites can be sources of valuable information about claimants and other parties to a loss. For example, a claimant alleging an immobilizing injury may post pictures that clearly contradict this on Facebook.

Various federal and state privacy laws regulate permissible conduct in investigations of social networking sites. Additionally, rules of evidence and ethical concerns surround reviewing individuals' social networking posts.

## Other Investigative Tools

Insurers and TPAs provide other investigative tools to their claims representatives to ensure consistent quality in claims handling. These tools can be fairly simple, such as programs that use room dimensions to calculate the amount of paint needed to repaint the walls. Others can be complex, such as expert injury evaluation tools that give the claims representative the benefit of many years' worth of historical data for use in evaluating an injury claim.

# CONFIRMING THE LOSS NOTICE INFORMATION WITH THE POLICY

The loss notice provides essential information about a claim. Matching the information on the loss notice to the relevant policy is the first step in confirming coverage.

An insurance claim is typically initiated when the insurer receives notification of a loss, which can come in several forms, ranging from a phone call to a transmission from an auto's telematics device.

**First notice of loss (FNOL)**

The initial report notifying the insurer of a claim.

An internal claims handler often transfers the information to the insurer's standard **first notice of loss (FNOL)** form, but sometimes the insured fills out the FNOL. However the loss notice form is completed, it will become the basis for the claim investigation. See the exhibit "Property Loss Notice."

If information obtained later contradicts statements on the loss notice form, additional investigation will be needed. Claims representatives should become familiar with the loss notice forms their insurer uses. ACORD forms are the industry's standard loss notice forms. For each line of insurance, claims information is entered into one of several fields, which include these:

- Agency
- Insured
- Loss or occurrence
- Policy information and preparer

## Agency

ACORD loss notice forms for property, auto, and general liability insurance contain a field at the top of the form for information about the insurance

# Property Loss Notice

**ACORD®**

## PROPERTY LOSS NOTICE

DATE (MM/DD/YYYY)

| AGENCY | INSURED LOCATION CODE | DATE OF LOSS AND TIME | AM |
|---|---|---|---|
| | | | PM |

### PROPERTY / HOME POLICY

| CARRIER | NAIC CODE |
|---|---|

| CONTACT NAME: | POLICY NUMBER | LINE OF BUSINESS |
|---|---|---|

PHONE (A/C, No, Ext):

FAX (A/C, No):

### FLOOD POLICY

E-MAIL ADDRESS:

| CARRIER | NAIC CODE |
|---|---|

CODE:    SUBCODE:

| POLICY NUMBER | |
|---|---|

AGENCY CUSTOMER ID:

### WIND POLICY

| CARRIER | NAIC CODE |
|---|---|

| POLICY NUMBER | |
|---|---|

## INSURED

| NAME OF INSURED (First, Middle, Last) | INSURED'S MAILING ADDRESS |
|---|---|

| DATE OF BIRTH | FEIN (if applicable) | MARITAL STATUS / CIVIL UNION (if applicable) |
|---|---|---|

| PRIMARY PHONE # | ☐ HOME ☐ BUS ☐ CELL | SECONDARY PHONE # | ☐ HOME ☐ BUS ☐ CELL | PRIMARY E-MAIL ADDRESS: |
|---|---|---|---|---|
| | | | | SECONDARY E-MAIL ADDRESS: |

| NAME OF SPOUSE (First, Middle, Last) (if applicable) | SPOUSE'S MAILING ADDRESS (if applicable) |
|---|---|

| DATE OF BIRTH | FEIN (if applicable) | MARITAL STATUS / CIVIL UNION (if applicable) |
|---|---|---|

| PRIMARY PHONE # | ☐ HOME ☐ BUS ☐ CELL | SECONDARY PHONE # | ☐ HOME ☐ BUS ☐ CELL | PRIMARY E-MAIL ADDRESS: |
|---|---|---|---|---|
| | | | | SECONDARY E-MAIL ADDRESS: |

## CONTACT        ☐ CONTACT INSURED

| NAME OF CONTACT (First, Middle, Last) | CONTACT'S MAILING ADDRESS |
|---|---|

| PRIMARY PHONE # | ☐ HOME ☐ BUS ☐ CELL | SECONDARY PHONE # | ☐ HOME ☐ BUS ☐ CELL |
|---|---|---|---|

| WHEN TO CONTACT | PRIMARY E-MAIL ADDRESS: |
|---|---|
| | SECONDARY E-MAIL ADDRESS: |

## LOSS

| LOCATION OF LOSS | POLICE OR FIRE DEPARTMENT CONTACTED |
|---|---|
| STREET: | |
| CITY, STATE, ZIP: | REPORT NUMBER |
| COUNTRY: | |

DESCRIBE LOCATION OF LOSS IF NOT AT SPECIFIC STREET ADDRESS:

| KIND OF LOSS | ☐ FIRE | ☐ LIGHTNING | ☐ FLOOD | | PROBABLE AMOUNT ENTIRE LOSS |
|---|---|---|---|---|---|
| | ☐ THEFT | ☐ HAIL | ☐ WIND | | |

DESCRIPTION OF LOSS & DAMAGE (ACORD 101, Additional Remarks Schedule, may be attached if more space is required)

| REPORTED BY | REPORTED TO |
|---|---|

ACORD 1 (2016/10)                     Page 1 of 3          © 1988-2016 ACORD CORPORATION.  All rights reserved.
The ACORD name and logo are registered marks of ACORD

agency. If no agency information is provided, the claims representative should review the policy to identify the agent or broker who submitted the application. This field does not apply to insurers that are direct writers.

The claims representative should investigate any discrepancy between the agency information provided on the loss notice form and the producer who submitted the application.

## Insured

It is essential for the claims representative to confirm that the insured is correctly listed on any notice of loss. If the name of the insured does not match that on the policy, a thorough investigation must be conducted to determine why.

Although an insured may move or change phone numbers without notifying the insurer, a claims representative must investigate any discrepancies between the address and phone number on the loss notice form and those on the policy. The insured can be questioned about other information from the insurance application to verify that he or she is the same person who filed the claim.

If there is a significant mismatch between the insured information on the loss notice form and in the application or policy that it cannot be easily resolved, the insurer may require an examination under oath, in which the insured provides documentation of his or her identity.

## Loss or Occurrence

Information about the loss or occurrence on the loss notice form is the starting point for the claim investigation. Documentation should be obtained to confirm the information provided during the course of the investigation.

A loss notice may be missing information that an insured omitted or discovered after completing the loss notice. During the claims representative's first contact with the insured, it is important to fill in any such missing information. For example, the insured may now have a copy of the police report, or a witness may have been identified.

## Policy Information and Preparer

All relevant policy information needs to be verified. For example, the policy number should be confirmed because a mistake could easily be made when entering it on the loss notice form. At the same time that the policy number is verified, the claims representative should also confirm the policy effective date to determine whether the loss or occurrence took place within the policy period.

If the person who prepares the loss notice form is not the insured or producer, the relationship of the preparer to the insured should be determined. Although a family member or friend may prepare a loss notice for someone who needs assistance, it is important to follow up directly with the insured to verify the accuracy of the loss notice.

# SUMMARY

Reserves can be established using any of these five methods: individual case method, roundtable method, average value method, formula method, and the expert system method. Regardless of the method chosen, reserving errors can result, and claims representatives should take all steps necessary to avoid these errors.

Using the individual case method of setting reserves, a claims representative analyzes the circumstances of the specific claim and determines, based on his or her experience with similar claims, how specific factors could potentially influence the claim settlement. Factors considered may include claimant profile, the nature and extent of the injury, special damages, claimant representation, liability factors, and miscellaneous factors.

An insurer has a duty to investigate a claim that has been reported. The investigation must be done with the insured's grant of authority and with reasonableness, good faith, promptness, and respect of privacy issues.

Claims representatives need to understand the important coverage aspects concerning the insured's duty to cooperate. Under most insurance policies, insureds' duty to cooperate requires them to comply with reasonable requests, produce documents and evidence, submit to examinations under oath and independent medical examinations, and suffer consequences for failure to cooperate.

If claims representatives wisely use all the tools at their disposal, they should be able to conduct thorough claims investigations. These investigations should produce sufficient information to make well-reasoned decisions about cause of loss, liability, and cost estimates of the loss.

It is important for claims representatives to become familiar with the loss notice forms used to report claims for any line of insurance that they manage. Verifying the information provided on the loss notice form is the essential first step of a coverage investigation.

# ASSIGNMENT NOTE

1. Form PP 00 01 09 18, copyright Insurance Services Office, Inc., 2017.

# Segment B

# Direct Your Learning ▶▶

# Documenting Claims

## Educational Objectives

After learning the content of this assignment, you should be able to:

▷ Demonstrate the importance of these types of representational documentation and how they are useful in claims investigations:

- Photos
- Videos
- Maps
- Diagrams

▷ Describe the following considerations related to spoliation of evidence:

- The insurer's obligation to preserve evidence
- What constitutes spoliation of evidence
- Available defenses to a spoliation claim
- Remedies in a spoliation claim

▷ Compare the advantages and disadvantages of audio, written, and video statements in documenting claims.

▷ Explain the following regarding sworn statements:

- Why they are used
- What forms they take
- How they are obtained
- When and how they are used

▷ Given a claim, determine what statutory reporting must be made and what specialty reporting would be useful.

▷ Illustrate techniques or actions that inside and outside claims representatives use to ensure their personal safety when handling claims.

# Documenting Claims

## REPRESENTATIONAL DOCUMENTATION

When investigating a claim, a claims representative has several options for documenting each type of evidence in the claim file. Photographs, videos, maps, and diagrams are all useful means of documenting evidence, but for different reasons.

In property-casualty insurance, nearly every type of loss produces physical evidence that must be preserved or documented in the claim file. However, not all physical evidence can be directly preserved. For example, skid marks at an auto accident scene will be worn away over time, and the accident scene itself—the configuration of the streets, traffic signals, and surrounding buildings and vegetation—can change.

Representational documentation, such as photographs, videos, maps, and diagrams, can preserve such evidence and illustrate what a loss scene looked like, how an accident happened, and the extent of any property damage or bodily injuries. For example, in a claim resulting from a collision of two vehicles that damaged both vehicles and injured both drivers, the claim file might include photos of the accident scene, the vehicles, and possibly the drivers' injuries; video of any obstructed views the drivers may have had at the intersection; a diagram indicating how the accident occurred; and a map or drone footage of the intersection showing traffic flows.

## Photographs

Photographs may be used in a claim file for two different purposes, serving to document either a point relevant to the event that gave rise to the claim or an investigative technique. For example, a claims representative might include photos of the process of packaging a key piece of evidence to indicate that it was not further damaged when it was unpacked. Occasionally, photos can also provide evidence of ownership, such as a photo of the insured wearing a fur coat that has since been reported stolen or a photo of the dust ring around the spot where a now-missing television sat.

Photos in auto collision claim files might include images of the vehicles involved (both damaged and undamaged parts); the location where the collision occurred, from all directions; any skid marks on the road surface; shrubbery that may have obstructed the insured's view of an intersection; traffic signals; buildings and other identifying landmarks near the incident location; points of contact (not just on the vehicles but also on other objects, such as gouges in the road and damage to other vehicles or buildings); and the vehicles' final resting places. In some cases, aerial photos of the scene taken by drones may provide useful information.

Photos can also help in other types of liability claims. For example, if a claimant alleges injuries suffered in a fall in a darkened hallway, photos of the hallway, the location of any lights, the presence of handrails, and the condition of the floor may document evidence relevant to the claim.

To avoid the effects of changing conditions, claims representatives should arrange for evidence at accident scenes to be photographed as soon as possible after an accident. Photos should be taken at about the same time of day that the accident occurred and in the same weather conditions to provide evidence about lighting and visibility.

A disadvantage of photos is that they can be misleading. Camera angles can distort apparent distances or the proximity of one object to another. Lighting can cast shadows or make an individual look malicious or less than honest. It has also become much easier to digitally manipulate photographs. Claims representatives should avoid any deliberate attempts to distort photos. Photos electronically marked with the date and time are preferable; if that is not possible, the claims representative should label each photo. Digital photos should always be saved in their original file format and should be stored as read-only files with limited access.

For more serious claims, photos should be taken by a professional photographer, an experienced investigator, or a person who has no involvement in the claim. Such a precaution will help avoid challenges on the basis of bias. However, anyone who takes photos at an accident scene should be prepared to testify as to the type of camera; film, if applicable; lens; camera settings; and prevailing weather conditions.

## Videos

Videos can be a powerful means of explaining how an event occurred (by recreating the event) or of documenting damage or injury. For example, claims representatives can use videos to show the extent of damage in a large warehouse fire. A soundtrack can explain the visual evidence as it is viewed.

Videos can also show that a claim may be exaggerated or fraudulent; for example, a claimant who is claiming total incapacity could be shown painting a house after he or she filed the claim. Such videos, however, must be made carefully so as not to invade the privacy of the claimant. The objective of an activity check is to obtain information about the claimant's injuries and current activities, and the taping must be confined to that subject. To be useful in court, the video must clearly identify the claimant as the person engaging in the activity. The person taking the video must be able to establish the date, time, and place of the activity. Claims representatives should hire only licensed, ethical investigators who would make a good impression on a jury.

Claims representatives and lawyers also increasingly record witness interviews and depositions. Recorded statements from parties to the claim at the loss scene could be useful. For example, a homeowner going through his storm-damaged house and describing the damaged and destroyed items can document the extent of the loss being claimed.

Claims representatives may be able to obtain videos of accidents and/or their aftermath from other sources, such as television stations or individuals who captured videos on their smartphones. If surveillance cameras are posted in the areas, they may have video images of the incident that would be helpful to the claims representative. Drones can also be used to obtain footage of the scene where a loss occurred, providing views of large areas and perspectives that might not otherwise be available.

## Maps

A map can be used to show the location of places that are relevant to the case. Depending on the situation, claims representatives may use official survey maps, road maps, or computer-generated street maps. Maps drawn to scale can indicate relevant distances, locations of landmarks, topographical features, and even GPS coordinates in case the specific location could affect the outcome of the claim (for instance, in a matter contingent on where an incident occurred in relation to state lines).

Maps should be prepared by professionally trained surveyors or engineers. If a map is introduced as evidence, the professional preparer may be called to testify about the method of measurement, the scale, and his or her qualifications. The claims representative, and possibly the defense attorney, should determine which issues the map will address—for example, those relating to causation, parties' conflicting contentions, and how topography and landscape features may have contributed to the accident. As with photos, a court will admit a map as evidence only when satisfied that it is a faithful representation of what it seeks to portray. Therefore, the claims representative should instruct the preparer as to what relevant information the map should convey.

## Diagrams

Diagrams included in a claim file can communicate or clarify the events that gave rise to a claim. A diagram of an auto accident scene, for example, may be far more succinct than a written report describing how the accident occurred.

A claims representative may also use diagrams in interviewing witnesses. Some witnesses may find it much easier to explain what happened when referring to a diagram or when drawing their own diagram.

In an auto accident investigation, diagrams may be included with the police report, or the claims representative may produce one. Such diagrams usually show the accident scene, including the streets, the direction of the vehicles before the accident, their position just before impact, and their position when they came to rest. The diagram might also show any possible obstructions to views; the grade of the street; and the location of traffic signals, skid marks, utility poles, and landmarks. Diagrams could also indicate camera angles for any photos taken. Because roadway layouts in accident scene diagrams on police reports are sometimes hastily drawn and imprecise, satellite imagery of the location, available online, may be used to verify their accuracy. See the exhibit "Diagram of Auto Accident."

## Diagram of Auto Accident

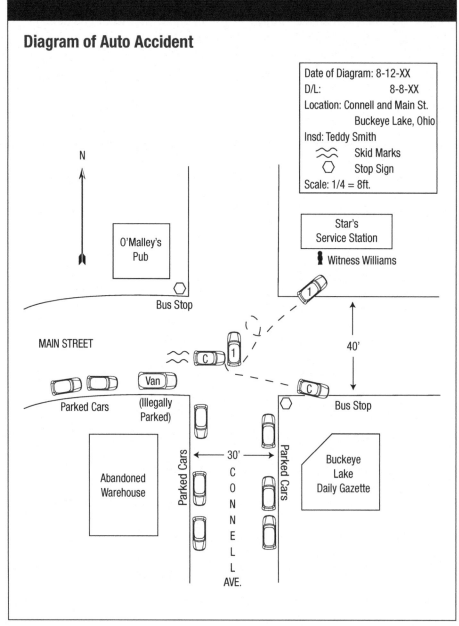

[DA04505]

Claims representatives often use accident investigation diagram templates as an aid to preparing diagrams, along with stencils of appropriate symbols. Software is also available for electronic diagramming, and some websites or mobile apps provide simple diagramming functions free of charge.

### Apply Your Knowledge

Linnea is a claims representative who was assigned a claim file regarding an auto accident. At the start of her investigation, she realizes it's important to capture a reliable representation of the conditions under which the accident occurred. What sort of photographic evidence should she consider for inclusion in the claim file?

*Feedback:* Linnea should aim to capture images of any vehicles involved in the accident, all angles of the location where the accident occurred, any skid marks on the road surface, shrubbery or signs that may have obstructed the insured's view of the road, nearby traffic signals, and buildings and other identifying landmarks near the incident location. Any points of contact—not just on the vehicles but also on other objects—should be photographed as well, along with the final resting places of any vehicles involved. In addition, she could try to obtain photos taken by a drone, to provide an overall view of the accident scene.

# SPOLIATION OF EVIDENCE

An insurer's failure to preserve evidence relating to potential litigation can adversely affect its position in lawsuits, lead to sanctions, and even be grounds for an independent lawsuit against the insurer.

Preservation of evidence is important for thorough claims investigation and to protect the interests of the insured and the insurer. Claims representatives should be aware of what evidence related to a loss should be preserved, and for how long, to avoid exposing the insurer to allegations of spoliation of evidence. Such allegations can delay claims resolution, complicate litigation, lead to court sanctions against the insurer, and influence jury verdicts.

Spoliation—the failure to preserve property for another's use in litigation—is often raised in relation to the destruction of documents or electronic files relevant to a court proceeding. Spoliation claims against insurers usually arise from the diminished chances of success of an insured, a third-party claimant, or another party in litigation as a result of the insurer's failure to preserve evidence from a claims investigation. Such cases may include subrogation proceedings or lawsuits that arise after a claim has been settled.

For example, after an auto accident liability claim is settled with the injured third party, an insurer sells the insured's auto for salvage. The insurer later decides to bring a subrogation claim against the auto manufacturer, alleging that the auto's brakes were defective. The manufacturer files a pre-trial motion to dismiss the case based on the insurer's spoliation of evidence necessary to the manufacturer's defense.

Similarly, the injured third party may consider suing the auto manufacturer for damages beyond what the insurance settlement covered. Because the insurer would not be a party to that lawsuit, the third party would likely address the spoliation allegation in an independent lawsuit against the insurer rather than through a pre-trial motion. In this case, the third party would charge that the unavailability of the evidence (the auto with defective brakes) compromises its ability to prove its case against the car manufacturer. Depending on the state, the court may allow the third party to consolidate the lawsuit against the manufacturer and the spoliation lawsuit into one case.

The law relating to spoliation continues to evolve. While recognizing an insurer's duty to preserve relevant evidence, courts differ on what evidence is considered relevant, how long it should be preserved, and to whom the duty is owed. Available defenses to a spoliation claim, as well as remedies and sanctions, can also vary depending on the facts of a case and the jurisdiction in which the claim is brought.

## The Insurer's Obligation to Preserve Evidence

An insurer has a duty to preserve relevant evidence in claims investigations. Without physical evidence of the cause of the loss, the chances of successfully defending an insured or pursuing a subrogation claim against a third party are significantly diminished.

Storage of physical evidence can be costly. Preservation of some evidence at a loss scene may be impractical or could even increase the amount of a claim by delaying an insured business's ability to resume operations. Insureds usually want to clear damage and rebuild, and businesses may need to put damaged machinery back into use.

How long evidence should be preserved depends, in part, on to whom the duty to preserve is owed. The insurer's duty extends to the parties in a claim but may also extend to others not involved in the claim, such as the car manufacturer in the previous example. The general rule is that the insurer's duty is to preserve evidence that is relevant to any contemplated litigation related to the claim. Some courts use terms such as "pending and future litigation," "reasonably foreseeable litigation," or "the potential for litigation."

For loss scenes that contain relevant evidence that cannot be preserved for an extensive period—for example, a fire scene at a home that the owners want to rebuild—insurers can take the precaution of identifying any foreseeable potential defendants in litigation arising from the event (such as manufacturers of products that may have caused the fire) and giving them an opportunity to view the loss scene. These parties should be notified as soon as possible after a claim is filed and invited to inspect the accident scene within a reasonable time (such as fourteen days).[1]

In spoliation cases, courts consider insurers to be professional litigants that should, therefore, be aware of the need to preserve evidence. As such, insurers may be held to a higher standard of care than parties who may be less familiar with litigation.

## What Constitutes Spoliation of Evidence

Spoliation claims are most often raised as a defense in court proceedings, although either party can raise such a claim. Such claims may be entered as motions submitted before or during trial for dismissal of the case or summary judgment, exclusion of evidence, specific jury instructions, or other sanctions against the alleged spoliator. Some jurisdictions allow separate causes of action in tort for spoliation.

The unavailability of evidence is not in itself sufficient to support a claim of spoliation. Although courts vary in the proof required in a successful spoliation claim, in general, they require proof that the evidence has been improperly lost or destroyed, that the alleged offender had ownership or control of the evidence, that the evidence is relevant or material to a claim in litigation, that the loss or destruction was the accused party's fault, and that the unavailability of the evidence is prejudicial to the other party.

Some states allow independent tort actions for spoliation only as an intentional tort; others allow claims based on negligent spoliation.

Courts generally agree that, for spoliation to apply, the evidence in question must be relevant and material to a case. In determining relevance, courts may analyze the extent to which the absence of the evidence prejudices the opposing party's case and the fault or degree of bad faith of the party responsible.

Several state courts have held that spoliation occurs when "crucial" evidence is destroyed or altered. Crucial evidence may include a product that malfunctioned and caused injury or a heater that exploded and caused extensive property damage.

At issue in some of these cases is how much of the evidence must be preserved—for example, whether it is sufficient to preserve a machine's component that caused damage or whether the entire machine must be preserved. In products liability cases, some courts have held that the entire product is crucial evidence. In some cases, an entire loss scene may be considered crucial evidence.

Because an insurer's determination of the cause of a loss may be contested in court, an insurer may face a spoliation claim if it has failed to preserve potential alternative causes of a loss. For example, an insurer's fire investigators may have identified a space heater as the cause of loss; however, a toaster oven in the same room may be a potential alternative cause of the fire. If the toaster oven has not been preserved, the heater manufacturer in a subrogation action may accuse the insurer of spoliation, alleging that its defense has been compromised by its inability to offer evidence that something other than the space heater may have started the fire.

An insurer's duty to preserve evidence does not extend to items that are not essential to proving a case. If a party can prove its case or defend itself without the evidence, a spoliation claim is not likely to prevail. See the exhibit "Examples of Spoliation Claims."

## Examples of Spoliation Claims

Here are some examples of spoliation claims:

- A fire inspector determines that a fire was started by an appliance in one corner of a room. The appliance and other items in that area were preserved. The extensive testing the insurer conducts causes it to fall to pieces and destroys some of its components. The appliance manufacturer, in a subrogation claim, raises a spoliation claim. The court determines that nondestructive testing could have been performed and rules that the results of the insurer's tests on the appliance are not admissible as evidence.

- A business destroys documents relevant to a court case a week before the court orders parties to the case not to destroy any documents. In defense of a spoliation motion, the business argues that the documents were destroyed in compliance with an established records retention policy. In general, courts are reluctant to permit this defense. Even when legal proceedings have not yet begun, a court may find that a business would have been aware of the pending case.

- After a woman is injured by a defective product in her home, she throws the product away. The product manufacturer, in a subsequent lawsuit, alleges spoliation. The court delivers an adverse inference instruction to the jury.

- Evidence in a products liability case is lost during shipping. The manufacturer, in defense of a spoliation claim, points out that it was not in possession of the evidence when it was lost. The court rejects the defense because the evidence was improperly packed and the shipment was not monitored.

- An injured employee sues his employer and its workers compensation carrier, alleging that the employer refurbished the machine that caused his injury, leaving him with no evidence on which to base a third-party lawsuit against the machine's manufacturer. The defendants state that workers compensation law, as the exclusive remedy for employee injury, precludes the lawsuit. The court rejects that defense.

[DA07294]

# Available Defenses to Spoliation

The party that claims spoliation bears the burden of proof. Available defenses, which vary according to the facts of the case and the jurisdiction in which the claim is brought, may include these:

- The evidence that has gone missing or has been destroyed is not relevant to the case or is not prejudicial to the other party's case—If the party alleging spoliation can successfully present its case or its defense without the missing evidence, the spoliation claim may be defeated.

- The evidence can be reconstructed—For example, copies of destroyed documents are available and can serve the same evidentiary purpose as the originals.

- The party claiming spoliation was given a reasonable opportunity to examine the evidence before it was lost or destroyed—Courts recognize that not all physical evidence or entire loss scenes can be preserved indefinitely. Whether or not the complaining party examined the evidence when it was available, the fact that it was given an opportunity may be a sufficient defense in some cases.

- Litigation was not contemplated when the evidence was destroyed—Courts generally rule that the mere fact that a loss or an injury has occurred is not sufficient to require the preservation of evidence for a potential lawsuit. Courts apply standards of reasonableness to determine whether litigation should have been contemplated or foreseeable.

- The evidence was destroyed in the regular course of business or for another valid reason—For example, a television station's practice of erasing digital videos after broadcast or an insured's clearing a fire scene in order to resume business operations may constitute valid defenses. This defense is not valid if, at the time of destruction of the evidence, a court order (called a litigation hold) was in effect prohibiting destruction of evidence in connection with the case.

- In a workers compensation case, a spoliation action in tort is precluded by the "exclusive remedy" rule—Workers compensation laws are designed to be the exclusive remedy for workplace injuries, precluding tort lawsuits. However, some courts have ruled that because a spoliation case does not relate to the injuries, the exclusive remedy rule does not apply.

# Remedies for Spoliation

Courts have imposed remedies or sanctions for spoliation to deter future spoliation, to place the risk of an erroneous judgment caused by the lack of evidence on the party who created the risk, or to restore an innocent party to the same position it would have been in had the evidence been available.

In court proceedings, the most severe sanction is dismissal of a case. If the nonspoliating party can prove that it cannot adequately defend itself without the evidence, the court may dismiss the case. Lesser remedies, such as exclusion of any evidence relating to the missing evidence, are designed to remove any unfair advantage the spoliator might gain from using the evidence. For example, a court may bar a plaintiff's expert witness from testifying about the evidence that is not available to the defendant.

Courts may also seek to eliminate a spoliator's unfair advantage with an "adverse inference" instruction to the jury. The jury is allowed to infer that, had the evidence been available, it would have been adverse to the spoliating party's interests. Such an inference may influence a jury to favor the opposing party.

Some courts impose sanctions only if the spoliation was intentional or in bad faith. Other courts impose less severe sanctions for negligent or innocent spoliation, depending on the degree of prejudice suffered by the nonspoliating party.

Courts may impose monetary sanctions on spoliating parties to cover the costs of investigating the spoliation charge, preparing and monitoring motions related to the claim, and the court's time and resources consumed by the claim. In rare cases, courts have imposed significant punitive fines.

In independent tort actions for spoliation, sanctions may include monetary damages. Federal law and a few states allow criminal charges for spoliation.

# TAKING STATEMENTS

Claims representatives interview witnesses, claimants, and insureds to obtain evidence during their claims investigations. To preserve the information gathered in these statements, claims representatives may record them.

Three types of statements are taken during claims investigations:

- Audio statements
- Written statements
- Video statements

Whichever kind of statement is used, effective questions are crucial to gathering the most complete and relevant information regarding a particular loss.

## Audio Statements

Audio statements, also known as recorded statements, can be taken in person or by telephone. The advantages of audio statements for claims representatives include saving time and having an account of the loss in the interviewee's own words. Also, audio statements allow the interviewer to ask additional questions to clarify or expand on information provided by the interviewee.

In some cases, an attorney may agree to an audio statement only if the claims representative will waive the right to a later deposition of the interviewee.

It is almost never advisable to waive the right to a subsequent deposition in exchange for an audio statement. If an interviewee is represented by an attorney, it may be wise for the claims representative to consult with defense counsel prior to taking a statement.

Before the start of an audio statement, the claims representative should ensure that the recording equipment is working. He or she should also spend some time making the subject of the interview comfortable with the process.

The audio statement should begin with the interviewee's acknowledgment that the statement is being recorded and that he or she has granted permission for the recording. The statement should conclude with the claims representative asking the interviewee whether he or she gave permission for the statement to be recorded and to verify that the facts are true to the best of the interviewee's knowledge.

Any interruptions that occur should be acknowledged in the recording, and the recorder should be turned off for the duration of the interruption. For example, the claims representative could state that the recording is being interrupted while the interviewee answers the door, noting the time, and then state for the record the time that the interview is resuming.

Audio statements are usually summarized in the claim file, and many insurers have templates to use for these summaries. If the interviewee requests a copy, or if the statement will be used in legal proceedings, the audio statement can be transcribed.

## Written Statements

A written statement may be either a free-flowing description of events by an interviewee or, more commonly, an interviewee's answers to questions on a form provided by the insurer. If the interviewee is represented by an attorney, the attorney may insist on a written, rather than an audio, statement so that he or she can review it before submission.

Written statements should contain signed consent from the interviewee, in addition to the interviewee's signature on each page. If an attorney is present, the attorney should also sign a statement indicating that he or she was present, has read the statement, and verifies that it accurately reflects the interview. A copy of the statement should be provided to the interviewee, and any corrections within it should be initialed by the interviewee. See the exhibit "Advantages and Disadvantages of Audio Statements as Compared to Written Statements."

Written statements are usually more easily admitted into evidence in legal proceedings than audio statements. As long as a statement is signed by the interviewee, it is typically admissible. Audio statements, in comparison, usually require testimony that the recording device was working properly and that no edits or changes were made to the recording before the statements can be admitted as evidence.

### Advantages and Disadvantages of Audio Statements as Compared to Written Statements

**Audio Statements**

**Advantages**

- Recording is less time consuming.
- The interviewee can be observed (if the interview is in person).
- Exact wording is recorded.
- Illegible handwriting is not an issue.
- Telephone or video call interviews are an option, saving additional time.
- Recorded statements can be transcribed if written record is needed.

**Disadvantages**

- Equipment may fail.
- Recordings must be stored (electronically or physically).
- Transcription adds to costs.
- Transcript must be reviewed for accuracy.

**Written Statements**

**Advantages**

- Interviewees may be less anxious.
- Claims representative has more control.
- Transcription is not required.
- Interviewee's signature may be easier to obtain (because a written document exists).

**Disadvantages**

- Handwriting may be illegible.
- Producing a written statement takes more time.
- Interviewees may claim they were misquoted.
- Paraphrasing may lead to challenges of inaccuracy.

Adapted from "Effective Statements: A One-Day Course to Improve Investigative Interviewing" by Claims Training Services, 1999, pp. 58–59, 69–70. [DA02436]

## Video Statements

When it is feasible to do so, taking a video statement adds significantly to the interview by revealing physical characteristics of the interviewee, including visible injuries, body language, and expressions. If a video statement is planned, the claims representative should consult with an attorney regarding the rules of the relevant jurisdiction for the admissibility of video statements.

The procedures for taking a video statement, other than the operation of the equipment, are the same as those for an audio statement. The statement should open and end with acknowledgment that it is being videotaped and should include permission from the interviewee for this type of recording.

# Statement Content

Effective statements exhibit these qualities:

- Coherence—The statement follows a logical sequence.
- Completeness—The statement is thorough.
- Objectivity—The statement contains facts relevant to the loss expressed in the interviewee's own words.

With few exceptions, the content of a statement should be the same whether it is written or recorded and should generally follow a pattern to ensure that all relevant information is included. The seven-part method can be a good guide for this. See the exhibit "Seven-Part Method."

---

### Seven-Part Method

1. Permission and introduction—date, time, and location of the interview, names of the parties involved in the interview, and an affirmation from the interviewee that the interview is given with permission

2. Identification—identifying information about the person being interviewed, such as name, address, phone number, Social Security number, and driver's license number

3. Setting—answers to questions such as who was involved in the loss, what was involved in the loss, when the loss occurred, where the loss occurred, and why the loss occurred

4. Incident—a step-by-step description of how the loss occurred

5. Post incident injuries/damages—description of the property damage and bodily injuries to individuals

6. Miscellaneous—any information the interviewee wants to add

7. Conclusion—reaffirmation that the statement was taken with permission

Adapted from Effective Statements: A One-Day Course to Improve Investigative Interviewing (Jackson, N.J.: Claims Training Services, 1999), p. 45. [DA02431]

---

The body of a statement should be adapted for different types of losses and should contain information specific to each type of loss. Whether the statement is written or recorded, the claims representative should have an outline of the questions that need to be asked. For this purpose, many insurers have statement guides.

The questions that a claims representative asks should reflect the specifics of the claim. For example, questions for an auto accident will differ from those for a slip-and-fall claim, and questions for an insured may be different from those for a claimant or witness. Additionally, the investigation could uncover facts or concerns that the claims representative will need to clarify in the statement.

## Types of Questions Used in Statements

Claims representatives should develop statement-taking skills that encourage cooperation and elicit facts about the loss. A key aspect of producing effective statements is an understanding of three different types of questions: direct, open-ended, and leading.

**Direct question**

A question that seeks specific information and that can often be answered with a short phrase or a yes or no response.

**Open-ended question**

A question that seeks an answer that explains or elaborates on the circumstances under consideration.

**Direct questions** specifically and objectively address an issue and are typically used to clarify an interviewee's statements. An example of a direct question is, "Was the car stopped at the traffic light when you approached the intersection?" The answer is direct and objective, and it would be difficult for an interviewee to change such an answer later.

**Open-ended questions** require explanation or elaboration, seeking detailed answers in the interviewee's own words. Open-ended questions tend to relax the interviewee and can make the statement-taking process feel less intimidating. See the exhibit "Examples of Open-Ended Questions."

---

### Examples of Open-Ended Questions

- How did the accident occur?
- What happened next?
- What was the condition of the premises?
- How did the fall occur?

---

[DA02424]

Open-ended questions allow the interviewee to be flexible in his or her response. Also, open-ended questions can lead to new follow-up questions. If a claims representative asks, "How did the fall occur?" (an open-ended question), the claimant may respond, "I slipped on some water on the floor of the warehouse." Then, the claims representative can follow up, asking, "Did you see the water on the floor before you fell?" (a direct question). Here, the open-ended question leads to a direct question asking for specific information.

One potential problem with open-ended questions, however, is that they can be time consuming and allow the interviewee to wander to topics that are either unrelated or do not follow the interview sequence. For example, an interviewee may veer into a discussion of issues related to his injuries while the claims representative is attempting to gather information about how the accident occurred. Keeping open-ended questions specific and using direct questions as follow-ups to open-ended questions may help avoid this problem.

**Leading question**

A question that seeks or suggests a particular answer.

The third type of question used in statements, **leading questions**, may require a yes or no answer and may prevent the interviewee from explaining the answer. See the exhibit "Direct, Open-Ended, and Leading Questions."

## Direct, Open-Ended, and Leading Questions

| Direct Question | Open-Ended Question | Leading Question |
| --- | --- | --- |
| Did you see the red Toyota stop at the stoplight? | What was the red Toyota doing? | The red Toyota stopped at the stoplight, didn't it? |
| At what speed would you estimate the Toyota was traveling before impact? | Can you tell me what you observed regarding the Toyota? | Did you see the Toyota traveling at a high speed? |

[DA02427]

Leading questions undermine the admissibility and credibility of statements. Also, interviewees may feel intimidated by leading questions and become less cooperative during the interview as a result.

Some circumstances require special considerations when taking statements. See the exhibit "Special Considerations When Taking Statements."

## Special Considerations When Taking Statements

- Hospitalized interviewee—Many states prohibit or restrict taking statements from people who are hospitalized after an accident. Even if the statement is permitted by law, such statements can later be challenged if the interviewee was experiencing shock or pain or was under the influence of medication.

- Injured interviewee—It is usually advisable at the beginning of a statement to ask a person who is claiming injuries after an accident whether he or she is taking medication. Additional questions may include whether he or she feels up to giving a statement or has significant discomfort.

- Illiterate interviewee—People who cannot read or write can give recorded statements. Alternatively, the claims representative or a field investigator can write out a statement with the answers provided by the interviewee. It is usually advisable for a disinterested party, such as a notary, to be present during such statements.

- Minor interviewee—Laws regarding statements from those who have not reached the age of majority vary by state. Most states require permission from a parent or guardian before the minor is interviewed. Some states require that the parent or guardian be present.

- Foreign language interviewee—The claims representative will usually arrange for an interpreter to assist in interviewing a person who speaks a foreign language and is not fluent in the language of the interviewer. The interpreter can either be a professional or a member of the interviewee's family.

[DA06798]

Taking a statement when there are special circumstances could result in the statement's being deemed inadmissible. Also, taking a statement when an interviewee is hospitalized, in pain, or otherwise vulnerable risks compromising the future cooperation of the interviewee. Insurers often have policies and procedures for handling statements when special circumstances exist.

### Apply Your Knowledge

Carol is preparing to interview Gary regarding a recent auto accident. Gary rear-ended the car in front of him at an intersection with a four-way stop sign. The interview will be recorded to video, and Gary's lawyer will be present. What sort of questions should Carol prepare before starting the interview?

*Feedback*: The questions Carol asks should reflect the specifics of the claim. For example, she could ask what Gary was doing as he approached the intersection (was he looking at his phone?), whether the car in front of him was standing still or had started to move forward, and how soon he hit his brakes before the collision.

# USING SWORN STATEMENTS

Sworn statements can play a sizable role in claim settlements. Claims representatives should familiarize themselves with the process of recording a sworn statement, as well as with the statement's uses, for the best chance of obtaining fair and equitable settlements.

**Sworn statement**

A signed record of events surrounding an event as told by the interviewee that contains language attesting that it is true.

**Sworn statements** can be valuable tools for claim investigations. Different forms of sworn statements are used for different types of claims. To be able to use these statements effectively, claim representatives need to understand why, when, and how to obtain and use the various forms of sworn statements.

## Why Sworn Statements Are Used

To be admissible as evidence in legal proceedings, statements must typically contain a declaration by the person giving the statement that the information provided is true under penalty of perjury. This legal requirement is the major reason for obtaining a sworn statement.

Another reason to obtain a sworn statement is that many insurance policies require the insured to provide a sworn statement at the request of the insurer. Although almost all policies require an insured to cooperate after a loss, an insurer can more readily persuade a court to compel an insured to provide something that is specifically required by the policy, such as a sworn statement.

Additionally, a sworn statement may provide more complete and accurate information than a statement in which there is no sworn declaration attesting to the truth of the statement. In addition to encouraging people whose intentions are basically honest to be forthright, a sworn statement also permits an insurer to pursue legal penalties for perjury if a person knowingly gives false information.

# The Forms Sworn Statements Take

The forms that sworn statements take may vary according to the policy and the circumstances of the claim.

## Recorded Statements

All recorded statements should contain a verbal declaration by the person giving the statement that the statement's contents are truthful to the best of that person's knowledge. However, most recorded statements do not contain an affidavit by a third party, such as a notary public, that the person giving the statement swore to the truth of the statement. Also, recorded statements do not contain the signature of the person giving the statement unless the claim representative has the statement transcribed and sends it to the person who provided the statement with a request for signature.

Recorded statements are adequate for many claims. In certain lines of insurance, such as workers compensation and commercial general liability, recorded statements may be the only type of sworn statement available to a claim representative during the investigation phase of the claim.

## Affidavit

An affidavit in a claim is essentially a sworn written statement. The person who is making the statement swears to the truthfulness of the facts, usually before a notary public, who then notarizes the affidavit.

Each state has a form and procedure for affidavits. Insurers may provide forms for affidavits that comply with appropriate state regulations. If a form is not provided by the insurer, the claim representative should consult with an attorney regarding the appropriate form and procedure to ensure that the information provided in the affidavit will be admissible in legal proceedings.

An affidavit can be added to a recorded statement if the statement is transcribed. The claim representative can then send the transcript to the person giving the statement along with an affidavit to be signed before a notary attesting to the truthfulness of the statement.

## Proof of Loss

Many insurance policies require a sworn proof of loss. For example, the Insurance Services Office, Inc. (ISO) Homeowners 3—Special Form policy contains this duty of an insured after a loss:[2]

> Send to us, within 60 days after our request, your signed, sworn proof of loss which sets forth, to the best of your knowledge and belief:
>
> a. The time and cause of loss;
>
> b. The interests of all "insureds" and all others in the property involved and all liens on the property;
>
> c. Other insurance which may cover the loss;
>
> d. Changes in title or occupancy of the property during the term of the policy;
>
> e. Specifications of damaged buildings and detailed repair estimates;
>
> f. The inventory of damaged personal property…;
>
> g. Receipts for additional living expenses incurred and records that support the fair rental value loss; and
>
> h. Evidence or affidavit that supports a claim under E.6. Credit Card, Electronic Fund Transfer Card or Access Device, Forgery And Counterfeit Money under Section I—Property Coverages, stating the amount and cause of loss.

The sworn proof of loss typically requires the insured to have the form notarized after the insured completes it.

## Examination Under Oath

Many insurance policies require the insured to submit to an examination under oath at the request of the insurer. For example, the ISO Personal Auto Policy coverage form states that "A person seeking coverage must…submit, as often as we reasonably require…to examination under oath and subscribe the same."[3]

An examination under oath is more formal than a recorded statement. It is typically taken at the insurer's office with a court reporter present or at the court reporter's office. An attorney representing the insurer usually asks the questions. Although the insured has the right to have an attorney present, that attorney may not ask questions or participate in the examination.

The attorney for the insurer will notify the insured of the time and place for the examination under oath. Failure to appear for the examination under oath will usually give the insurer the right to suspend any benefits to the insured under the policy until the insured cooperates with the examination under oath.

## Deposition

As in an examination under oath, the person who is deposed is required to swear to the truthfulness of the information he or she provides during the deposition. A deposition is typically part of the discovery in a lawsuit. It takes place at the office of an attorney, a court reporter, or the insurer and is usually conducted by an attorney for any party in a legal proceeding. An attorney for the other party or parties has the right to object to questions and to conduct a cross-examination.

# How Sworn Statements Are Obtained

The methods of obtaining sworn statements vary considerably. They may involve adding a verbal attestation to a recorded statement, an affidavit or a proof of loss sent by mail, or a formal examination with attorneys and a court reporter. See the exhibit "How Sworn Statements Are Obtained."

## How Sworn Statements Are Obtained

| Types of Sworn Statements | How They Are Obtained |
|---|---|
| Recorded statement | • Claim representative takes statement over the phone (or sometimes in person). <br>• Addition of verbal statement, under penalty of perjury, that the facts in the statement are true. <br>• Statement may be transcribed and sent to the person who gave the statement with an affidavit to be signed before a notary. |
| Proof of loss | • Proof of loss form is mailed. <br>• Insured signs form before a notary attesting to its truthfulness, then mails it back to the insurer. |
| Affidavit | • Affidavit form is mailed. <br>• Insured, claimant, or witness signs the form before a notary attesting to the truthfulness of the statement, then mails it back to the insurer. |
| Examination under oath | • Notice issued to insured to appear at office of insurer, attorney, or court reporter. <br>• Attorney for insurer administers the examination. |
| Deposition | • Part of discovery in a lawsuit. <br>• Attorney for either party can require deposition; attorney for other party can participate. |

[DA07415]

The cost of obtaining a sworn statement varies according to the type of statement. A sworn proof of loss typically involves only the cost of postage to send the form to the insured. However, an examination under oath involves fees for the attorney representing the insurer, in addition to court reporter fees and the costs of transcripts.

## When and How Sworn Statements Are Used

Because the requirements and costs for different types of statements vary significantly, it is important for claim representatives to understand when and how these statements are used. Most policies contain a section describing the insured's duties after a loss. This section of a policy typically contains a general provision regarding the insured's duty to cooperate with the insurer, along with specific requirements, such as providing a sworn proof of loss or submitting to an examination under oath. It is critical that a claim representative consult the policy before making a decision to obtain a sworn statement.

Although most policies require the insured, and sometimes third-party claimants, to provide sworn statements, there are significant exceptions. For example, a workers compensation policy typically contains only a general duty of the insured to cooperate. Most state workers compensation laws contain no requirement for a claimant to provide a recorded statement or submit to an examination under oath. However, many states require a claimant to attend a deposition under certain circumstances.

Recorded statements, written statements with affidavits, and sworn proofs of loss are usually used during a claim investigation. These types of sworn statements have little cost associated with them, and they provide a valuable method of obtaining and preserving information about the facts of a loss.

An examination under oath should be used whenever serious questions exist about the validity or extent of injury or damages in a claim. If there are contradictory statements about the circumstances of a loss, an examination under oath should be considered. If there is litigation in a claim, an examination under oath provides the insurer with an opportunity to assess how the insured will perform as a witness during the litigation process. In a routine, straightforward claim involving no litigation, an examination under oath may add to the expenses of a claim without providing any significant benefit. Under most policies, the insurer usually has the right to an examination under oath of the insured at any time. The circumstances of each claim determine when it is appropriate to obtain an examination under oath. In some cases, it is appropriate to obtain it during the investigation of a loss. In other claims, it may be more appropriate to obtain it before a scheduled court hearing.

Depositions are part of the discovery during a lawsuit. An attorney for any party to the suit may require a deposition.

# STATUTORY AND SPECIALTY REPORTING OF CLAIMS INFORMATION

State and federal governments require insurers to meet statutory reporting requirements for certain types of claims and insurance information.

Aggregated insurance information supports the development of auto, property, and safety regulations on state and federal levels; can deter insurance fraud; and creates a basis for education and safety programs. There are a number of data-reporting service organizations that help insurers and others comply with statutory reporting requirements.

## State and Federal Casualty and Property Reporting

Individual states have their own casualty and property claims reporting requirements to meet regulatory and information needs. The federal government has its own reporting requirements. Because of this, there are several types of casualty and property reporting.

### Bodily Injury Reporting

State and federal reporting on bodily injury claims enables the injury information to be aggregated to develop statistics that are then used to develop safety regulations or laws. For example, states may use statistics on workers compensation bodily injury claims to properly staff workers compensation regulatory offices and to develop state safety codes for various workplaces. Some may use statistics on bodily injury from other types of claims to develop appropriate liability laws associated with bodily injuries, to support education and safety programs, and for other purposes. The federal government uses workers compensation statistics to develop laws for the United States' Occupational Safety and Health Administration (OSHA), as well as general safety requirements and recommendations training programs and publications on workplace safety. Most reporting is handled through the National Council on Compensation Insurance, Inc. (NCCI).

State and federal reporting on bodily injury claims from all sources also helps reduce fraud. For example, nationwide databases and query services can alert insurers to claims made for a single injury through multiple sources, such as workers compensation, auto liability, and health insurance claims.

The support organization Insurance Services Office, Inc. (ISO) has developed a comprehensive database and protocols to help with bodily injury reporting and other types of data services.

### Auto Accident Reporting

ISO provides various data collection, aggregation, and other services for reporting auto accident claims. Auto claims reporting can be used for a variety of purposes, and requirements vary among states. Some states require reporting of all auto claims, while others require reporting only on specified types of auto claims or claims of specified amounts, such as those exceeding $2,500.

Auto claims data is aggregated and used for statistics that form the basis of laws regarding minimum auto liability limits, no-fault laws, and similar auto regulations. These statistics can also guide development of motor vehicle regulations and road and traffic management design, such as deciding whether a traffic signal should be installed at a particular intersection.

## Fire Reporting

Many state fire marshals collect information regarding fire losses, which helps states determine the number of fire stations and amount of equipment needed to protect communities and business owners. These statistics can also be used for numerous other purposes, such as assigning public fire protection classes, developing fire protection codes, and investigating and tracking arson. ISO provides services to help insurers and others comply with state-mandated fire reporting.

## Child Support Enforcement Reporting

Several states use claims reporting to redirect claim payments from individuals who are delinquent on their child support obligations.

State child support reporting requirements vary among states. For example, one state might require the report only if a claim payment exceeds $5,000, while another state might require reporting if a payment is $500 or more. States also determine whether the origin of a claim payment is relevant— for example, whether such payments can stem from workers compensation, auto accidents, or other liability claims or from property damage claims. ISO provides state-specific reporting services that streamline reporting and compliance for subscriber organizations.[4]

## Fraud Reporting

Many state governments and the federal government require insurers and special investigation units (SIUs) to report suspected fraudulent claims. These government entities use insurance fraud statistics to develop fraud detection, investigation, and prevention services.

Auto and mobile equipment fraud reporting helps detect stolen motor vehicles and mobile equipment, thereby deterring thieves from bringing them into the marketplace. It also helps aid recovery efforts around such stolen property. Auto fraud reporting protects consumers from title fraud as well and provides some consumer protection from unsafe vehicles.

The reporting of crime that is suspected or detected in auto, other property, and bodily injury claims is used to develop fraud detection and enforcement programs, public safety programs, and educational materials.

### *Apply Your Knowledge*

Which one of the following types of reporting involves using data for statistics that form the basis of laws regarding minimum auto liability limits and no-fault laws?

a.  Fraud reporting

b.  Child support enforcement reporting

c.  Auto accident reporting

d.  Fire reporting

*Feedback:* c. Auto accident reporting uses data for statistics that form the basis of laws regarding minimum auto liability limits and no-fault laws.

## Office of Foreign Assets Control Reporting

Certain claim payments and other insurance transactions must be reported to the federal government as required by the U.S. Office of Foreign Assets Control (OFAC). OFAC administers and enforces economic sanctions against foreign countries, organizations, and individuals that are involved in terrorism, international narcotics trafficking, and activities related to developing weapons of mass destruction. The sanctions can be comprehensive or selective and can apply to a country's regimes, wholly or partially state-owned organizations, front companies, high-ranking officials, and agents.

OFAC maintains a list of "specially designated nationals (SDNs) and blocked persons" and other targeted entities, including variations on the names of those targeted. It blocks assets of targeted entities and implements trade restrictions in order to meet foreign policy and national security goals.

Companies are required to follow "due diligence steps" to determine whether a transaction is prohibited by OFAC; otherwise, they may face federal fines, several years in jail, and severe civil penalties.

Conducting business under an insurance policy with an SDN or targeted entity without an OFAC license is illegal. This includes issuing the policy or payment of a claim to that party or on behalf of that party. In the case of a payment ordinarily owed to an innocent third party, such as the victim of an auto accident for which an SDN was responsible, OFAC would likely work with the insurer, issuing a license to make payment to the innocent party.

## Medicare Secondary Payer Reporting

The U.S. Medicare, Medicaid, and SCHIP Extension Act of 2007 (MMSEA), Section 111, details mandatory reporting requirements for liability insurers, no-fault insurers, workers compensation insurers, self-insureds, and group health plan (GHP) arrangements.

When a bodily injury claim is filed by a Medicare-eligible claimant or plaintiff, the insurer or self-insured organization is required to electronically submit information on the identity of that claimant to the Centers for Medicare and Medicaid Services (CMS). After such a claim is settled, or a judgment, award, or other payment is determined, insurers must electronically submit information on the claim to coordinate benefits.

Support organizations often help their insurer subscribers comply with MMSEA. For example, ISO provides Medicare secondary-payer reporting service.

## Specialty Reporting

Specialty reporting has been established for specific purposes and is not government mandated. It helps deter theft of high-value property, such as works of art, antiques, mobile equipment, and marine hulls and machinery. Some specialty reporting is beneficial in attempts to recover lost or stolen high-value property.

Marine reporting helps deter bodily injury fraud from marine workers who are not subject to federal workers compensation statutes. For-profit and not-for-profit specialty reporting organizations have emerged to manage the data collection in these specialty areas and to provide various services to their members and to law enforcement authorities. Some specialty service providers include the Art Loss Register (ALR), the National Equipment Register (NER), and the Marine Index Bureau (MIB).

## Data-Reporting Service Organizations

A number of data-reporting service organizations assist with statutory reporting compliance. These organizations aggregate the data reported and maintain databases on many types of loss information and premium information, offering additional services to member organizations, including statistical reporting developed from aggregated data; programs to assist with risk control, loss, and theft recovery; and numerous educational programs and materials to help deter fraud and other crimes.

### ISO

ISO offers services and products to support insurers and risk management organizations. These include providing statistical, actuarial, underwriting, claims, and compliance information to organizations that subscribe to the appropriate services. For example, ISO offers claims information services and solutions through its comprehensive database system, ClaimSearch, which contains claim information from every type of insurance business.

ClaimSearch participants include property and casualty insurers, self-insured organizations, and claims administrators. In addition to its participating organizations, ClaimSearch serves state workers compensation insurance funds, third-party administrators (TPAs), state fraud bureaus, and law-enforcement agencies.

The database is developed through insurers and other participants submitting their claim information through their own claim information systems or through direct entry into the ISO web interface. When an organization submits a claim to ClaimSearch, the system searches its database by the individual's or organization's name (as claimant or insured) and returns any matches in the identifying information, such as the name, address, vehicle identification number (VIN), Social Security number (SSN), or tax identification number (TIN). The system returns exact and similar name matches.

In addition to claim inquiry services, ClaimSearch provides a variety of core and optional services, including statutory and regulatory reporting, VIN decoding, OFAC reporting, crime and fraud reporting, child support enforcement agency (CSEA) reporting, and National Motor Vehicle Title Information System (NMVTIS) reporting, among many others. Participants receive core services through a subscription to ClaimSearch, but they can subscribe to optional services as well.

ISO has collaborated with a number of data collection associations and other organizations to collect required data and update information in appropriate databases and to enable those organizations to access information stored in ISO databases. The ClaimSearch system automatically provides federal- and state-required statutory and regulatory reporting. Some specialty uses of ClaimSearch include fraud detection and investigation, OFAC compliance, ALR and NER services, MIB reporting, and Medicare secondary payer reporting services. SIUs, claim personnel, and law enforcement personnel can use the ClaimSearch system to research prior loss histories, identify claim patterns, and investigate suspected fraud and other crimes.

## NCCI

NCCI manages the nation's largest database of workers compensation insurance information, providing a Bureau Compliance Statistical Service (BCSS) that assists insurers in submitting unit report data for all states. NCCI also transmits electronic data to state bureaus, analyzes industry trends, prepares workers compensation insurance rate recommendations, and determines the cost of proposed legislation.

## NMVTIS

At least forty-five states participate to some degree in NMVTIS,[5] which aims to help prevent the introduction or reintroduction of stolen motor vehicles into interstate commerce, to protect states and consumers from automobile title fraud, to reduce the use of stolen vehicles for illicit purposes, and to provide consumer protection from unsafe vehicles.

NMVTIS reporting requirements are imposed on junkyards, salvage yards, and insurers in participating states. State titling agencies use NMVTIS to prevent fraud by verifying the motor vehicle and title information, information on whether the motor vehicle has been reported stolen, and labels that may indicate a vehicle is unsafe, as in a "flood vehicle."

Insurers and others in states that participate fully in NMVTIS submit to a national database the VIN, year, make, and model information of stolen or damaged autos. Before a title is issued, the titling agency uses the NMVTIS database information to obtain a full record of title from the last titling jurisdiction.

## National Insurance Crime Bureau

The National Insurance Crime Bureau (NICB) is a not-for-profit organization exclusively dedicated to preventing, detecting, and defeating insurance fraud and vehicle theft through data analytics, investigations, training, legislative advocacy, and public awareness. Information in the NICB database is submitted by member organizations, including commercial and personal property and casualty insurers, self-insured organizations, rental car companies, parking service providers, and transportation-related firms. The data is used by local, state, federal, and international law enforcement agencies to help deter vehicle, property, and workers compensation insurance fraud and vehicle theft.

NICB coordinates collection of questionable claims with ISO through ISO's claims database. NICB members submit data on questionable claims to ISO, which are then added to NICB's questionable claims database.

### Apply Your Knowledge

Which one of the following is not a service provided by the NCCI?

a.    Transmit electronic data to state bureaus

b.    Analyze industry trends

c.    Prepare workers compensation insurance rate recommendations

d.    Deter bodily injury fraud from marine workers

*Feedback: d.* Deterring bodily injury fraud from marine workers is not a service provided by the NCCI, but rather a feature of marine reporting, which is a type of specialty reporting.

# PERSONAL SAFETY FOR CLAIMS REPRESENTATIVES

Claims representatives encounter many issues while handling claims, which requires thoughtful preparation and analysis and good communication and customer service skills. To prepare accordingly, they should understand how to respond to potential stressors and personal safety risks, as well as familiarize themselves with their employers' guidelines and protocols regarding personal safety.

Claims handling can be a stressful occupation. Absorbing heavy daily workloads; interacting with people who have experienced varying levels of loss and injury; and managing claims with adverse effects on policyholders and claimants can be exhausting. Moreover, claims representatives can face physical and emotional hazards while handling claims. Being able to recognize and respond to these hazards can help claims representatives perform their work appropriately and safely.

## Physical Hazards

Both inside and outside claims representatives can be exposed to physical hazards such as or related to these:

- Emotional or irate customers
- Crime-prone areas
- Roads
- Animals or insects
- Property inspections
- Boat and trailer inspections
- Auto physical damage inspections
- Catastrophe claims handling

## Emotional or Irate Customers

When an insured or a claimant is emotional or irate after a loss, the claims representative risks being verbally or physically threatened. The claims representative can mitigate this risk by thoroughly reviewing loss-related documents to understand the claimant's emotional state before initiating phone conversations or visits. This will prepare the claims representative for potential reactions so he or she can maintain control of the conversation.

Actively listening and demonstrating an understanding of the situation by paraphrasing the customer's concerns can also help calm a highly charged claimant. By expressing empathy, the representative shows that he or she can relate to the customer's frustration—which may, in turn, temper the customer's reaction.

A claims representative who believes the situation is beyond control should advise the customer that he or she will review the customer's concerns and be in contact later. Common sense and a professional demeanor are crucial during a potentially explosive situation, and any perceived threat should be reported to management.

## Crime-Prone Area Hazards

Outside claims representatives, also called field reps, may conduct investigations or inspections in crime-prone areas and must immediately leave such areas if they feel unsafe. If you, as a claims representative, find yourself in a situation where safety is or will be an issue, you may also wish to employ these techniques:

- Be sure that a manager, co-worker, or family member knows where you will be.
- Schedule an appointment with your contact person and confirm where and when to meet beforehand; be sure to have his or her contact information with you.
- Locate the nearest police and fire stations before arriving.
- Ensure that your vehicle is in good working order and has enough fuel.
- Have a spare tire and know how to change it or have the phone number of a service that can assist.
- Keep the car doors locked and the windows up at all times.
- Check both the back and front seats upon returning to the vehicle.
- Keep any costly equipment, such as laptops and mobile devices, in the trunk of the car or otherwise hidden from view.
- Keep a fully charged cell phone within easy reach at all times.

Claims representatives who encounter would-be robbers should surrender any property demanded. Maintaining personal safety is far more important than securing physical items.

## Roadside Hazards

If a claims representative conducts an accident investigation requiring that he or she exit a vehicle and stand on a road, then all rules of the road should be observed, including the use of parking or hazard lights. Additionally, the claims representative should wear a safety vest while working in a high-traffic or high-speed area.

## Animal or Insect Hazards

The claims representative should always survey the area for domestic and wild animals, including insects. If pets are present at an inspection site, the claims representative should ask the owner to restrain them, or the appointment should be rescheduled to a time when the animals will not be present.

While inspecting a damaged site, including autos, claims representatives should be aware that animals may hide or nest in the damaged property. When inspecting auto physical damage at a repair or salvage facility that uses animals for security purposes, the representative should request that animals are properly restrained before beginning an inspection.

## Property Inspection Hazards

Claims representatives need to be aware of potential safety hazards when completing a property inspection, such as these:

- Clutter or debris
- Uneven surfaces
- Weak floors and compromised structures
- Liquid spills resulting in slippery conditions
- Chemical or dust pathogens
- Sharp objects and protruding surfaces
- Live electrical wires

A claims representative should conduct an inspection only if he or she believes the area is safe and the property has been properly secured. If cleanup or repair work has already begun on the property, protective glasses, a disposable dust mask, and protective gloves should be worn to ensure physical safety. A hard hat may be appropriate to prevent head injury from falling debris.

If a ladder is needed to inspect roof damage, special precautions should be observed to prevent injury. The ladder should be approved by the Occupational Safety and Health Administration (OSHA) and meet requirements for the weight and height of anyone using it.

The claims representative should also use common sense to ensure his or her safety. For example, if the type of roof, its condition, or additional hazards are a threat to the claims representative's safety, he or she should not complete the inspection.

## Boat and Trailer Inspection Hazards

Many of the same hazards that affect property inspections are present when inspecting a boat or trailer, such as debris, slippery surfaces, and sharp objects or protruding surfaces. A claims representative who needs to inspect a boat in the water should wear appropriate clothing and footwear, as well as a life preserver.

## Auto Physical Damage Inspection Hazards

Claims representatives should be wary of these hazards when working in auto repair facilities, drive-in facilities, and towing and salvage yards:

- Clutter or debris
- Damaged parts with sharp or protruding edges
- Liquids and spills
- Repair equipment in use
- Paint booths in use that emit toxic fumes
- Uneven ground or surfaces
- Poor accessibility of the damaged vehicle

As with property inspections, claims representatives should complete auto physical damage inspections only if they believe the area is safe; further, they should wear appropriate footwear and be careful to avoid surfaces or debris that may cause a slip or fall. Contact with liquids or spills should be avoided because of potential chemical contaminants.

An auto body shop should make available a Safety Data Sheet, sometimes referred to as a Material Safety Data Sheet, advising what to do if contact is made with any hazardous material.

## Catastrophe Claims Handling Hazards

Handling claims during or after a catastrophe presents some unique additional hazards. Severe storms and other catastrophic events result in widespread damage and debris, which could call for claims representatives to wear protective clothing and use safety equipment. Suitable housing may be an issue, exposing the claims representative to airborne or waterborne contaminants, and the claims representative may have to obtain precautionary inoculations that prevent certain infections and diseases.

Catastrophe work can result in sleep deprivation, poor nutrition, and improper hydration when claims representatives are not cognizant of their physical well-being. To combat these conditions, claims representatives should adhere to normal sleeping and eating patterns as much as possible.

### Apply Your Knowledge

If the conditions are not clear or a claims representative believes that his or her personal safety is at risk while handling a claim, which one of the following actions would be best to employ?

a.  Wear protective gear, such as safety glasses, protective gloves, and a disposable dust mask

b.  Make sure all pets and animals are secure before entering the premises

c.  Leave the area and postpone the appointment

d.  Wear shoes that cover the entire foot to protect against debris

e.  Keep the auto in good repair with a full tank of gas

*Feedback:* c. All of these actions are appropriate techniques in certain situations, but if the conditions are not clear or the claims representative believes his or her safety is at risk, then leaving the area and postponing the appointment is always the best course of action.

# Emotional Hazards

Emotional hazards can affect the claims representative's demeanor, sometimes even causing depression. On a daily basis, claims representatives are required to demonstrate empathy, good communication, and customer service skills and to remain calm in stressful situations, as most claims involve policyholders or claimants who may be emotional and under stress.

Regardless of the circumstances, claims representatives are expected to remain professional while representing insurers, whose interests may be at odds with an insured's.

Catastrophe situations involving widespread damage, loss of life and property, and human suffering can create considerable stress for claims representatives. Working long hours, handling heavy caseloads, and dealing with claimants and communities that have suffered devastating losses can take an emotional toll on anyone. Claims representatives should be aware of the signs that trigger emotional problems resulting from job-related stress, including fatigue, inability to sleep, changes in eating habits, and unusual irritability.

Claims representatives should try to maintain a healthy work/life balance, and discuss any concerns about stressors and emotional hazards with a manager. Managers, meanwhile, should watch for warning signs in their representatives, such as personality or demeanor changes, and take appropriate actions, which may include temporary assignment changes for affected claims representatives.

## *Apply Your Knowledge*

All of the following signs indicate that a claims representative is struggling with the emotional hazards associated with a catastrophe, EXCEPT:

a.  Fatigue and complaints of an inability to sleep

b.  Sudden changes in weight

c.  Inappropriate outbursts or atypical irritability

d.  Demonstration of a calm, professional demeanor

*Feedback:* d. Fatigue and complaints of inability to sleep, sudden changes in weight, inappropriate outbursts or atypical irritability, and changes in demeanor or personality may indicate that a claims representative is struggling with the emotional hazards associated with a catastrophe situation. The manager should be aware of the stressors involved and monitor the effect that these stressors have on claims representatives assigned to handle catastrophes.

# SUMMARY

Claims representatives use photographs, videos, maps, and diagrams to illustrate what a loss scene looked like, how an accident happened, and the extent of the property damage and bodily injuries. Photos may be used to document a point relevant to the event that gave rise to the claim or to document an investigation technique. Videos can be used to recreate an event, document damage or injury, or record witness statements and depositions. Maps can indicate relevant distances, locations of landmarks, and topographical features that may be relevant to a claim. Diagrams serve as visual aids to communicate or clarify the events that led to a claim.

Spoliation of evidence claims against insurers often arise in subrogation proceedings or in litigation initiated after a claim has been settled. Insurers have a duty to preserve relevant evidence. Although courts vary in the proof required in a successful spoliation claim, in general, they require proof that the evidence has been improperly lost or destroyed, that the alleged offender had ownership or control of the evidence, that the evidence is relevant to a claim in litigation, that the loss or destruction was the accused party's fault, and that the unavailability of the evidence is prejudicial to the other party.

Available defenses to a spoliation claim can vary depending on the facts of a case and the jurisdiction in which the claim is brought. Remedies for spoliation include dismissal of the underlying case, exclusion of evidence relating to the missing evidence, an adverse inference instruction to the jury, and monetary sanctions.

Statements, which can be written or recorded, provide a foundation for claims investigations. They should be organized consistently, and the seven-part method is useful for structuring the content of statements. Questions asked in statements should be either direct or open ended, not leading, and vary according to the type of loss.

Sworn statements can be valuable tools for obtaining and preserving accurate information in a claim. It is important for claim representatives to understand why these statements are used, what forms they take, how to obtain them, and when and how to use to them.

State and federal governments impose regulatory reporting requirements on property-casualty insurers and related organizations to meet statistical and other needs. Insurers also complete voluntary reporting that assists in their claims functions. A number of data-reporting service organizations have emerged to assist insurers and others in complying with statutory reporting requirements.

Claims representatives may need to face physical and emotional hazards when handling claims. Physical hazards can cause bodily injury to the claims representative, while emotional hazards can affect the claims representative's demeanor or cause depression. Using appropriate techniques and actions to respond to these hazards ensures that a claims representative can handle claims appropriately and safely.

## ASSIGNMENT NOTES

1. Richard Boyd Jr., "Getting Burned by Missing Evidence," Claims Advisor, Summer 2010, p. 47.

2. Includes copyrighted material of Insurance Services Office, Inc., used with its permission. Copyright, ISO Properties, Inc., 1999.

3. Personal Auto Policy, Insurance Services Office, Inc. (Jersey City, N.J.: ISO Properties, Inc., 2003).

4. ISO ClaimSearch Compliance Office, "ISO ClaimSearch® Mandatory— Statutory Reporting for the Industry" (Jersey City, N.J.: Insurance Services Office, Inc., 2010), pp. 1-4.

5. National Motor Vehicle Title Information System, www.vehiclehistory.gov/ nmvtis_states.html (accessed July 2, 2018).

# Direct Your Learning

# Communicating Effectively

## Educational Objectives

After learning the content of this assignment, you should be able to:

▷ Examine the role of the claims representative in using the communication process model to improve the quality of interactions with insureds, claimants, and other stakeholders in claims handling activities.

▷ Explain how claims representatives employ active listening skills.

▷ Given a claims situation that requires a written communication, plan a document that addresses the following:

- Intended audience

- Purpose

- Content, including accuracy, tone, and organization

- Specific requirements based on the type of document

▷ Apply effective verbal communication techniques to claim-related verbal exchanges.

▷ Interpret the nonverbal cues, given a claim-related discussion.

# Communicating Effectively

# 5

## USING THE COMMUNICATION PROCESS IN CLAIMS HANDLING

Accurate and clear communication is fundamental to all aspects of the claims process. During claims investigation and resolution, claims representatives communicate with various parties, including insureds, claimants, witnesses, attorneys, experts, and other insurance professionals.

Some official written claims communications, such as acknowledgment letters and status letters, may be legally prescribed. Claims representatives write reports and summaries to document claims investigation and settlement activities, and those documents become part of the permanent claim file. Claim files may be reviewed by insurance managers, regulators, and attorneys, and they may be used as evidence in legal proceedings. Claims representatives also communicate verbally with others—at meetings, in casual conversations, and over the telephone.

An understanding of the communication process can help claims representatives plan and develop effective communications that contribute to effective claim resolution. The communication process has two phases: the transmission phase, during which the sender shares information, and the feedback phase, during which the receiver responds.[1] Each phase has various components that lay the foundation for effective claims communication.

The communication process also has four main components:

- The sender
- The message
- The medium
- The receiver

Each of these components is present in both the transmission phase, during which information is shared, and in the feedback phase, during which the information is interpreted and acted on. An understanding of these components can help claims representatives communicate effectively. See the exhibit "The Communication Process."

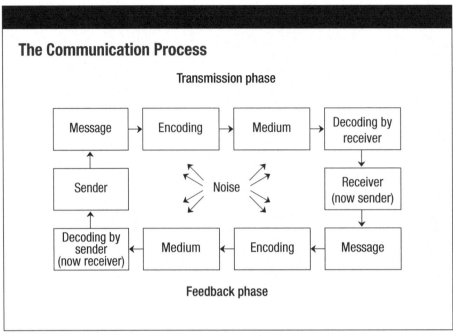

The Communication Process

Transmission phase

Gareth R. Jones and Jennifer M. George, Contemporary Management, 6th ed. (Boston: McGraw-Hill/Irwin, 2009), p. 569. [DA07632]

**Sender**

The person who initiates the communication process.

**Receiver**

The person who chooses from the verbal and nonverbal symbols in the sender's message to interpret the message's meaning.

**Initial credibility**

The degree of credibility an individual has before interpersonal communication begins.

**Derived credibility**

An individual's perceived credibility during interpersonal communication.

**Terminal credibility**

An individual's perceived credibility after interpersonal communication in a given situation has occurred.

# Sender

The **sender** and the receiver are the primary components in the communication process. When a claims representative requests information from an insured or a claimant regarding a claim, the claims representative is the sender and the insured or claimant is the **receiver**. This initial communication takes place in the transmission phase of the communication process, in which the sender (the claims representative) shares information (a description of the needed information) intended for the receiver (the insured). The claims representative must create a cooperative environment in which effective communication can occur in order to obtain the specific information needed to investigate the claim.

The credibility of the sender is an important consideration. Three types of credibility can affect claims communication:

- **Initial credibility**—Initial credibility depends partly on the individual claims representative's reputation and experience and partly on the perceived status of the profession of claims handling.

- **Derived credibility**—Claims representatives can improve their derived credibility based on the type of communication and by projecting a confident and concise approach to communication.

- **Terminal credibility**—Terminal credibility is the sum of the sender's initial credibility and derived credibility.

For example, in investigating a claim for damages against an insured, a claims representative contacts the claimant, who alleges that her injuries were caused by the insured. The claims representative's initial credibility may be based on the claimant's distrust of insurance companies in general as well as her distrust of the claims representative, who represents the party who caused her injuries. By clearly explaining the claims investigation and resolution process and communicating professionally, objectively, and empathetically, the claims representative can begin to establish a foundation of trust, which leads to derived credibility. Claims representatives should evaluate the effect of credibility when communicating with insureds, claimants, attorneys, and persons within their own organization.

## Message

The **message** is the second component of the communication process. In **encoding** a message, the sender must make a number of decisions that determine the message's effectiveness. For example, the sender must choose words that express the intended meaning most clearly and arrange them to conform reasonably to grammatical rules. When communicating in writing or speech, claims representatives should orient the level of communication to the intended audience. Technical terms and phrases that are clearly understood by insurance professionals and producers may be incomprehensible to insureds and others outside the industry, resulting in miscommunication.

Miscommunication may also result from ambiguity in the message. For example, a claims representative may request an inventory of items lost or damaged in a fire. The inventory will ask for the value of each item. Depending on the type of coverage available, the claims representative may need the original cost, the replacement cost, or both. To avoid any ambiguity, the claims representative must be specific about what cost is needed in the inventory.

**Message**
The words a sender uses in the communications process and their underlying theme.

**Encoding**
The process of translating a message into words.

## Medium

The **medium** is the message's shuttle from sender to receiver. Speech and writing are both vital means of communication for claims representatives, who may use letters; telephone conversations; e-mails; and face-to-face communication, such as meetings with the parties to a claim. Organizations are increasingly using technological communication media such as teleconferencing, video or Web conferencing, Webcams, and instant messaging.

Each communication medium has advantages and disadvantages. Telephone contact can be advantageous when a quick response is needed or the receiver is too far away for a face-to-face meeting. Webcams and conferencing technologies may be expensive but can also facilitate bringing distant parties together for communication purposes. Use of these technologies and e-mail has decreased the use of written letters in claims handling and in business in general. However, letters and memos are still appropriate for many purposes,

**Medium**
The means by which a message is transmitted from sender to receiver.

such as to relay detailed or complex information and to establish a permanent record of the communication.

All message types fall into two categories: verbal and nonverbal. Verbal messages include both oral and written communication. However, individuals communicate not by words alone; many sensory mechanisms play a vital role in interpersonal communication. Nonverbal communication can include eye movement, kinesics, appearance, and time and space.

## Receiver

The receiver is the fourth component of the communication process. The receiver chooses from the verbal and nonverbal symbols in the sender's messages, selects the symbols that seem to convey the sender's intended meaning, and interprets the message's meaning through **decoding**. These activities occur in the feedback phase of the communication process, during which the receiver responds to the sender's message. Claims representatives can use the feedback phase both to assess the adequacy of their message and to determine the receiver's understanding of the message.

**Decoding**

The process by which a receiver interprets a sender's message.

One of the most critical skills for effective communication is the receiver's ability to listen and understand what is being communicated. Good listening skills can help the claims representative clearly interpret information required to evaluate, investigate, and settle a claim. Claimants and insureds who have recently experienced loss may not communicate as clearly as they would under normal circumstances when describing how the loss occurred. Investigation involves interviewing witnesses and experts and accurately interpreting their answers. Negotiating settlements requires a clear understanding of the positions of insureds, claimants, and attorneys.

**Active listening**

The process of listening with mental and physical openness to more clearly determine a message's meaning.

Claims representatives who engage in **active listening** may establish better rapport with insureds, claimants, and witnesses and, in turn, receive better cooperation during investigative interviews and claim negotiations. By carefully listening and responding, the claims representative may think of additional questions to expand the information provided, resulting in a more complete investigation.

A successful listener must have a mental attitude open to listening and free of distractions so that full attention can be given to the speaker. The listener must avoid the temptation to interrupt. A listener who is waiting to speak or thinking about what to say next is not actively listening.

Allocating adequate time for communication is also essential to maintaining a good mental attitude. Feeling rushed can jeopardize active listening because it fosters impatience, and the listener may tend to interrupt to hasten the conversation. Interruptions can cause the speaker to lose his or her train of thought and omit important information.

# Effective Claims Communication

Claims communication involves gathering information and disseminating information. For example, claims representatives gather information during the claims investigation and disseminate information regarding claim settlement or denial.

When a claim is filed, it may provide general information about the loss. Acquiring additional information from parties to the claim, witnesses, and experts is often necessary to complete an investigation. When interviewing parties and witnesses, claims representatives should make certain that their questions will be understood by the person to whom they are directed. When obtaining the information by phone, e-mail, or another medium, claims representatives should prepare an outline of needed information before initiating the call or completing the e-mail message. This outline can assist claims representatives in focusing their thoughts, reducing the need for additional follow-ups.

After a decision is reached regarding claim settlement or denial, the claims representative must inform the parties to the claim. If the decision is negative, good-faith claims handling requires the claims representative to explain the rationale behind it. Careful drafting of a denial message is an important component of good-faith claims handling.

Another aspect of claims communication relates to persuading or influencing others. The persuasion function is intended to move the receiver to some specific action or behavior. For example, a claims representative might persuade a supervisor that additional settlement authority is needed on a specific claim. The influence function, which pervades all communication, is intended to effect a general change. The impression that claims representatives make on insureds, claimants, and others reflects either favorably or unfavorably on the insurer. A conscious attempt to create the most favorable impression possible, within the constraints imposed by sound claims handling, enhances the influence function of communication.

## Apply Your Knowledge

You are investigating an auto accident claim and have scheduled an interview with a witness to the accident. Which of the following should you consider in preparing for the interview?

a.   How the witness views your initial credibility

b.   How you will decode your questions to the witness

c.   Whether to use nonverbal communication in the interview

d.   How to word your questions to the witness

e.   How to get the witness to listen actively to your questions

*Feedback: a. and d.* By being aware of how the witness may view your initial credibility, you can make an effort to change it on meeting the witness, thereby building trust for the interview (a.). Carefully wording your questions helps ensure that the witness will understand them and answer accurately. Option b. is not correct because, as the sender of the message (your interview questions), you do not decode it; you encode it. The recipient decodes the message. Nonverbal communication (c.) occurs in all face-to-face communications. Although you cannot decide not to communicate nonverbally, you can be aware of your nonverbal cues and, to an extent, choose them to make your communication more effective. Observing the witness's nonverbal cues can help you interpret her answers. Although it is important to word your questions so that the witness will understand them, it is not your task to persuade the witness to listen actively (e.). However, your use of active listening can help ensure that you have interpreted the witness's answers correctly and encourage the witness to expand on her answers.

# EMPLOYING ACTIVE LISTENING SKILLS IN CLAIMS HANDLING

Given that a claim settlement can hinge on the smallest of details, effective claims representatives will rely on specific listening techniques to ensure successful communication throughout the claims handling process.

Claims representatives receive much of the information regarding a claim via the spoken word. Although all messages must be interpreted by their receivers, interpreting spoken messages poses particular challenges. Developing skills in active listening can help a claims representative interpret spoken messages accurately, build a rapport with claimants and insureds, and ensure the overall accuracy of claims information.

## Use of Active Listening

To effectively investigate and resolve a claim, a claims representative must establish a foundation of trust with an insured or a claimant, beginning with the first encounter. This encounter often occurs soon after a loss, when emotions such as shock, grief, anger, or uncertainty may hamper the insured's or claimant's ability to communicate clearly and may foster a general distrust of others. Strong listening skills can contribute to a claims representative's successful first encounter with an insured or a claimant.

Claims representatives may find the active listening technique particularly useful, not just at the beginning of the claims process but throughout it, as they gather investigative information, speak with experts about losses and damages, possibly deal with a claimant's attorney or a defense attorney, and negotiate claim settlement. An active listener provides feedback to the speaker to verify that the listener is interpreting the message correctly. Active listening requires the listener to set aside his or her own emotions or preconceptions, suspend judgment, overcome environmental distractions, and focus attention on the speaker. The listener should try to understand the speaker's point of view in order to empathize.

Use of active listening during investigative interviews can help claims representatives accurately record statements of parties and witnesses. By indicating a willingness to listen and understand, a claims representative may encourage cooperation from witnesses. Careful listening can reveal additional lines of questioning or investigating that, in turn, can result in more thorough investigations.

The empathy, concern, and desire to understand called for by the active listening technique are appropriate only if they are sincere. An insured or a claimant who has been traumatized by a loss may already be distrustful and is likely to detect any sign of insincerity, feigned concern, or false empathy. If the insured or claimant does detect such a sign, the claims representative will find it difficult to establish the rapport necessary to efficiently handle the claim.

## Active Listening Techniques

An active listener sets aside his or her own judgments and opinions and attempts to understand the speaker's frame of reference and to empathize with the speaker's situation and concerns.

A cornerstone of active listening involves "reflective listening," a technique that helps listeners correctly interpret messages. Using this technique, the listener periodically paraphrases, or restates, what the sender has said to verify that the listener's understanding matches the sender's intended message. Use of the technique also indicates the listener's desire and willingness to understand and reassures the speaker that the listener is fully engaged in the conversation. If the listener has misinterpreted the message, the speaker has the opportunity to clarify, correct, and possibly expand on the original message.

Reflective listening responses should be accepting rather than challenging. For example, responding with "Why?" may put the speaker on the defensive by appearing to seek justification for a statement. A more appropriate active listening response might be, "That is interesting; can you tell me more about it?" While offering respect and acceptance, the listener's replies should indicate neither agreement nor disagreement.

Nonverbal cues are also important in active listening. Direct eye contact and an open, relaxed posture can encourage open communication. The claims representative can also observe the speaker's nonverbal cues. See the exhibit "Examples of Common Responses and Active Listening Responses."

People being questioned about an accident or loss often give noncommittal replies that may be overlooked in the course of an interview. Use of active

### Examples of Common Responses and Active Listening Responses

| Insured's Statement | Claim Representative's Possible Response | Better, Active Listening Response |
|---|---|---|
| Then I got to the top of the hill, and it was so bright. I didn't expect that, and I didn't even have time to put down my visor. I couldn't see a thing. Then, blam! And that was it. | What was it? | I'm not sure I understand you. Are you saying that the collision occurred just after your car cleared the hilltop and you were blinded by the sun? |
| You big insurance companies are all alike. I lost my home, but I'm sure you'll find some reason not to pay me any money. | You can trust us. We're professionals. | You're concerned that you won't be treated fairly. |
| I just don't know how I'm going to survive this. I've lost everything. | Your house isn't a total loss. And you're fortunate no one was hurt. | You've just had a traumatic experience, and you're worried about where you go from here to get back on your feet. |
| Part of my house just burned down and now you're asking me to list everything that was destroyed and how old it was. How am I supposed to remember all that? | If you don't tell us what you lost, we can't pay for it. | It sounds as though you're feeling overwhelmed with the loss and with the paperwork required to document the loss. |

[DA07800]

listening can help a claims representative detect such vague or indefinite replies and seek immediate clarification. For example, in response to a question such as "Did you hear the ambulance's siren before you pulled out from the stop sign?" an insured might answer, "Not really." The claims representative can ask additional questions (such as "When did you first become aware of the siren?") to determine whether the insured did not hear the siren, cannot remember hearing it, heard it but didn't think it was so close, or ignored it.

## Barriers to Effective Active Listening

Like the communication process itself, active listening is subject to barriers that can reduce its effectiveness. The setting in which the conversation takes place can produce environmental barriers. Barriers can come in the forms of noise, distracting activities, interruptions from others, and even uncomfortable temperatures or chairs. For example, a claims representative who repeatedly checks his muted cell phone for incoming calls during a meeting with an insured indicates giving less-than-complete attention to the insured's concerns.

These actions or attitudes can raise barriers to effective active listening:

- Using the same wording for each response—Repeatedly starting reflective responses with phrases such as "I hear you saying…" or "You feel that…" can begin to sound insincere.

- Pretending to understand—Communication is rendered ineffective if a listener pretends to understand rather than seeking clarification. Instead, the listener can say, "I'm sorry, I didn't get that. What are you saying?"

- Overreaching—A listener who ascribes meaning far beyond what the speaker has expressed can frustrate the speaker. For example, a claimant might say, "As I passed my co-worker's cubicle, I said hello. Suddenly there was this cart being pushed in front of me from behind the cubicle, and I crashed into it." A claims representative's response, "You weren't paying attention to where you were going and ran into the cart" might be considered overreaching.

- Underreaching—Similarly, a listener who repeatedly understates the significance of a speaker's intended message can cause the speaker to withhold information. For example, an insured might say, "I was paralyzed in terror that the car was going to hit my child." A claims representative's reply that begins, "So you were worried about your child" minimizes the speaker's feelings.

- Engaging in long windedness—Long or complex responses from a listener can interrupt the flow of information and overwhelm or confuse the claimant or insured.

- Ignoring nonverbal cues—By ignoring cues such as the speaker's gestures, posture, and facial expressions, the listener may miss important information and, as a result, misinterpret a message. If a speaker's nonverbal cues appear to be incongruent with the spoken message, the listener can request clarification.

- Violating the speaker's expectations—Giving reflective responses that are clearly not appropriate to the situation is a violation of the speaker's expectations. For example, an insured might say, "We really need money right now to carry us over until the house is repaired." The claims representative's reply, "I can recommend a good motel" does not address the speaker's concerns.

- Exhibiting boredom or loss of focus—Active listening implies attention on the speaker and the speaker's intended message. A listener whose mind wanders is no longer actively listening.
- Conveying insincerity—A claims representative who feigns concern or empathy for an insured or a claimant may be going through the motions of active listening but is not using the technique effectively.

### *Apply Your Knowledge*

Andrew and Lisa arrived home after work to find many of their electronic devices, jewelry, and collectors' items missing from their home. As a claims representative, you are interviewing the couple in their home to get more information about the loss. Soon after you introduce yourself, Lisa says, "I feel violated by this break-in." Andrew adds, "What is really weird is that we can't figure out how they got in or how they got everything out." In your attempt to build rapport with the couple and lay the groundwork for acquiring information, which one of the following responses is the most appropriate?

a.   "We can't rule out that it was an inside job."

b.   "If you can provide a list of the missing items, it will speed up the claims process."

c.   "Why would you say that?"

d.   "It can be a shock when someone enters your personal space and takes your possessions."

*Feedback: d.* This statement indicates that you heard and empathize with Lisa's feelings of being violated. The other statements are not appropriate at this stage in the interview. Choice a. sounds accusatory. Even if you suspect that the couple staged the burglary, you would need much more information before voicing your suspicions. At this point, you should be suspending judgment. Choice b. ignores both Lisa's and Andrew's comments in an apparent effort to get to the business of settling the claim. Choice c. appears to demand either that Lisa defend her feelings or that Andrew explain why it is important to him to know how the burglars entered and left the house. Such a question may put the couple on the defensive.

# EFFECTIVE WRITTEN CLAIMS COMMUNICATION

The emails, text messages, letters, and reports that claims representatives write while handling a claim are not only crucial to clear communication with other parties but also become a claims investigation's primary record. That's why documentation must be clear, concise, accurate, objective, and professionally written.

What are the keys to effectively written communications? Thinking about these aspects of a document while writing can ensure a clear, accurate result:

- Intended audience
- Purpose
- Content, including accuracy, tone, and organization
- Specific requirements

## Intended Audience

Written communication may be directed toward those associated with the insurer (such as claims supervisors or underwriters) or outside parties (such as insureds, claimants, or attorneys). Defining and understanding a message's intended audience helps ensure effective wording.

For example, a message to an external reader who has little insurance knowledge should avoid using technical terms. So while an internal memo to a claims supervisor might state, "The payments can be recovered through subrogation," a letter to an insured could instead note that "The insurer will recover the funds from the person who caused the loss."

Defining the intended audience for a message may also indicate a need to learn more about that audience before the message is composed. For example, taking time to learn about a claimant's culture, job or profession, and community can help the writer achieve the overarching goal and build trust through the communication. Such information may also help the writer anticipate and answer the claimant's objections or questions and influence the tone of the message.

Additionally, written communication may have more than one audience. For example, the primary audience for a claims status report might be a claims supervisor or claims examiner. Secondary audiences can include anyone else who may read the claims file, including underwriters, the insurer's defense attorney, insureds' or claimants' attorneys, regulators, and courts of law.

A claims representative may direct an email to an insurer's defense attorney (primary audience) and copy on it the insured and the claims supervisor (secondary audience). Because multiple audiences may view a particular piece of writing, those who compose communications should be aware of and consider all potential audiences when writing messages.

## Purpose

A written message's purpose should be clearly defined. This can be as simple as asking questions such as, "Why am I writing this message?" and "What should this message accomplish?"

In general terms, most written business communication is developed to either inform or persuade. An informative written claims communication may include an email or a letter to an insured reporting on the status of an investigation or claim. A persuasive written claims communications may include a letter asking an insured to provide additional information regarding a loss by a specified date or an internal memo to a claims supervisor recommending a reserve amount for a claim.

## Content

Writing an effective message is a process. Defining the message's intended audience and purpose is part of the planning stage, which also includes generating ideas or topics for the content of the communication and outlining or organizing those topics. For a complex message, a formal outline can help the writer organize topics and subtopics. For short messages, a topic sentence and a list of supporting ideas may be sufficient for planning purposes.

A rough draft is the first attempt to put ideas into sentences and arrange them in logical order. The focus is on organization and flow, not on correct grammar, spelling, and phrasing. The writer should keep in mind the purpose, audience, appropriate length and tone, and organization and flow of ideas.

The revision stage involves adding, deleting, and correcting. The writer reviews the message to ensure that it contains all the information needed to accomplish its purpose. Unnecessary verbiage should be deleted and word choice refined. Tone should be adjusted with the intended audience in mind, and jargon and technical terms the receiver may not understand should be eliminated or, if necessary, defined. Grammar and spelling should be checked and corrected. Sentences should be honed for clarity and coherence and rearranged for logical flow and organization. In the final edit, the spelling of all names should be thoroughly checked, and numbers should be verified.

The tone that business writers adopt reflects their attitudes about the subject and toward the audience. Readers may react personally to tone and may also build an image of the sender and the sender's organization based on the tone of a written communication.

The appropriate tone for most business letters is businesslike; friendly; courteous; polite; sincere; and, if need be, firm but tactful. Emotional extremes; flippancy; sarcasm; and demanding, demeaning, or argumentative language should be avoided. Light humor may be appropriate in some circumstances.

During revision, it may be helpful to ask, "How would I react if I received this message?" Reading the message aloud can reveal awkward or ambiguous wording. Asking a co-worker to read the message can also provide useful feedback.

# Specific Requirements: Claims Communications With Legal Ramifications

The importance of clarity and accuracy of written communication is particularly important for documents required by law or that may be material to legal proceedings.

## Reservation of Rights Letters and Nonwaiver Agreements

Reservation of rights letters and nonwaiver agreements, if improperly worded, can be costly to an insurer. Consequently, the language of such agreements is often mandated by case law or individual insurers. Before writing either type of document, a claims representative should consult with counsel to obtain the language for a specific state.

Reservation of rights letters and nonwaiver agreements should be clear and unambiguous. While striving to meet legal requirements for such documents, claims representatives should avoid using jargon in order to communicate with insureds in a nonthreatening, understandable manner. The documents should set forth the specific coverage part, provision, or exclusion that applies to the situation in question.

A reservation of rights letter should do more than identify the named insured and policy, describe the claim, and discuss the relevant policy provisions. It should also convey that the letter is not a denial of coverage, state that any actions taken by the insurer do not constitute a waiver of rights or admission of coverage, and reserve the right to add to or modify the insurer's coverage position based on additional coverage issues that may be discovered.

Further, reservation of rights letters include wording allowing the insurer to reserve the right to raise other coverage issues later if they become known. Claims representatives should make sure that these letters include any language recommended or required by the insurer.

Nonwaiver agreements can present special communication challenges because the claims representative must obtain the insured's signature. A claims representative who becomes aware of a coverage problem or defense will fill out a specific nonwaiver agreement form, entering the reasons for the coverage question and referencing the specific policy provisions or exclusions that raise the coverage questions.

In most cases, claims representatives meet personally with insureds to acquire their signatures on nonwaiver agreements, but in some cases, signatures are acquired by mail. In such cases, a letter accompanying the agreement should explain the reasons for requesting it and ask the insured to sign and return it. A carefully worded cover letter can make the difference in whether an insured signs or rejects a nonwaiver agreement.

## Denial Letter

Claims denials may be based on lack of liability, lack of coverage, or breach of a policy condition. Because they can trigger bad-faith lawsuits, claims denials must be presented with great care. Many insurers have strict guidelines regarding claims denial, often requiring approval from underwriters and claims managers before issuing denial letters.

Many denial letters are drafted by attorneys to ensure compliance with the relevant jurisdiction's legal requirements; however, this responsibility is often assigned to claims representatives.

Denial letters differ from most other letters in that the purpose is not stated in the first sentence. Generally, a denial letter should start with a positive or neutral statement related to the fact that the claim has been reported and then build toward the denial. The denial should be clearly stated, and an explanation should follow. Specific policy language should be quoted, and its location in the policy should be designated; for example, "p. 2 of 14 of the BPP, A. Coverage, 2. Property not covered, c. Automobiles held for sale." The policy provisions should then be related to the facts of the loss.

The letter's closing should invite a claimant or insured who disagrees with the denial to submit additional information that might cause the claim to be reevaluated. A general reservation of rights paragraph is also included in the letter.

## File Status Notes

File status notes (also called log notes or file notes) provide a chronological account of the claims representative's activities as well as those of claims supervisors and managers relating to the claim. These notes can include information about the progress of the claim, recommendations to change reserves, and requests for assistance and settlement authority. Status reports are one way to confirm that a claims investigation is progressing in a timely manner.

File status notes may contain short summaries of reports and information received from outside sources. Because lawyers and state regulators can obtain copies of claims files, file status notes and other file documentation must contain clear, concise, and accurate information that reflects these qualities of the investigation and its subsequent resolution:

- The claim was handled in a timely matter.
- The investigation was fair and balanced and took both the insured's and the insurer's interests into consideration.
- The investigation was conducted thoroughly and in good faith.

The tone of file status notes should be straightforward, factual, and objective. The notes should not leave the reader with the impression that the claims representative is taking sides, such as in this statement: "The claimant obviously wasn't paying attention."

File notes should not express prejudice of any sort, avoiding remarks about race, religion, weight, or sex. Humor is also out of place in file notes. A note that seems innocuous when written can be devastating when read to a jury.

Claims representatives should avoid using personal shorthand in file status notes because they may not be available to interpret them later. Some insurers have guidelines that include acceptable abbreviations for frequently used terms, such as "PR" for police report or "s/s" for stop sign.

## Emails

Because emails live forever, claims representatives should take special care when writing them. An email related to a claim could end up in court. Carefully written messages also contribute to efficient and effective claims handling.

Emails should be brief. As with all written communications, an email's author should define the purpose and audience before composing the message, clearly stating the purpose in the first sentence.

The writer should consider both primary and secondary audiences when choosing language and tone. Jargon and technical terms should be used judiciously and explained when necessary. An email writer should always carefully read a message before sending it, checking for correct grammar, missing words, and misspelled words that can be overlooked by spell checkers.

Although many email messages are internal and may, in some cases, have a more relaxed tone than formal business letters, symbols, emojis, email abbreviations, excessive punctuation (for example, multiple exclamation points), and under-punctuation should be avoided.

---

### Apply Your Knowledge

As a claims representative, you are investigating a liability claim against an insured. The claimant, an immigrant who speaks little English, was injured when she tripped on a cracked paving stone on the city-owned sidewalk in front of the insured's home. You have reviewed the accident report and the insured's homeowners policy and have determined that the insured is not responsible for maintaining a sidewalk owned by the city and is therefore not liable for the claimant's injuries. Your claims supervisor agrees and advises you to inform the claimant of the decision. Which one of the following choices describes the best approach for preparing to communicate the denial of liability to the claimant?

- Locate a claims denial form letter, fill in the details of the claim and the conclusions, and mail it to the claimant
- Find out more about the claimant's native culture and language to determine how best to communicate the information.

- Write a handwritten note expressing empathy
- Send the claimant a reservation of rights letter

*Feedback: b.* You should find out more about the claimant's culture and language to ensure that the claimant will be able to understand the message. Your letter should explain that the insured does not own the sidewalk in front of his home and is therefore not responsible for maintaining it. You may decide to have the letter translated into the claimant's native language.

# VERBAL CLAIMS COMMUNICATION

The ability to communicate effectively is essential to a claims representative's success.

Most of a claims representative's work involves communicating with different types of people for various purposes. Effective claims communication involves understanding several key components of those communications:

- The types of people engaged in claims communications
- The purpose of claims communications
- Methods for effective claims communications
- Barriers to effective claims communications

Claims representatives who practice purpose-oriented communications, using language and methods appropriate for each person, will produce positive business outcomes for their insurers.

## Types of People Engaged in Claims Communications

Different types of people routinely participate in verbal exchanges with claims representatives:

- Insureds
- Agents and brokers
- Claimants
- Attorneys
- Service providers
- Internal management

Claims representatives must be able to communicate effectively with different types of people. Effective communication involves understanding the perspective of each person and the communication tools and techniques most likely to be understood by that person. See the exhibit "Perspectives of People Engaged in Claim Communications."

## Perspectives of People Engaged in Claim Communications

| Types of People | Perspectives |
|---|---|
| Insured | **First-Party Claims**<br>• May be injured and/or under emotional stress<br>• May be unfamiliar with the claim process or the language of insurance<br><br>**Third-Party Claims**<br>• May be concerned about liability and cost as well as the condition of the person(s) alleging injury or damage<br>• May be unfamiliar with the claim process or the language of insurance |
| Agents and Brokers | • Understand the language of insurance and the claim process<br>• Usually communicating on behalf of the insured |
| Claimants | • Typically do not understand the claim process or insurance terminology<br>• May be injured and/or under emotional stress<br>• May be wary or frightened |
| Attorneys | **Plaintiff Attorneys**<br>• Usually negotiating benefits or settlements<br>• Usually familiar with the claim process and insurance terminology<br>• May be verbally provocative<br><br>**Defense Attorneys**<br>• Represent insurer and/or insured<br>• Understand the claim process and insurance terminology<br>• Usually bill for telephone conversations |

| Service Providers | Medical Providers |
|---|---|
| | • Important to understand different perspectives of treating physicians, physicians conducting independent medical examinations (IME), and expert witnesses |
| | • Nurse case managers have different focus than claim representatives, even if employed by the same insurer |
| | **Investigators** |
| | • Need to clearly communicate purpose and parameters of investigation |
| | **Others** |
| | • Have varying levels of understanding of claim process and insurance terminology |
| **Internal Management** | • Type, method, and style of communication varies with level of management |
| | • Have varying levels of understanding of the claim function—for example, a claim manager versus an underwriting manager |

[DA07271]

While maintaining a consistently professional approach to communications, claims representatives should adjust their style and terminology according to the type of person involved in the verbal exchange. For example, it is important to be able to communicate differently with a claimant than with an attorney. Effective communication requires understanding the perspective of the other person.

How could a claims representative approach a telephone conversation with an insured who has been injured in a severe auto accident?

The claims representative could begin by asking the insured how he or she feels and allow the insured to express those feelings. The claims representative can maintain a sympathetic yet professional tone throughout the conversation by using phrases such as, "I understand."

## Purpose of Claims Communications

There are four major purposes of claims communications:

- Investigation
- Evaluation
- Negotiation
- Resolution

Just as it is important for claims representatives to understand the perspective of the other person in a verbal exchange, it is also important to understand the purpose of each communication. How might the method of communication change depending on the purpose of the communication?

A claims representative, for example, may choose to conduct a telephone interview or take a recorded statement when speaking with an insured during a claim investigation because the purpose is to obtain information. In other situations, when possible and permissible, the claims representative may choose to meet with the insured or claimant in person.

The style of the claims representative's communication may change according to the purpose. During an investigation, the claims representative may be more casual in tone and style than during a negotiation, where the language and tone may be more formal.

How could a claims representative approach an insured when investigating an auto accident?

The claims representative could begin with a conversation that puts the insured at ease. The claims representative could make statements and ask questions that express concern such as, "This seems to be a difficult experience for you," or "How are you doing?" If a statement is to be taken, the claims representative can explain its necessity using simple language that reassures the insured that it is routine and express a sincere apology for any inconvenience this may cause the insured.

## Methods for Effective Claims Communications

Because claims representatives conduct many of their activities by telephone, it is important that they employ effective spoken communication techniques for the person and purpose involved in each verbal exchange. Effective communication in phone conversations, as well as in meetings, begins with understanding the perspective of the other person and the purpose of the communication. If the claims representative initiates the conversation, a plan for the phone call or interview will focus the conversation.

The claims representative should maintain a courteous and professional telephone manner even when dealing with angry or upset people. Expressions of consideration and understanding may help the insured remain calm and be cooperative. For example, statements such as, "I understand you're upset, however, if you can help me with some information, I will be better able to help you," can convey sincere concern. Communication should always be sincere and display a positive attitude.

Whenever possible, communication should be a collaborative process that involves working with others to attain mutual goals. For example, a claims representative should work together with an insured or claimant to reach a mutually agreeable outcome on claims decisions. When attorneys are involved, the same process can be used to expedite mutually acceptable settlements.

Claims representatives should avoid jargon unless they are certain that the other person is completely familiar with that language. The purpose of the discussion should be a focal point throughout any conversation or meeting to avoid rambling that does not produce results. At the end of each conversation or meeting, it is helpful to summarize the results and any necessary follow up. For example, a claims representative might tell an insured, "We agree that your property damage from the fire is covered under your homeowner's policy. I am going to send you a proof of loss form. When you receive it, you should itemize the damaged property, have it notarized, and send it back to me."

## Barriers to Effective Claims Communications

It is important for claims representatives to recognize potential barriers to effective claims communications. These are four major barriers that are often encountered:

- The telephone
- Hostility
- Language
- Culture

Although the telephone is used for many different types of claims communications, it can present a barrier to effective communication. The recipient of the phone call may be involved in another activity and perceive the call as an intrusion. There can be interruptions, distractions, and noisy surroundings during the phone conversation that affect the nature or flow of communication. Additionally, there is the disadvantage of not being able to see the other person during a phone call. Nonverbal expressions, such as a smile or nod, which could provide an understanding context for the dialogue, are not available. Practicing techniques such as smiling while talking on the phone (which has an effect on voice tone), patient listening, and the use of affirming phrases such as, "I see" or "Please go on," can help overcome barriers presented by the telephone.

A hostile insured, claimant, witness, or plaintiff attorney can be a barrier to a claims representative's attempt to effectively communicate. While it is important for claims representatives to be calm and professional and try to elicit cooperation when the other person is hostile, it is also important to determine when hostility escalates or threatens the claims representative or others. Claims representatives should be aware of their insurers' procedures for handling threats. Claims representatives should also guard against becoming angry with or hostile to people who are rude or hostile to them. An essential skill for a claims representative is to be able to respond professionally in those situations.

Claims representatives will often encounter people who do not have the same native language. It is important in these situations to determine whether a meaningful conversation can take place without an interpreter. If an interpreter is used, another decision must be made as to who should provide the interpretation. Family members can often assist an insured or claimant; however, this assistance could create a relationship that may present problems. For example, the spouse of a claimant may take on the dominant role in the claim. Professional interpreters are available, but this service can be costly and may need to be scheduled in advance.

Cultural barriers can be subtle but significant in claims communications. These can vary from slang that is used in verbal communications to how roles are perceived. Some cultures may foster distrust or resentment of those outside the community. Claims representatives may be able to consult colleagues who come from similar cultural backgrounds to develop techniques for resolving these barriers. If the cultural barrier occurs with an insured, the account representative, underwriter, or loss control representative may be able to assist with the communication.

# NONVERBAL CUES IN CLAIM COMMUNICATION

Many experts say that nonverbal communication is more effective in delivering a message than verbal communication.

Face-to-face meetings, whenever possible and practical, can provide excellent claim information because these interactions include nonverbal, as well as verbal, communication. In order for claim representatives to achieve good results from in-person claim conversations, it is important for them to understand these aspects of nonverbal communication:

- What is nonverbal communication
- The importance of nonverbal communication
- Messages communicated with nonverbal language
- Nonverbal cues

## What Is Nonverbal Communication

During in-person meetings, information is conveyed by **nonverbal communication** in addition to verbal communication. Nonverbal communication can

**Nonverbal communication**
Communication that is not spoken or written, including eye movement, kinesics, appearance, and time and space.

enhance, illustrate, confirm, or contradict verbal communication. Nonverbal communication can also facilitate communication or create a barrier to communication.

Eye contact and facial expressions are common methods of nonverbal communication. In the United States, eye contact is usually considered an important aspect of communication. Failing to make eye contact can convey an impression of avoidance, disinterest, or even dishonesty. "Shifty eyes" is an expression that describes someone whose eye movements convey a lack of sincerity. Smiling typically conveys warmth and friendliness. Frowning may convey displeasure or a lack of understanding. Sadness or grief can often be observed in a person's eyes or overall expression.

Posture and gestures are used either intentionally or unconsciously when people communicate. A hand extended for a handshake is an intentional gesture of a friendly greeting. Waving one's arms while speaking may express enthusiasm. Fiddling with fingers or other objects can convey nervousness. Finger tapping can be either a conscious or unconscious expression of impatience.

A person's appearance involves his or her clothing, grooming, and overall demeanor, including posture and facial expression. A clean, neat, and conservatively attired appearance typically expresses professionalism. Erect posture may convey self-esteem and confidence, while a slouched posture may convey a careless attitude or lack of confidence.

An important aspect of communication is personal space. People will often instinctively back up from another person if that person gets too close to them during communications. The time of arrival and time spent with another person are also types of nonverbal communication. Late arrival for a scheduled meeting can convey an impression that the person does not view the meeting as important or is avoiding the meeting (even if the person arriving late was unavoidably detained). Taking more than the time allotted to complete a meeting may convey that the organizer thinks the meeting is more important than the attendees' prior commitments or that the organizer is disorganized.

All aspects of nonverbal communication combine with verbal communication to create an overall impression. For example, someone who is late for a scheduled appointment cannot make eye contact, fiddles with his fingers, turns his head to look away, and is hesitant when speaking may convey that he is not being honest and straightforward. A person whose office is cluttered, who shuffles through papers to locate a form, and whose speech is rambling may convey disorganization.

It is important to recognize that different cultures may have different types of nonverbal communication. For example, the common greeting in some European countries is a kiss rather than a handshake, while in Japan it may be appropriate to bow. It can be as important to provide interpretation for the nonverbal language of other cultures as it is for the verbal language.

# The Importance of Nonverbal Communication

Face-to-face communication provides more information than any other medium because of the nonverbal communication that occurs.[2] Therefore, it is important in any in-person claim communication for the claim representative to be attentive to the other person's nonverbal communication.

One of the disadvantages of most telephone communications is the inability to see the other person. Does a pause indicate that the other person is uncomfortable with the conversation or is distracted by something else? This type of information can be immediately conveyed during an in-person conversation through nonverbal communication.

The adage that "one picture is worth a thousand words" summarizes the benefits of face-to-face communication compared with telephone communication. A wince of pain can express how an injured person is feeling more eloquently than a five-minute verbal description of symptoms. Another adage is that "actions speak louder than words." A person's body language may contradict his or her spoken language. Conflicts between these two different types of messages can indicate to a claim representative a need for additional lines of questioning or investigation.

# Messages Communicated With Nonverbal Language

Claim representatives need to understand their own nonverbal communication and the information it conveys to others. They also need to understand other people's nonverbal communications and how these may be significant in claim communication.

---

### Apply Your Knowledge

Amy, a claim representative, has scheduled an appointment with Mark at his home to interview him after an accident in which he injured his back when he slipped and fell at a store. Amy arrives five minutes before the scheduled time. Mark answers the door. He does not respond verbally when Amy tells him who she is, but he gestures for her to enter and holds the door open.

Mark silently leads Amy into the living room, He walks quickly without any apparent difficulty and sits on the sofa; Amy sits in a chair across from him. When Amy asks him how he is doing, he brusquely says, "About as well as I can be, I guess."

Amy sits erect on the chair and takes a leather-bound notebook from her briefcase. She plans to record the interview, but she decides to try to establish a more cooperative framework first. She asks Mark whether he would like to discuss what happened in the accident. Mark looks away from her toward the window. Finally he says, "I guess that's what you're here for."

What types of nonverbal communication occur in this setting? How is the nonverbal communication important for the claim?

*Feedback:* Amy's nonverbal communication as described is professional. She arrives slightly ahead of the scheduled time. Her posture is erect, indicating confidence. She uses a leather-bound notebook that she takes from a briefcase to make notes about the interview; these accessories are likely to convey an impression of professionalism and organization. She follows Mark's lead and does not immediately start the recorded interview. This is conscious nonverbal communication on Amy's part to attempt to make Mark feel comfortable and elicit his cooperation.

Mark's nonverbal communication creates an impression of evasiveness. His silence is brusque and unwelcoming when Amy arrives. He walks without apparent discomfort, which conveys the impression that he is not in pain from his alleged injury. His nonverbal response to Amy's question conveys a reluctance to answer questions.

Claim representatives should be just as alert for nonverbal messages as they are for verbal messages. It is important to respond to others' nonverbal messages with appropriate physical, as well as verbal, responses. For example, if another person looks away and is hesitant in the verbal description of how an accident occurred, the claim representative may want to ask more detailed questions and to lean forward to engage the person.

## Nonverbal Cues

A cue is "a signal…to begin a specific speech or action."[3] Each person involved in a conversation or discussion typically responds to the other person's verbal cues. If the conversation takes place face to face, each person will also respond, consciously or unconsciously, to the other person's nonverbal cues.

Most people are familiar with the contagious yawn. If one person in a group yawns, another person often follows, then another. This is an unconscious physical response to another person's nonverbal message.

It is important for claim representatives to understand what other people's nonverbal cues indicate and to respond to those cues consciously and deliberately rather than unconsciously. For example, if another person displays aggressive gestures, such as staring and clenching fists, it is natural to respond defensively or aggressively, by folding arms across one's chest or drawing back. However, claim representatives can be most effective by responding with purposeful and thoughtful nonverbal, as well as verbal, messages. Leaning slightly toward a person who has adopted an aggressive posture and saying in a soft tone of voice, "You seem to be upset about the accident," for example, may allow the other person to relax and share additional information.

Best practices for the claim representative include maintaining an attitude of relaxed and attentive listening while observing the other person's overall communication, including how the nonverbal cues relate to the verbal messages.

Nonverbal claim communications provide cues that lead a claim representative to the next steps in a claim, such as the direction of questioning or further investigation.

## SUMMARY

The communication process consists of two phases: the transmission phase and the feedback phase. Within these phases, the process also has four components:

- The sender
- The message
- The medium
- The receiver

An understanding of these components can help claims representatives communicate effectively.

Claims representatives can use active listening to build a rapport with claimants, insureds, and others involved in the claims process. As part of active listening, claims representatives can use the reflective listening technique to correctly interpret messages and to indicate a desire and willingness to understand others' spoken messages. Active listening requires listeners to set aside their own emotions or preconceptions, suspend judgment, and overcome environmental distractions. Environmental factors and listeners' actions and attitudes can raise barriers to effective active listening.

The ability to communicate effectively in writing is fundamental to good-faith claims handling and effective claims resolution. Before writing a message, a claims representative should define its intended audience and purpose. The process of developing written communication includes planning, drafting, and revising. Claims representatives should be aware that some claims documents they write may have legal ramifications, including reservation of rights letters, nonwaiver agreements, claims status reports, claims denial letters, and email messages.

Effective claims communications begin with understanding the perspective of the other person engaged in the verbal exchange and the purpose of that exchange. Selection of the appropriate communication method and technique will produce good claims investigations, evaluations, negotiations, and resolutions. Finally, recognizing and overcoming any barriers to consistently effective communication will help claims representatives achieve success.

To be effective during face-to-face meetings, it is important for claim representatives to understand nonverbal communication. Developing skills in this type of communication will enable claim representatives to obtain a greater depth of information about a claim than verbal communication alone provides.

## ASSIGNMENT NOTES

1.    Gareth R. Jones and Jennifer M. George, Contemporary Management, 6th ed. (Boston: McGraw-Hill/Irwin, 2009), p. 569.

2.    Gareth R. Jones and Jennifer M. George, *Contemporary Management* (New York: McGraw-Hill, 2009), p. 573.

3.    *Merriam-Webster's Collegiate Dictionary*, 11th ed. (Springfield, Mass.: Merriam-Webster, Inc., 2004), p. 303.

# Dealing With Fraud

## Educational Objectives

After learning the content of this assignment, you should be able to:

▷ Explain why the following factors are important to insurers when detecting and preventing insurance fraud:

- Public attitude toward insurance fraud

- Cost of insurance fraud to the insurance industry

▷ Given a claim, determine the types of fraud involved.

▷ Using a balanced claim investigation, evaluate any fraud indicators present in the claim.

▷ Evaluate the anti-fraud efforts made by:

- Insurers

- State government

- Federal government

- Industry organizations

▷ Explain how network analysis and clustering can be used to detect claims fraud.

# Dealing With Fraud

**6**

## IMPORTANCE OF DETECTING AND PREVENTING INSURANCE FRAUD

Insurance fraud is often described as a victimless white-collar crime because it involves deception rather than violence and because the victim is a company instead of an individual. Though untrue, this perception is part of the environment in which claims representatives operate.

Claims representatives are on the front line of detecting and preventing **insurance fraud**. To do so effectively, it helps to understand the public's attitude toward fraud and the cost of insurance fraud to the industry.

### Public Attitude Toward Insurance Fraud

Insurance fraud is common in auto insurance, workers compensation, and health claims. While most people realize that insurance fraud leads to higher insurance rates, some nonetheless tolerate some forms of claims fraud, such as slightly increasing the amount of a claim to make up for deductibles or past premiums paid (called padding).[1] See the exhibit " Attitudes Toward Insurance Fraud."

**Insurance fraud**
Any deliberate deception committed against an insurer or an insurance producer for the purpose of unwarranted financial gain.

### Attitudes Toward Insurance Fraud

| | Strongly Agree | Agree | Probably Agree | Probably Disagree | Disagree | Strongly Disgree |
|---|---|---|---|---|---|---|
| It's all right to increase claim amount to: | | | | | | |
| Make up for premium | 3% | 5% | 10% | 13% | 24% | 45% |
| Make up for deductible | 3 | 6 | 15 | 13 | 23 | 40 |

Insurance Research Council, Insurance Fraud: A Public View, 2013 Edition (Malvern, Pa.: Insurance Research Council, 2013), p. 7. [DA12784]

Attitudes toward fraud vary with age, gender, and other factors. Insurance professionals should try to raise overall public awareness of the costs and ramifications of insurance fraud, which include criminal penalties. Public awareness can reduce tolerance of fraud, which in turn helps insurers detect and deter it.

# Cost of Insurance Fraud

Insurance fraud is one of the costliest white-collar crimes in the United States, second only to tax evasion.[2] The Insurance Information Institute estimates that insurance fraud accounts for 10 percent of the property-casualty insurance industry's incurred losses and loss adjustment expenses.[3] Fraud costs roughly $80 billion per year across all lines of insurance, with about $34 billion from property-casualty lines.[4]

Insurers also lose needed funds through rate evasion, which occurs when insureds make false statements on insurance applications. For example, some insureds report false Social Security numbers to hide bad credit scores. Others apply for auto insurance and claim that their vehicles are used only for leisure when they are actually used in long commutes to and from work in urban areas.

The cost of fraud does not fall on insurers alone; it is shared by everyone. Fraud results in higher insurance premiums, taxes, and costs of goods and services. In fact, insurance fraud costs the average family in the United States hundreds of dollars per year in increased premiums.[5] The more that insureds and the public realize its negative consequences, the less likely they will be to commit or tolerate fraud.

---

## Apply Your Knowledge

Samantha, an insurance professional, is home for the holidays when she overhears her cousin, Karl, talking about how a co-worker inflated a workers compensation claim. Karl is sympathetic to his co-worker, saying that he is owed for all the time he has given the company. Which one of the following best describes how Samantha should respond to help change Karl's opinion of insurance fraud?

a.   Samantha could explain that fraud results in higher insurance premiums, taxes, and costs of goods and services.

b.   Samantha should not respond because Karl will think that she is biased because of her role in the insurance industry.

c.   Samantha should ask the extent to which Karl's co-worker inflated his claim; if a claim is just slightly exaggerated, no harm is done.

*Feedback: a.* Samantha could explain that fraud results in higher insurance premiums, taxes, and costs of goods and services.

---

# TYPES OF INSURANCE FRAUD

Insurance fraud is any deliberate deception committed against an insurer or an insurance producer for the purpose of unwarranted financial gain. It can occur during the process of buying, selling, or underwriting insurance, or making or paying a claim.

To identify the types of insurance fraud, it is important to understand what constitutes fraud. Fraud occurs when all of these elements exist:

- An individual or an organization intentionally makes an untrue representation.
- The untrue representation concerns an important or a **material fact** or event.
- The untrue representation is knowingly made.
- The untrue representation is intended to deceive.
- The victim relies on and acts on the untrue representation.
- The victim suffers some detriment, such as loss of money and/or property, as a result of relying on and acting on the untrue representation.

**Material fact**
In insurance, a fact that would affect the insurer's decision to provide or maintain insurance or to settle a claim.

Insurance fraud can be committed by anyone—insured, claimant, doctor, lawyer, mechanic, claim representative—involved in the insurance transaction or in a claim. For example, an applicant for workers compensation insurance may deliberately underreport the amount of payroll to the insurance agent, broker, or underwriter. The underwriter relies on the payroll information provided by the applicant to set the premium amount. The applicant's misrepresentation causes the underwriter to charge a workers compensation premium that is lower than the premium appropriate for the risk, and the insurer thereby suffers a loss of premium income. An agent, in collusion with an applicant, may overreport the square footage of a commercial building, permitting the applicant to purchase higher insurance limits with the intent of burning the building, collecting the insurance money, and splitting the proceeds with the agent. Or, an underwriter may provide an agent with a low premium quote in exchange for a payoff. Fraudulent claims may include **staged accidents**, inflated medical bills, and the intentional burning of an insured property. These are all examples of insurance fraud.

Insurance fraud can be classified as either hard or soft. **Hard fraud** involves actions that are undertaken deliberately to defraud. False claims or intentional losses are examples of hard fraud. **Soft fraud**, also known as opportunity fraud, occurs when a claim is exaggerated. The perpetrator uses the "opportunity" of a legitimate claim to obtain unwarranted personal gain.

**Staged accident**
An accident deliberately caused by a person who intends to feign injury and collect on the ensuing claim.

**Hard fraud**
Actions that are undertaken deliberately to defraud.

## Hard Fraud

Hard fraud involves schemes to defraud insurers by filing false claims for losses that have not occurred or by intentionally creating losses. Hard fraud can be a staged or invented accident, injury, or theft that results in a false claim. Hard fraud can also be an intentional loss, such as that resulting from arson.

**Soft fraud, or opportunity fraud**
Fraud that occurs when a legitimate claim is exaggerated.

## False Claims

False claims arise when an insured pursues a claim for property damage or injury that has not actually occurred. Many types of false claims involving many types of insurance coverage can be made. For example, an insured may file a homeowners claim for stolen jewelry when no jewelry was stolen, or an employee may pretend to have a back injury to get paid time off under a workers compensation policy.

**Misrepresentation**

A false statement of a material fact on which a party relies.

**Concealment**

An intentional failure to disclose a material fact.

False claims can also include **misrepresentation**, **concealment**, or distortion of a material fact.

For example, store patrons who intentionally pull display items on top of themselves and then file bodily injury claims commit misrepresentation. Also, restaurants are frequently the victims of people who falsely claim injury or illness from improperly prepared food, another act of misrepresentation.

Some false claims can involve the insured's collusion with others. For example, an auto body shop may prepare a repair estimate for alleged damage to an auto when no damage exists. Workers at vehicle salvage yards may collude with others to purchase insurance on unrepairable vehicles; after the insurance is in effect, the "owner" files a false claim for damages when, in fact, the vehicle was already damaged at the time it was insured. See the exhibit "Examples of False Claims."

### Examples of False Claims

- An insured obtains a pre-damaged vehicle, insures it, and then claims she is a victim of a hit-and-run vehicle. The police are called to verify the property damage.

- An insured buys an expensive vehicle for a minimal down payment and sells it overseas. He reports it stolen and then collects on the insurance as well as the sales price of the vehicle.

- An insured collects fine jewelry from his friends and family. He has it appraised and schedules it on his homeowners policy. He returns the jewelry to the owners and reports it stolen. He then collects on the insurance.

[DA07278]

## Intentional Losses

Another type of hard fraud is an intentional loss, one that is not accidental or fortuitous and that results from an intentional act. Intentional losses can be distinguished from exaggerated and false claims. An exaggerated claim is based on an actual loss, but the value of the loss is inflated. In a false claim, no loss has actually occurred. In contrast, intentional losses involve an actual incident with resulting damage. In this case, however, the incident is not accidental, and the damage is intended. See the exhibit "Staged Accidents."

**Staged Accidents**

An insurer sued to recover more than $4.6 million in claim payments from participants in a staged car-accident ring in Texas. Most of the claims arose from collisions resulting when a car stopped suddenly in front of an innocent victim's auto, allegedly causing injuries. Lawyers, law-office employees, medical clinics, and others participated in the scheme.

[DA05568]

Arson committed by an insured or at an insured's direction is an example of an intentional loss. A business owner may burn his own warehouse and file a claim to recover the insurance proceeds. Another example of intentional loss is a staged accident. The intent of those who stage accidents is to defraud an insurer. Typical staged accidents include rear-end automobile collisions. When the collision occurs, the scammer claims to be severely injured and to require transportation to a hospital by ambulance, while feigning great pain. Alleged injuries from staged accidents vary, but the most common involve soft-tissue injuries to the neck and back because they are harder to medically disprove. See the exhibit "Examples of Intentional Losses."

**Examples of Intentional Losses**

- The claimant's vehicle swerves quickly in front of the insured's vehicle and stops abruptly, causing the insured to rear-end the claimant's vehicle. The claimant asserts he is severely injured.

- An insured buys multiple fire insurance policies on the same house, then intentionally burns it until it is a total loss and collects the policy limits on several policies.

- An insured is in default on her car loan for failing to remit several months of loan payments. She drives the car into a lake and claims it was stolen to collect on the insurance.

[DA07282]

# Soft Fraud

Soft fraud, or opportunity fraud, is the exaggeration or padding of a legitimate claim for the purpose of receiving greater reimbursement than would be received for the actual loss. Such claims may exaggerate the value of property or the severity of an injury. For example, an insured may state that a stolen computer is six months old rather than its actual age of two years to increase the value of the claim.

Injury claims can be exaggerated or padded in several ways. Some medical providers exaggerate claims by overtreating patients. Overtreatment involves performing more procedures, or more expensive procedures, than are medically necessary to treat an injury. These treatments may include additional or unnecessary diagnostic tests, such as x-rays, CT scans, or MRIs; extra office visits; or extended physical therapy. Overtreatment or unnecessary treatment by medical providers can occur with many insurance coverages, including automobile liability, workers compensation, and homeowners liability.

Overtreatment is a form of medical provider fraud—that is, fraud that occurs when healthcare professionals help insureds file insurance claims for treatment that is unnecessary, is not related to the injury, or has not been rendered. For example, a doctor may recommend that a patient receive physical therapy three times per week for twelve weeks when three times per week for eight weeks would suffice. The patient may be aware of the deception and go along with it, or the patient may be unaware of the scheme and may simply be following the doctor's orders. The unnecessary treatment "pads" or exaggerates the true value of the claim, costing the insurer more money. The medical provider increases revenues by overtreatment. See the exhibit "Examples of Exaggerated/Padded Claims."

---

### Examples of Exaggerated/Padded Claims

- Overstated value of property
- Overstated severity of injury
- Overtreatment for injuries
- Unnecessary treatment for injuries

---

[DA02658]

It is a valuable skill to be able to determine what type of fraud has occurred in a set of facts. See the exhibit "Practice Exercise."

---

### Practice Exercise

**Facts:** An employee injures his back over the weekend while helping his brother-in-law put a new roof on his house. He goes in to work Monday morning. Within a few minutes of arriving at work, and while out of sight of his co-workers, he calls out in pain. When his co-workers come to help, he claims he injured his back lifting a heavy box.

**Question to consider:** What type of fraud has occurred to make this workers compensation claim not legitimate?

**Answer:** This is fraud as each of the elements exists. It is not a hard fraud false claim because the employee did actually injure his back. It is not a hard fraud intentional loss because he did not intentionally injure his back. It is a soft fraud because he was actually injured and the injury was accidental. However, he misrepresented when and where the injury occurred to obtain workers compensation benefits.

---

[DA07283]

# INDICATORS OF POSSIBLE INSURANCE FRAUD

Claims representatives should be trained to look for fraud indicators that can help detect fraud before a claim is paid. Paying only legitimate claims protects other insureds as well as the insurer. When fraudulent claims are not paid, other insureds pay lower premiums and the insurer can better maintain its solvency. It is also important to recognize that insurance fraud usually increases during difficult economic times.

Insurers rely on claims representatives to notice indicators of possible fraud in claims and to conduct appropriate investigations. The claims representative must also conduct a balanced investigation once fraud is suspected, because fraud indicators are not proof of fraud. Fraud-fighting organizations such as the National Insurance Crime Bureau (NICB) publish lists of claim-fraud indicators. Some insurers develop their own lists of indicators.

Many insurers now use computer programs to detect characteristics that are common to fraudulent claims. Such programs can analyze vast amounts of data across different lines of insurance to identify claim patterns and other similarities that may indicate fraud. Several organizations, such as the Insurance Services Office (ISO), offer electronic antifraud databases that contain claim-related records or provide access to public records that may be used to gather evidence of fraud.

Claims representatives who are aware of fraud indicators can more readily recognize cases that warrant review by a special investigation unit (SIU) or, when appropriate, referral to the NICB or to law enforcement agencies.

## Conducting a Balanced Investigation

Claims representatives must balance a suspicion of fraud with the possibility that a claim is legitimate despite the presence of one or more indicators of possible fraud. To achieve this balance, a claims representative can frame an investigation around these questions:

- Given the circumstances of the loss, what are reasonable or expected actions/responses of the affected party?
- Is part of the reasonable action or response missing?
- Has something been added to the reasonable action or response?
- Is there physical evidence to support the reported version of the loss?
- Is the loss as reported physically possible?
- Are records available from a third party, such as a governmental agency or retailer, that can confirm or refute the insured's version of the loss?
- Is there a witness to the loss, and, if so, is the witness reliable?
- Is the fraud indicator based on conjecture or assumption?
- Is there a rational explanation for the fraud indicator?

The claims representative is responsible for meeting both insurer- and state-mandated time frames for resolution of certain types of claims. The investigation of suspected fraud can be time consuming, and the claims representative in many states will have to justify extending the deadline for claim resolution with specific evidence in order to continue an investigation.

A claims representative's detection of fraud fits into a broader framework of efforts on the part of government, the insurance industry, and the public to detect and prevent insurance fraud. For example, many state governments have enacted laws that help claims representatives by providing some form of protection and guidance.[6]

Two protections are commonly found in the laws. The first involves extending the time limit within which an insurer's investigation of a claim must be completed and the claim must be either accepted or denied. The second protection allows an insurer not to disclose to an insured that fraud is suspected if there is evidence that the insured has committed fraud. A common element in the laws is a requirement that evidence of fraud be documented in the claim files and available for inspection by state authorities.

## Fraud Indicators

Claims representatives should be alert for fraud indicators when a claim is first assigned and address these indicators during the course of their investigation. Valid reasons may exist for any of the possible fraud indicators listed in this section.

When indicators are present, claims representatives should be aware of an increased risk of fraud but should also avoid jumping to conclusions. Nothing surpasses the value of a good investigation in determining the validity of a claim.

These are some common indicators of possible fraud:[7]

- Parties involved supply vague information.
- Conflicting information appears in documentation or witness accounts.
- Known attorney/medical provider combination is present.
- Database indicates multiple similar losses for the same individual.
- Loss occurs soon after policy inception.
- Insured or claimant is uncooperative or evasive.
- Insured or claimant is eager to accept blame for an accident or demands a quick settlement.
- Insured or claimant is unusually familiar with medical or insurance terms and procedures.
- Claimant threatens to hire an attorney unless claim is settled quickly.
- No police report exists for an auto accident or theft.
- Attorney letter of representation is received shortly after the accident.

- All of the people involved in an accident report similar injuries and use the same doctor or clinic.
- The only address for the claimant is a post office box or a motel.

There are many additional fraud indicators, and each insurer typically has internal procedures for identifying and handling suspected fraud cases. It is important for claims representatives to be aware of their insurers' practices and to follow these practices when investigating claims with possible fraud. For example, an insurer's SIU may be investigating a suspected staged auto accident ring, and a new suspicious claim that is promptly reported to the SIU may assist in that investigation.

## Apply Your Knowledge

Marie, a claims representative, is investigating a homeowners claim for the theft of personal items from the trunk of an auto the week before Christmas. The insured submitted a lengthy list of toys and sports equipment that were stolen from the trunk. The insured stated that the items were all Christmas presents for his family and that the trunk was the only place that no one in the family would look to discover the gifts. The insured also said that he paid cash for most of the items and left the receipts in their respective bags in the trunk. The insured claims that the total value of the items in the trunk exceeds $10,000.

Marie's conversations with the insured raise her suspicions about the veracity of the list of stolen items. Although she believes that hiding Christmas presents in an auto's trunk and keeping the receipts with the items could be considered reasonable behavior, she questions whether reasonable behavior would include paying cash for these items. She also questions whether physical evidence would support the claim that all the items, in their original boxes, could fit into the trunk of the insured's 2018 Ford Fusion.

Marie asks the insured whether there is a police report. The insured states that he lost the police report. He does not recall which police precinct responded.

What additional investigation can Marie perform to conduct a balanced investigation based on her suspicion? Select all that apply.

a. Have a physical examination conducted of the vehicle, including whether the allegedly stolen items would fit in the trunk

b. Schedule an examination under oath of the insured, and require receipts documenting the source of the cash used to purchase the items

c. Ask for a list of stores where the items were bought and contact those stores regarding purchases made

d. Conduct interviews with family members of the insured to find out whether they were aware of the purchase of the gifts

*Feedback: a; b; and c.* Physical evidence and records from third parties can confirm or refute the conjecture of fraud. Interviews with family members are not likely to be helpful. It would be expected that family members would either state they did not know of the gifts or corroborate the insured's story.

# ANTI-FRAUD EFFORTS

Because insurance fraud results in an enormous cost to insurers, it is important for claims representatives to understand the resources available in the fight against fraud.

Insurers, state and federal governments, and insurance industry organizations all play a part in the United States' efforts to detect and deter fraud as well as prosecute and punish those who commit it.

## Insurers

Insurers are the first line of defense against insurance fraud because they are most likely to detect and report it.

### Special Investigation Units

**Special investigation unit (SIU)**

A division set up to investigate suspicious claims, premium fraud, or application fraud.

To assist claims representatives in detecting and reporting insurance fraud, insurers have created **special investigation units (SIUs)** to investigate claims that raise suspicions of fraud. Many states now mandate that insurers maintain an SIU as part of their anti-fraud efforts.

Many SIU personnel have law enforcement and investigative experience, and some have criminal justice degrees. Such qualifications help SIU personnel conduct the intensive investigations that are often necessary to substantiate claim denials based on fraud.

Claims representatives refer claims to SIUs based on criteria that vary by insurer. Some insurers refer every claim that raises suspicions to an SIU. Others refer claims based on the extent of the suspected fraud, the prospects of obtaining proof of the suspected fraud, the size of the claim, or the type of coverage.

Insurers can also help combat fraud by educating individual consumers about the costs associated with insurance fraud. Some insurers are making efforts to bring awareness of the problem to schools, organizations, and consumer groups.

### Technology

Technology provides multiple ways to detect fraud and is used by insurers as well as organizations that support them. Databases maintained by insurance-related organizations, such as Insurance Services Office, Inc. (ISO) accumulate information about insurance fraud. These databases cross-index claims to pinpoint multiple filings and provide historical information about claimants.

Predictive models are also used to increase the accuracy of fraud detection and to avoid false positives. Some of the more comprehensive models rely on an insurer's expert claims representatives to determine which variables (such as occupation, number of doctors seen, and injury type) are most useful in detecting fraud. An insurer can work with data scientists to create a database of closed claims that are known to have been fraudulent. The key is to assign a weight to each variable to arrive at a score that represents the probability that a claim is fraudulent. The weights are tweaked as the model is used to predict fraud using the database of known fraudulent claims. The model may run through the database of hundreds or even thousands of such claims. As the model learns how to weigh each variable, it becomes increasingly accurate. Eventually, a predictive model reduces the number of improper referrals to an SIU. However, predictive models must be revised as criminal behavior evolves.

By enabling insurers to share fraud-related information, blockchain offers ways to combat fraud. Blockchain provides visibility of transactions and can be used to manage identities of insureds and histories of insured items. A public ledger associated with a particular risk could provide a record of its value, past claims, and previous owners. For example, an individual may purchase an auto and insure it with six different insurers under six different names and addresses. By having a transparent ledger associated with the car, insurers can identify fraud that would be difficult to detect otherwise.

Additionally, **telematics** and the **Internet of Things** offer insurers increasing amounts of data, some of which can be used to prevent fraud. For example, telematic devices can gather data about a driver's history and habits for use in preventing auto claims fraud. As another example, data from employees' wearables has the potential to prevent workers compensation fraud. If an employee's movements are tracked by a GPS-enabled vest connected to the IOT, the employer and insurer will have a record to compare to an employee's version of events. However, employee privacy must be considered as well.

**Telematics**
The use of technological devices to transmit data via wireless communication and GPS tracking.

**Internet of Things (IoT)**
A network of objects that transmit data to and from each other without human interaction.

# State Government

Responsibility for legal efforts to combat insurance fraud lies with a variety of city, state, and federal regulatory bodies, including state insurance departments, state fraud bureaus, and law enforcement agencies. Many states have enacted anti-fraud legislation, such as expanding the definition of insurance fraud to include reckless conduct; increasing civil and criminal penalties for committing insurance fraud; requiring insurers to cooperate with law enforcement authorities in cases of suspected fraud; giving broad immunity from civil lawsuits to insurers that share information about suspected fraud; and requiring insurers to form SIUs, develop anti-fraud plans, and place fraud warnings on all applications and claims forms. See the exhibit "States That Require Mandatory Insurer Fraud Plan."

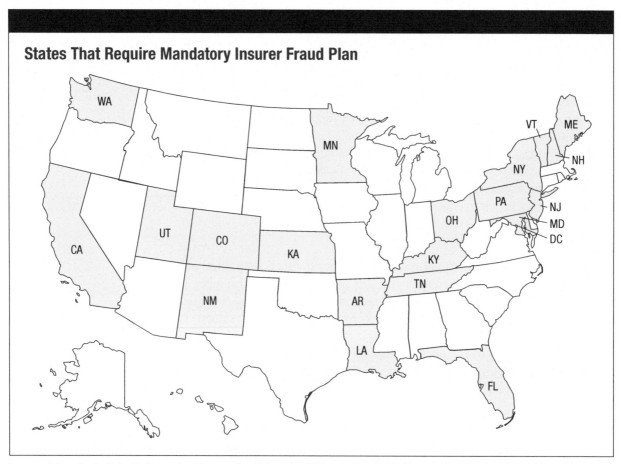

**States That Require Mandatory Insurer Fraud Plan**

Insurance Information Institute, "Background on: Insurance Fraud," November 2017, www.iii.org/publications/insurance-handbook/regulatory-and-financial-environment/background-on-insurance-fraud (accessed July 3, 2018). [DA12783]

Let's examine some anti-fraud efforts at the state level:

- Pre-inspection laws—To combat the dual problem of auto theft and fraudulent auto-repair facilities, some states require insurers to physically inspect vehicles as a prerequisite to providing insurance. Pre-inspection programs are effective in reducing theft claims for nonexistent or phantom vehicles and can deter inaccurate reporting of drivers and vehicle garaging locations that results in lower-than-adequate premium. Some states require photographic documentation as part of pre-inspection.

- Mandatory reporting—Cooperation and information sharing between insurers and law enforcement are essential in fighting insurance fraud. Most states have laws requiring insurers to report claims that raise suspicions to law enforcement or other authorities. Without these mandatory reporting laws, insurers may be hesitant to report fraud because they could face a civil suit if they were unable to prove the allegation.

- Immunity laws—To further protect insurers who report potentially fraudulent claims, states have adopted immunity statutes. Most statutes grant immunity if an insurer reports information but it turns out there is no fraud, malice, or criminal intent. Statutes vary by jurisdiction, and each should be reviewed before a report is made.

- Civil and criminal penalties—Anti-fraud efforts increasingly involve civil or administrative action to punish people who make fraudulent insurance claims. The advantages of this include the potential recovery of civil damages and the ease of civil versus criminal prosecution.

- Fraud prevention bureaus—State fraud bureaus evaluate potentially fraudulent cases submitted by insurers. After the referrals have been evaluated and enough evidence has been gathered, the information is presented to a prosecutor. Prosecutors can become involved during any phase of the investigation; when they become involved depends on the particular case. State fraud bureaus' scope of operation may vary—for example, a state insurance fraud bureau that is part of the state police department may have a relatively broader scope of operation than a similar bureau that is a division of the state department of insurance. Fraud bureaus have proved to be effective, and fraudsters tend to target states where tracking and monitoring systems are weak or nonexistent (a practice known as migrating fraud).

## Federal Government

Several federal statutes were enacted to help in the fight against insurance fraud:

- Motor Vehicle Theft Law Enforcement Act of 1984—Congress passed this act to reduce the incidence of motor vehicle thefts and facilitate the tracing and recovery of stolen motor vehicles and parts of stolen vehicles. To enable identification of stolen vehicles and parts, it required manufacturers of certain high-theft passenger car lines to inscribe or affix the Vehicle Identification Number (VIN) onto the engine, the transmission, and twelve major body parts. As an alternative, manufacturers could install anti-theft devices as standard equipment in these car lines.

- Anti Car Theft Act of 1992—The Anti Car Theft Act of 1992 built on the Motor Vehicle Theft Law Enforcement Act in several ways, including increasing the number of vehicle lines covered by the acts and making dealing with stolen marked parts a federal crime. The act also created the National Motor Vehicle Title Information System to help in the collection and dissemination of theft and recovery information.

- U.S. Mail Fraud Statute—This statute defines fraud as a scheme that uses the United States mail to obtain money or property by means of false or fraudulent representations. To obtain a mail fraud conviction, a prosecutor must prove that facts surrounding the offer were intentionally misrepresented and that U.S. mail was relied on to carry out the scheme.

- False Representation Statute—The False Representation Statute is a civil law used to protect the public (including insurers) from aggravated monetary loss when proving fraudulent intent is difficult. If the Postal Service sues the fraudster based on evidence obtained by postal inspectors, it need only prove that a particular representation was made, that it was false, and that money or property was sought through the mail.

## Industry Organizations

Many industry organizations are dedicated to the reduction of insurance fraud. Most provide services such as access to a shared database or education and training to strengthen an insurer's ability to fight fraud:

- Insurance Services Office, Inc. (ISO)—ISO provides a proactive fraud detection software tool, ISO ClaimSearch, for claims representatives. The software can find hidden connections between claims files, such as several claimants from different claims files using the same address or Social Security number.

- National Insurance Crime Bureau (NICB)—NICB fights auto insurance crime through data analytics, investigations, training, legislative advocacy, and public awareness.[8]National Insurance Crime Bureau, "About NICB," www.nicb.org/about-nicb (accessed July 4, 2018). Members that support NICB are primarily commercial and personal lines property-casualty insurers, self-insured organizations, rental car companies, parking services providers, and transportation-related firms.

- Coalition Against Insurance Fraud (CAIF)—CAIF is a diverse group that includes consumers, insurers, legislators, and regulators. It advocates measures to detect, prosecute, and deter fraud.

- International Association of Special Investigation Units (IASIU)— IASIU offers professional development for special investigators, who typically are employed by insurers, self-insurers, or third-party claim administrators. In addition to organizing an annual educational conference, the IASIU created and administers the Certified Insurance Fraud Investigator (CIFI) certification.

### *Apply Your Knowledge*

Dylan works as a claims representative for an insurer. The insurer asks Dylan to help determine which variables, such as occupation and injury, have been most useful in detecting fraud in the claims Dylan has worked on. The insurer will then weight the variables and, using a database of proven fraudulent claims, develop a method of identifying fraud before a claims representative investigates a claim. The insurer Dylan works for is most likely developing which one of the following?

a. Blockchain

b. Predictive modeling

c. Telematics

d. Mandatory reporting

*Feedback: b.* Dylan's insurer is developing a predictive model, based on variables and claims, to predict fraud in future claims. Claims representatives often help determine which variables should be included in the model.

# DETECTING CLAIMS FRAUD WITH NETWORK ANALYSIS AND CLUSTERING

Insurers have incorporated the expanding field of data analytics into many aspects of their operations, but they've been especially quick to embrace its use in fraud detection. **Network analysis**, made possible by data analytics, is a particularly useful method of detecting and preventing ever-evolving fraud schemes.

About 10 percent of the property-casualty insurance industry's incurred losses and loss adjustment expenses stem from fraud.[9] Insurers attempt to detect fraud by identifying patterns, controlling underwriting at the points of sale, and using special investigation units (SIUs). Advances in **data mining** techniques—including network analysis and clustering—are enabling insurers to more effectively identify patterns in fraudulent claims activity. Insurance and risk management professionals therefore benefit from understanding how to analyze links in a social network and clusters of data points.

Suppose that a regional insurer is concerned about its auto-related claims. In particular, this insurer has experienced a significant increase in the number and settlement amounts of auto physical damage claims. While its claims representatives and SIU currently identify 1 percent of its auto claims as fraudulent, the insurer's upper management believes, based on industry data, that the number of fraudulent claims is actually much higher. The insurer is hesitant to spend its resources on increasing its claims staff, nor does it want to continue to raise its auto rates because of the increase in claims. Investing in data mining and predictive modeling seems to be the best long-term solution.

**Network analysis**

The study of the nodes (vertices) and edges (lines) in a network.

**Data mining**

The analysis of large amounts of data to find new relationships and patterns that will assist in developing business solutions.

The insurer will conduct these activities to identify fraudulent claims:

- Detect claims fraud through traditional fraud indicators and through mining social media data
- Apply network analysis by examining links and suspicious connections
- Apply cluster analysis to discover claims characteristics that might indicate fraud

## Detecting Claims Fraud

The insurer's claims representatives were already following the insurer's protocol for identifying fraudulent claims. Insurers rely on claims representatives to notice indicators of possible claims fraud and to conduct appropriate investigations. Examples of fraud indicators include an insured or a claimant who pushes for a quick settlement or has too much or too little documentation. However, the claims representative must conduct a balanced investigation once fraud is suspected because fraud indicators are not proof of fraud.

Fraud-fighting organizations, such as the National Insurance Crime Bureau, publish lists of claims-fraud indicators. In addition, the insurer has developed its own lists of indicators and uses a computer program to detect characteristics common to fraudulent claims. Such programs analyze vast amounts of data across different lines of insurance to identify claims patterns and other similarities that may indicate fraud. Several organizations, such as Insurance Services Office, Inc., offer electronic antifraud databases that contain claims-related records or provide access to public records that may be used to gather evidence of fraud. Based on which indicators are identified, claims representatives decide whether a case warrants review by the SIU.

Although the insurer is already taking many of the appropriate steps to identify fraudulent claims, some fraud still goes undetected. One reason for this is that the insurer is using fraud indicators, the traditional approach to fraud, which means that it's depending on fraud that has happened in the past. Intelligent and innovative fraudsters will change their approaches and patterns, limiting the usefulness of these indicators.[10] The traditional approach to detecting fraud is also highly subjective and depends on claims representatives' experience in the field. A more automated approach would allow for greater objectivity and enable new claims representatives to be more effective in less time.

The insurer has begun encouraging its claims representatives to search social media for any indicators of fraud, and it will continue to do so. Claims representatives can often find evidence that someone may be lying by comparing his or her social media posts with his or her statements in a claim. For example, a car could be reported as stolen on Thursday while photos show it in the insured's driveway the next day. Or a claimant could complain of extreme back pain but post a status update about dancing.

As useful as these methods may be, however, truly efficient use of data mining and predictive modeling to detect fraud goes a step further and analyzes not only social media posts but connections within a network as well.

## Applying Network Analysis

Network analysis can be applied to social media through **social network analysis** as well as to claims files to detect possible fraud. Certain situations indicate possible fraud, such as multiple people living at the same residence claiming an auto accident in one month or numerous claims involving the same auto repair shops and/or doctors. While a claims representative might be able to pick up on these signs, it would likely be by chance. A particular street address or a doctor's last name would not be included among traditional fraud indicators. By using a machine to analyze the networks, connections are readily detected.

The insurer conducts a network analysis and discovers a fraud ring in which a relatively small number of drivers and auto body shops have participated. The repair shops have been marking up their claims for repair times and parts used to make a profit. All the participants in the fraud ring—the drivers, witnesses, and auto repair shop owners—know each other and are in the same social network. The exhibit shows a simplified diagram of a fraud ring. See the exhibit "Network Analysis of Fraud Ring."

Social network analysis

The study of the connections and relationships among people in a network.

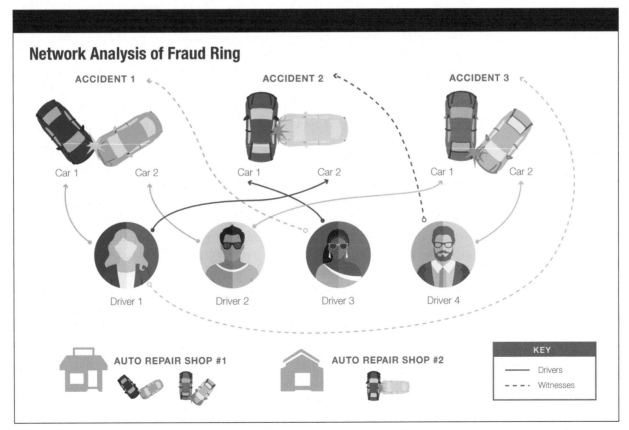

**Network Analysis of Fraud Ring**

ACCIDENT 1   Car 1   Car 2

ACCIDENT 2   Car 1   Car 2

ACCIDENT 3   Car 1   Car 2

Driver 1   Driver 2   Driver 3   Driver 4

AUTO REPAIR SHOP #1

AUTO REPAIR SHOP #2

KEY
—— Drivers
- - - - Witnesses

## Applying Cluster Analysis

The insurer wants to train a predictive model to help identify fraudulent claims as they are submitted. It has the attributes it has already used as fraud indicators, and it has identified a fraud ring through the use of network analysis. However, the insurer believes that some fraud has still gone undetected. One of the limitations in building predictive models is that they are based on historical information—attributes the insurer has already identified as being associated with fraud.[11] This creates several problems. First, because insurers do not identify all fraudulent claims, they often do not have all the historical information needed to develop an effective predictive model. In addition, fraud is ever evolving, with fraudsters constantly changing their tactics and targets, so the predictive model may quickly become outdated. The insurer needs a way to identify new fraud trends as they emerge.

A solution to the problems inherent in predictive models—and an alternative to the already performed network analysis—is **unsupervised learning** by means of **cluster analysis**. The cluster analysis will use **k-means** to group data into clusters of claims closest in distance (and therefore similar) to each group's **centroid**.

Suppose that the regional insurer performs a cluster analysis on all its auto physical damage claims. The results show a cluster of claims amounts ranging from $8,000 to $10,000. This cluster draws the claims department's attention because it is removed from the other auto physical damage claims clusters, the amounts of which are primarily either under $2,000 or from $3,000 to $4,000. Several of the claims in the outlier cluster are confirmed fraudulent claims. A claims representative confirms that several of the other claims in the cluster were flagged as suspicious. It is highly unlikely that all the claims in the cluster will be found to be fraudulent; most likely, one or more other attributes, in combination with the claims amount, will distinguish the fraudulent claims. Essentially, the fraudulent claims are outliers within the already outlying cluster.

The insurer's SIU now has sufficient reason to investigate this cluster of claims. If a significant number of claims are confirmed to be fraudulent, the insurer has just discovered another attribute (or attributes) it can include in its predictive model. Claims likely to be fraudulent will be referred to an experienced claims representative or the SIU. However, the fraudulent activity identified by this cluster analysis will eventually be suppressed, and fraudsters will develop other schemes to defraud the insurer. The insurer must be prepared to reevaluate the attributes in its predictive model, and it will probably have to perform additional cluster analyses as time goes on. Doing so will allow the insurer to stay ahead of many fraudulent claims instead of relying on dated indicators.

**Unsupervised learning**
A type of model creation, derived from the field of machine learning, that does not have a defined target variable.

**Cluster analysis**
A model that determines previously unknown groupings of data.

**K-means**
An algorithm in which "k" indicates the number of clusters and "means" represents the clusters' centroids.

**Centroid**
The center of a cluster.

## Apply Your Knowledge

Karen is the claims supervisor for the homeowners insurance division of Millstone Insurance. She has instructed all the claims representatives who report to her to examine claimants' social media accounts for any indications of fraud. How could Karen best use information from social media to detect and prevent fraudulent claims?

*Feedback:* To best use social media data, Karen should work to implement technology that would allow her team to analyze not only social media posts from individual claimants but also connections within a network. Social network connections often reveal fraud rings and other useful information. However, the team must follow the insurer's policies and relevant laws regarding privacy.

# SUMMARY

To successfully detect and prevent insurance fraud, claims representatives should first understand the public's perception of fraud and its costs for the industry and society as a whole.

Two categories of insurance fraud are hard fraud and soft fraud. Hard fraud involves schemes to defraud insurers by filing false claims for losses that have not occurred or by intentionally creating losses. Soft fraud is characterized by claims that overstate the value of property or the severity of an injury, or claims that involve the overtreatment or unnecessary treatment of injuries.

Claims representatives should be trained to look for indicators of possible insurance fraud that can help detect fraud before a claim is paid. The claims representative must maintain a balanced investigation if fraud is suspected, because fraud indicators are not proof of fraud.

Anti-fraud efforts are made by insurers, state and federal governments, and insurance industry organizations. Each plays an important role in fraud detection and deterrence, and it is important for claims representatives to understand the resources they provide.

Data analytics is particularly helpful to insurers in the area of fraud detection and prevention. While many insurers already operate programs that automatically search for traditional fraud indicators, there are opportunities to expand into network analysis and cluster analysis and thereby catch more emerging fraud trends.

# ASSIGNMENT NOTES

1.  Insurance Research Council, Insurance Fraud: A Public View, 2013 Edition (Malvern, Pa.: Insurance Research Council, 2013), p. 9.

2.  National Insurance Crime Bureau, "Prevent Fraud & Theft," www.nicb.org/prevent-fraud-theft (accessed July 2, 2018).

3.  Insurance Information Institute, "Background on: Insurance Fraud," November 6, 2017, www.iii.org/article/background-on-insurance-fraud (accessed July 2, 2018).

4.  Coalition Against Insurance Fraud, "By the Numbers: Fraud Statistics," www.insurancefraud.org/statistics.htm (accessed July 2, 2018).

5.  Federal Bureau of Investigation, "Insurance Fraud," www.fbi.gov/stats-services/publications/insurance-fraud (accessed July 2, 2018).

6.  Tim Lynch and Anne Bandle, "Protecting Adjusters from Fraud Traps," Claims, October 2008, pp. 20–21.

7.  Gary Blake, PhD, "Twenty-Seven Fraud Indicators," Claims Advisor, Fall 2010, p. 61.

8.  National Insurance Crime Bureau, "About NICB," www.nicb.org/about-nicb (accessed July 4, 2018).

9.  Insurance Information Institute, "Insurance Fraud," January 2016, www.iii.org/issue-update/insurance-fraud (accessed June 13, 2016).

10. Roosevelt C. Mosely Jr. and Nick Kucera, "The Use of Analytics for Claim Fraud Detection,"http://support.sas.com/resources/papers/proceedings14/1837-2014.pdf, p. 4 (accessed June 14, 2016).

11. Roosevelt C. Mosely Jr. and Nick Kucera, p. 10.

# Segment C

# Negotiating Claims

## Educational Objectives

After learning the content of this assignment, you should be able to:

▷ Evaluate the suitability of the four different styles of negotiation for use by a claims representative.

▷ Describe the steps in the claim negotiation process.

▷ Demonstrate how claimant and claims representative variables affect claim negotiations.

▷ Evaluate the claim negotiation techniques that are:

- Common to all parties

- Used with unrepresented claimants

- Used with represented claimants

- Used by claimants' representatives

▷ Examine the reasons that claims representatives should avoid certain negotiation techniques.

▷ Given a claim, identify the common pitfalls in claim negotiation and how to avoid them.

# Negotiating Claims

**7**

## STYLES OF NEGOTIATION

Negotiation is a part of everyday life. People negotiate when they purchase cars, homes, and major appliances, and friends may negotiate which movie to see or in which restaurant to dine. Negotiation also plays a role in resolving claims, and a claims representative's familiarity with the proper techniques could be the difference between a quick resolution for a claim or a date in court.

Whether negotiations are formal or informal, individuals usually develop negotiation styles that reflect their attitudes toward the negotiation and the other parties. Successful claims representatives can adapt their negotiation style to a specific claim, choosing from one of these main four:

- Win-win
- Win-lose
- Lose-win
- Lose-lose

Individuals who have no clear dominant style may typically compromise in negotiations. For example, a negotiator who prefers compromise settlements may suggest that the two parties split the difference or may offer to increase a proposed settlement if the other party decreases the demand. Compromise is not a style of negotiation; rather, it is the lack of a clear, dominant style.

## Important Qualities in Negotiation

Effective claims negotiators engage in activities and exhibit traits that demonstrate concern for obtaining the best outcome, and they are skilled in achieving rapport. These qualities are important to claims representatives seeking to obtain the best outcome:

- Thorough knowledge of the claim file
- Persistence
- Firmness, coupled with fairness
- Thorough evaluation of the claim

These qualities contribute to rapport in a claim negotiation:

- Good listening skills
- Humor

- Empathy
- Friendliness

Most good negotiators have an integrated style of negotiation that simultaneously seeks to obtain the best outcome and build rapport with the other party. A claims representative may focus on obtaining the best outcome in one phase of the negotiation process and, at another phase, may find that achieving rapport is more important in seeking a successful claim settlement. The integrated style gives the claims representative flexibility to shift focus depending on the circumstances and the claimant's needs and reduce the potential for conflict.

In claims, obtaining the best outcome does not mean taking advantage of the other party, settling for an unusually low amount, or providing an otherwise unfair settlement. Obtaining the best outcome means arriving at a settlement that is favorable to the insurer but that is considered equitable and fair by the other party. Negotiating parties seeking to obtain the best outcome may use a more direct negotiating style and may be less likely to make concessions than when they are working to build rapport.

Claims representatives may often negotiate with the same parties on different claims; they may be insureds, salvage buyers, or lawyers, for example. Impressions from prior negotiations can influence the outcome of current negotiations. In this situation, the claims representative may be more concerned with building rapport than with obtaining the best outcome and may, therefore, use a less aggressive, more cooperative negotiating style.

With an awareness of the various negotiating styles, claims representatives can select and adapt the style that will contribute most to a successful settlement in each case. See the exhibit "Negotiation."

## Win-Win

A claims representative using the win-win negotiation style seeks both to obtain the best outcome and to achieve rapport with the other party, resulting in a settlement that is satisfying to all parties. Win-win negotiators are simultaneously assertive and cooperative. They approach disagreements not as destructive or as conflicts but as tools to better understand the other party's wants and needs.

These examples show how alternative repair proposals in property claims can be used in win-win negotiations:

An insured scorched her Formica countertop when she placed a hot pan on it. The undamaged part of the two-year-old countertop is in good condition. Matching the Formica for a section repair is impossible because the particular pattern is no longer made. The insured expects that a repair will entail removing all the kitchen countertops and replacing them with a similar grade of Formica.

## Negotiation

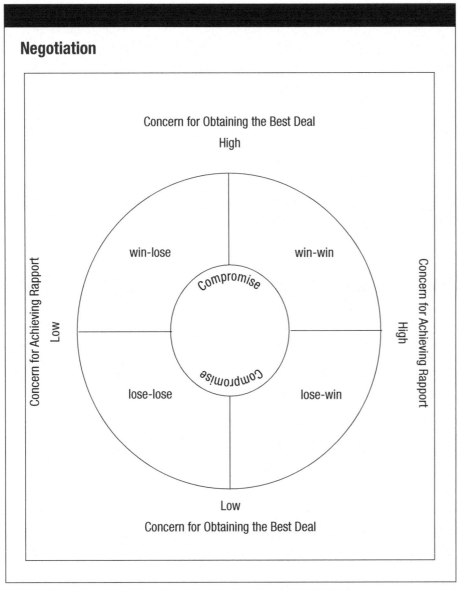

Reprinted with permission from William Stewart Associates, Inc., Jackson, N.J. [DA02927]

*Win-win solution*—Because the kitchen counters are otherwise in good condition, the claims representative offers to replace the damaged section of the counter with a built-in cutting board that will also serve as a hot pad for hot items from the stove. The claims representative may even offer to waive the insured's deductible as an added incentive to proceed with this repair.

Lightning strikes an insured's business office and damages the two-year-old telephone system, rendering it unusable. Because the telephone system is one of the insured's primary marketing tools, it must be replaced as soon as possible.

*Win-win solution*—Noting that it may be hard to locate the same make and model of equipment to replace the phone system, the claims representative offers to replace the system with a readily available newer model that has the same features, plus some enhancements. The insured will receive the phone system quickly and will benefit from an up-to-date system with additional features. The insurer will save not only the time it would have taken to replace the old system, but also costs because technological advances have resulted in lower prices for phone equipment.

Win-win negotiations can also occur in automobile physical damage claims, as this example illustrates:

The insured is driving her car when she strikes a large rock in the road, cracking the oil pan and causing an oil leak. As she continues to drive, the engine overheats and is damaged beyond repair. The car is four years old and has about 65,000 miles on it. A new engine will cost about $9,000. The insured's Personal Auto Policy, which has a $500 deductible, uses actual cash value (ACV, meaning the replacement cost less reasonable depreciation) as the valuation basis for a loss. Assuming that the car engine has a useful life span of 130,000 miles, the ACV of the engine would be 50 percent of the cost of a new engine, or $4,500. Half the engine's useful life has been used, so the insurer reduces the loss amount by 50 percent to allow for depreciation. With the deductible of $500, the net settlement amount is $4,000, leaving the insured to pay the remaining $5,000 for the new engine.

*Win-win solution*—The claims representative offers to replace the engine with a used engine of like kind and quality (LKQ) from a local salvage yard. Most repair shops provide a minor warranty on used auto parts. If the insurer has a direct repair program (DRP) and directs the claimant to a specific repair facility, most states' fair claims regulations require the insurer to guarantee the work. This solution eliminates the depreciation deduction and provides the insured with some warranty on the work performed.

Win-win negotiations may also be used in liability or workers compensation claims. This example is of a liability claim, but a similar approach can be used in workers compensation claims:

A six-year-old neighbor girl is playing with the insured's dog when the dog tries to grab a cap from the girl's head. One of the dog's teeth scrapes the girl's forehead, causing a cut that requires twenty stitches. Although the dog is not known to be vicious, a law in this state creates strict liability (meaning liability regardless of negligence or intent) on the part of the dog owners in such cases. About a year after the injury, the scar has healed fairly well and no plastic surgery is anticipated. The claims representative is aware that injury claims involving children with facial scarring usually settle at high dollar amounts.

*Win-win solution*—During negotiation, the claims representative asks the parents whether they want their daughter to attend college. Both parents say they do but express concerns about their ability to pay for a college education. The claims representative suggests a structured settlement that will pay equal sums to the claimant during her four college years between ages eighteen and twenty-one. Such a settlement will have to be approved by a judge, he explains. An advantage of the settlement is that the daughter would be receiving the payments in the year she would spend them. If, instead, the family were to receive a lump sum payment, they might invest it for their daughter's education; consequently, they would have to pay taxes on the investment income, if any, and there would be no guarantee that the investment would not be lost. The claims representative may be able to negotiate a settlement that will cost less than a lump-sum settlement, so the insurer would benefit as well.

Another example of a win-win negotiation is the offer to settle a claim with a release that allows future payments for a claimant who may need additional treatment. The claimant receives immediate funds, and the insurer agrees that, if the claimant decides to have further treatment (such as plastic surgery), the insurer will pay up to a specified amount within a specified time after the claimant completes the treatment.

Although a claimant may decline a win-win offer, the claims representative who seeks a win-win settlement, at the very least, demonstrates an interest in resolving the claim to the claimant's satisfaction and may help build rapport as negotiations continue.

## Win-Lose

Negotiators who use a win-lose style see negotiation as a contest between two opposing parties, each seeking to defeat the other. The parties' greatest concern is obtaining the best outcome for their side. They have little interest in achieving rapport with the other party. Negotiators may use this style of negotiation when other avenues of resolution have been exhausted, such as when a lawsuit has been filed and a trial is approaching. At that point, any rapport between parties has eroded because the settlement amount will ultimately be determined by the party that presents the best case to the judge and jury.

Claims representatives may use the win-lose style of negotiation in resolving claims that appear to involve fraud. While claims representatives must always act in good faith in all aspects of claims handling, they may be less concerned with achieving rapport with people they suspect of trying to defraud the insurer.

When fraud is suspected, insurers may require a formal proof of loss from the insured, followed by an examination of the insured under oath. Imposing these requirements does nothing to build rapport; however, this confrontational win-lose negotiation style can serve the insurer's need to prove or disprove suspected fraud.

# Lose-Win

A negotiator using the lose-win style of negotiation is primarily concerned with achieving rapport with the other party; obtaining the best outcome is a low priority. This approach may sometimes result in a more expedient and more cost-effective settlement than other approaches. Generally, the lose-win style is best used when it is highly likely that the other party will hire an attorney or other representative to help resolve the issue.

These examples illustrate the use of the lose-win negotiation style:

- The claimant is injured in an automobile accident with the insured, and the claimant's vehicle is not drivable. The claimant had no medical insurance. Assuming the insured is liable, the claims representative may offer to pay the claimant directly for a rental so that the claimant does not have to use his own money to rent the car and then submit the bills to the insurer for reimbursement.
- The insured's home is destroyed by fire, forcing the insured to stay in a hotel. The claims representative may offer the insured advance payment of part of the additional living expense claim while the claim investigation is pending rather than waiting until the entire claim can be resolved.

While the lose-win style initially meets the needs of the claimant, the insurer often achieves an equitable settlement in the long run because the claims representative began by engaging in rapport-building activities. Such activities may also shorten the amount of time that the claim is open.

# Lose-Lose

A negotiator who has little concern either for obtaining the best outcome or for achieving rapport may be using a lose-lose negotiation style. The negotiator may focus on a fast resolution without considering the other party's specific wants or needs. Used in claim negotiation, this approach can result in inequitable treatment of claimants and insureds. To avoid any inequity and potential bad-faith actions, claims representatives should normally avoid this negotiation style.

Claims representatives who use a lose-lose style may be trying to avoid confrontational settlement negotiations. They may give in to demanding claimants and settle claims more quickly than they would with less demanding claimants.

Occasionally, the lose-lose negotiation style cannot be avoided in claim settlement. For example, some claimants offer unrealistic demands in negotiation and may not understand the logic of the claims representative's offer. Any explanation the claims representative offers only irritates the claimant. As a result, the claimant withdraws from the negotiation process and hires a public adjuster or a lawyer to continue the negotiations. Ultimately, the involvement of a third party will prolong resolution of the claim and result in less money for the claimant.

This is an example of the use of the lose-lose negotiation style:

A small kitchen fire has damaged some of the insured's personal property and left a smoky residue and a persistent foul odor in the room. The claims representative offers to settle with the insured for the cost to replace the personal property and the curtains and to pay a restoration firm to clean the residue from the ceiling. The insured is satisfied with the payment for the damaged property but demands complete replacement of the ceiling material. The claims representative explains that replacement of the material is more costly than cleaning and suggests that the cleaning be completed, and if it is not satisfactory, then the insurer will replace the ceiling. The insured persists with the demand that the ceiling be replaced.

*Lose-lose solution*—The claims representative withdraws from settlement negotiations to give the insured time to consider the offer. The insured hires a public adjuster to handle the case on his behalf. The public adjuster charges a fee that, when subtracted from the final settlement amount, would reduce that amount to less than the cost to hire a restoration firm to clean the ceiling. The insured cancels the property policy. The result is that the insurer pays for the replacement of the ceiling material and the insured pays more of his own money for the repair than he would have had he accepted the initial offer. Both the insurer and the insured lose from this negotiation.

# CLAIM NEGOTIATION PROCESS

By being aware of and thoroughly completing each step in the claim negotiation process, claim representatives can work towards more effective negotiations.

Generally, all negotiators follow a process that breaks down into four steps:

1. Prepare
2. Develop and evaluate alternative outcomes
3. Identify and evaluate each party's interests
4. Make concessions and create appropriate resolutions

## Prepare

Preparation begins long before the negotiation itself begins. For a claim representative, the process begins when the claim is assigned. The claim representative assembles information about the claimant's lifestyle, expectations, preferences, and likely behavior; any previous claims handled by the current insurer or other insurers and their outcomes; and any information about the claimant's history that may be useful in the negotiation. For a commercial insured, the claim representative may assemble information about the claimant's business or employment policies, its supply contracts, and even its competitors. During this step, the claim representative also begins establishing rapport with the claimant.

## Develop and Evaluate Alternative Outcomes

In the second step of the negotiation process, both parties identify the settlement alternatives they consider appropriate and present the reasons why they are appropriate. The party with the greatest number of acceptable alternatives usually has the most leverage in the negotiation because the various alternatives can be used in making concessions that lead to satisfactory settlements.

To develop settlement alternatives, each party must identify the minimum and maximum dollar amounts acceptable for a claim resolution. Answering the questions in the exhibit can help the negotiating parties establish these amounts. See the exhibit "Negotiation Questions to Establish Dollar Amount."

### Negotiation Questions to Establish Dollar Amount

| Claim Representative | Other Party (Claimant) |
| --- | --- |
| What is the minimum amount I should accept for this claim in good faith? | What is the maximum amount I can demand without appearing outrageous? |
| What is the maximum amount for which I am willing to settle this claim? | What is the maximum amount the other party might pay for this claim? |
| What is the maximum amount the other party might demand for this claim without appearing outrageous? | What is the minimum amount the other party might pay for this claim without appearing outrageous? |
| What is the minimum amount the other party might be willing to accept for this claim? | What is the minimum amount I might be willing to accept for this claim? |
| What amount should I use for my starting offer? | |

Source: Judith Gordon, Organizational Behavior: A Diagnostic Approach (Upper Saddle River, N.J.: Pearson Education, Inc., 2002), pp. 336–337. [DA02926]

The values determined through the answers to the minimum and maximum questions can be used to develop a best alternative to a negotiated agreement (BATNA). A BATNA is a standard against which a negotiator can measure any proposed agreement. It can help a negotiator avoid accepting unfavorable terms and rejecting favorable terms.[1] Stated simply, a BATNA is the choice a negotiator can make if the negotiation direction seems unlikely to result in a favorable outcome. If the BATNA is better than the likely outcome of the negotiation, the negotiator can walk away.

To determine the best alternative, the claim representative should consider the costs of the BATNA as well as the likely outcome. Any offers can then be compared against the cost of the BATNA. If an offer is less costly than the BATNA, the claim representative should seriously consider the offer. If the offer is greater than the BATNA, the claim representative should reject it.

The claim representative should also consider the claimant's likely BATNA and should compare the insurer's offers against it. For example, the claimant's BATNA may be the net outcome (after legal costs) likely from litigation. The claim representative should estimate the likelihood that the claimant will file a lawsuit based on information from the investigation. If the claimant suggests that a lawsuit would render a better settlement, then the claim representative, while acknowledging the claimant's right to file a lawsuit, should point out the legal costs that would reduce the settlement amount. If the claim representative's offer for a negotiated settlement is greater than the claimant's BATNA, then the claimant would be more likely to accept the offer.

## Identify and Evaluate Each Party's Interests

In the third step of the negotiation process, each party's interests are identified. These interests can be based on essential needs, socialization needs, personal needs, or organizational needs. For example, an injured person's needs may include ongoing medical treatment, hospice care, income continuation, rehabilitation, social interaction, and financial provisions for dependents. A family's needs after a property loss can include temporary housing, food, clothing and personal necessities, toys or other entertainment, and allowance for public transportation of children to school. An organization's needs can relate to its reputation, relationships with its customers, organizational goals, and income.

Interests can be tangible, such as housing, or intangible, such as reputation, fairness, and socialization needs. Interests can be also subjective, that is, based on the claimant's perceptions. A claimant's interests can change intentionally or unintentionally during the claim settlement period.

## Make Concessions and Create Appropriate Resolutions

In the final step of the negotiation process, successful negotiators recognize the need to make concessions to create appropriate resolutions. Concessions are trade-offs. For example, a claim representative may offer to increase the claim amount by $2,000 if the claimant agrees to concede on $4,000 worth of personal property reported stolen but for which the claimant has no proof of ownership. The settlement, then, would pay for fifty percent of the reported value of the allegedly stolen property.

Negotiators can assess prospective concessions by considering the best and worst possible claim resolutions for each party. They can examine the effect a concession would have on the claim resolution, and then they can determine whether the resulting claim resolution would better serve the interests of the claimant and the insurer. The parties' perceived value of the concessions may vary, as in this example: An old vehicle is a total loss after an auto accident. The claimant, who repairs auto body damage as a hobby, values the car for sentimental reasons. As a concession, the claim representative offers to allow the insured to keep the damaged vehicle with a salvage title. If the insurer instead were to pay for a replacement vehicle, the claimant would have to pay sales tax on it. This concession can lead to a win-win resolution: the insured wins because he can keep a beloved car, and the insurer wins because it pays the value less the salvage to the claimant. The insurer also saves by not having to dispose of the salvage.

In another example of concessions that can lead to win-win resolutions, a tornado tears the roof off a school, and most of the school's computers are damaged by the building's sprinkler system or rain. The claim representative offers to replace the mismatched older computers and printers with equipment of similar makes, models, and software configurations, including some refurbished computers and printers, along with refurbished network hardware and software. The insurer benefits from the convenience of getting all the equipment from one source and by receiving discounts for volume purchases and refurbished equipment. The school benefits from new, updated equipment and compatibility to enable better networking capability.

Successful claim resolution requires reviewing all the needs of both the claimant and the insurer to determine an optimum resolution for both parties. Options such as refurbished or used equipment, like-kind auto parts, and structured settlements can be negotiating tools for developing mutually satisfying claim resolutions.

# CLAIM NEGOTIATION VARIABLES

Claim negotiation often focuses on the amount of money the insurer will pay for the claim. For example, if a roof requires replacement because of windstorm damage, an insured and a claims representative will negotiate the loss amount. However, like any negotiation, claims are affected by variables such as needs, timing, and setting.

No two claim negotiations are exactly the same. The facts of two different losses may be similar, but the characteristics of the negotiation and the parties, as well as the outcome, can be dramatically affected by the claimant's and claims representative's (rep's) variables.

# Claimants' Negotiation Variables

The variables the claimant brings into the negotiation influence the rep's choice of negotiation techniques and strategies. Let's examine how significant variables affect the rep's negotiating behaviors and the outcome.

## Negotiation Phase

Claimants experience three phases during the negotiation process: the crisis phase, the motivation phase, and the bargaining phase. The rep does not become involved until the second phase. Understanding these phases can help the rep respond appropriately, resulting in smoother negotiations and contributing to successful claim settlements.

During the crisis phase, most claimants are motivated more by a desire for life to be normal again rather than by the money they might recover through the claim settlement process. Although the rep does not become involved until later, understanding the claimant's experiences during this phase can help the rep work with the claimant in the remaining negotiation phases.

For example, suppose Joe's new car is hit by an insured making a left turn at an intersection. Joe had the right of way. Although nobody is injured, Joe's car is not drivable and must be towed from the scene. Joe is most likely wondering who will repair the car, how long he will be without his car, and how he will get to work. As the claimant's desire for normalcy shifts to finding ways to achieve normalcy, the motivation phase begins.

During the motivation phase of the negotiation process, the claimant recognizes that life will not be normal unless someone pays for the damage. Accordingly, the claimant files an insurance claim to seek payment for the damages. A quick response by the rep at this stage can establish that rep as an ally, as well as bolster the insurer's credibility.

Conversely, if the rep does not respond quickly, the claimant may begin to view the insurer as a hindrance or as unmotivated or indifferent. When a claimant experiencing a crisis feels ignored by the insurer, he or she may begin to approach the relationship as adversarial and act out, sometimes even exhibiting illegal behavior, such as inflating the claim or engaging in other forms of soft fraud. Because of this, most insurers adopt contact standards that are more stringent than statutory legal requirements (which may allow up to ten days for an insurer to contact a claimant).

During the bargaining phase, a claimant brings his or her impressions of the rep and the insurer that have developed during the previous negotiation phases. At this point, parties share their evaluations of the claim and determine any differences. Disagreements may arise, and any rapport previously built between the parties can disintegrate. In successful negotiations, the parties resolve their differences and settle the claim.

## Financial Needs

A claimant's need for money in order to return to normal is a major variable that determines how the rep should approach negotiations. For example, the rep can encourage an early and reasonable settlement. However, a claimant who has money or property available to meet temporary needs while damaged property is being repaired or replaced may wish to delay settlement. For example, a claimant who has a rental vehicle for use while his or her primary vehicle is being repaired may be slow to seek repair estimates and complete the necessary repairs, thus postponing the claim negotiation and settlement. In such instances, the rep may need to appeal to another of the claimant's needs.

## Time Pressures

Reps should be aware of time pressures on the claimant, such as around bills. Other examples may include the claimant's desire to repair a damaged home before an approaching holiday or to repair an automobile for a daughter to use at college before the term begins. With knowledge of such pressures, the rep can combine a reasonable offer with a promise of prompt payment to encourage the claimant to negotiate a settlement.

## Emotional Reaction

The rep should allow the claimant to express any fears, concerns, frustrations, and needs evoked by the loss. Empathizing with the claimant can help establish rapport.

Sometimes claimants will direct their emotions at the rep, through angry reactions or criticism. Such reactions should not be considered personal attacks.

By maintaining flexibility and a professional demeanor, the rep can turn differences with the claimant into opportunities to resolve the claim satisfactorily. For example, if the claimant expresses distrust of the insurer or the rep, the rep could regain trust by making a prompt and reasonable offer for an advance payment that would be credited to the ultimate claim settlement.

## Experience With or Knowledge of Insurance Claims

The claimant's experience with or knowledge of insurance claims can significantly affect the claim outcome. Reps should ask claimants whether they have ever filed a claim. Claimants, in turn, may respond with a variety of answers.

For example, if a claimant asks why the rep wants to know about previous claims, that claimant could be distrustful of the insurer. In such an instance, the rep could explain that many people do not understand the claims process and then reassure the claimant that any and all information will help the claimant return to normalcy as soon as possible.

In other cases, a claimant's previous bad claim experience may color his or her feelings about the present claim. To counter this concern, the rep can differentiate the insurer's claim service from the service the claimant may have previously experienced.

## Personality

A claimant's personality can have a significant effect on negotiations. If the claimant is self-assured and easy-going, the rep may be able to establish rapport and resolve the claim quickly and satisfactorily. On the other hand, claimants may be insecure or distrustful of businesses, or even arrogant or aggressive. In responding to personality traits that can complicate negotiations, reps can use empathy and patience and strive to establish rapport.

# Claims Representatives' Negotiation Variables

Negotiation variables for reps can differ from those for claimants, although the two parties are often affected by common variables. Let's review some of the most significant negotiation variables that can affect claims representatives.

## Knowledge of the Claim

The claims representative's knowledge of the claim is one of the most significant negotiation variables. The more the rep knows about the loss details, parties, and results of the claim investigation, the better prepared he or she is to negotiate a satisfactory claim settlement. Conversely, the rep's lack of knowledge about the claim can be a severe detriment to the claim negotiation.

## Authority Level

Before beginning claim negotiations, the claims representative should be given sufficient authority to settle the claim up to its estimated maximum value. If the rep lacks sufficient authority, the claimant is justified in negotiating with the rep's supervisor or someone with more negotiating authority. Delegating adequate negotiating authority to a rep demonstrates an insurer's good faith.

## Number of Alternatives Available for a Satisfactory Claim Settlement

Before reaching the bargaining phase, the rep should apply his or her knowledge of the claim and the claimant to devise as many settlement alternatives as possible. For example, if an insured's heirloom diamond necklace was stolen, but the matching bracelet and earrings were not, several alternatives may be available for settling this claim, including replacing the entire set with one of like kind and value, replacing only the necklace, or paying the insured the value of the necklace.

## Time Factors

Claims work often results in time management challenges. Time factors may be imposed by a claims manager or department guidelines, by the insurer or a reinsurer, or by insurance regulators and state laws. The claims representative's caseload is also a variable because it determines the amount of time available to devote to any particular claim.

A rep who faces deadlines in negotiating a settlement may be more flexible in accepting the claimant's demands and may take less time exploring alternative settlement options than one who has no deadlines. As with claimants, the rep's personal schedule can also influence the negotiation. Any factor that prompts the rep to settle the claim more rapidly or to reduce the time devoted to the bargaining step in the negotiation process is a negotiation variable.

## Claim Negotiation Settings

Many claims are settled entirely by telephone, email, or online communication; the rep and claimant may never meet in person. Although negotiating by telephone and online is efficient and effective for most claim settlements, reps may find that certain claims are better negotiated in person.

When people communicate in person, words, tone, and body language all contribute to the message. Of these three, the words used may be the least significant, and the major component of face-to-face communication is body language. When a person's words, tone, and body language appear in conflict, body language usually conveys the communicator's true meaning. A potential disadvantage of in-person negotiation is that the claimant can observe the rep's body language and form an opinion of his or her credibility.

Reps should follow some basic rules when conducting in-person negotiation, such as arriving on time, if not early; becoming familiar with the negotiation site; bringing only necessary confidential documents; assuring portable electronic devices are secure; and being prepared to deal with a large number of opposing negotiators.

An advantage of in-person negotiation relates to physical evidence. When the claims representative and the claimant see evidence such as photos or diagrams of the accident scene or visible scarring, they may change their opinions of the claim's value.

For reasons of convenience and efficiency, many claim negotiations are conducted by telephone. Telephone negotiators must rely on words, tone, and active listening skills. With active listening, the rep periodically paraphrases the other party's communication. For example, the rep could say, "From our discussion, Mr. Brown, I understand that you are satisfied with the amount of the settlement we have offered for your totaled car, but we disagree on the value of contents of your car that were also damaged. Is that correct?"

Telephone negotiations are generally quicker and more convenient than in-person negotiations. While on the phone, people tend to get to the point more quickly and avoid casual conversation that often occurs in person; however, even in telephone negotiations, claims reps should take the time to develop rapport. They should also be aware that telephone conversations may be more prone to conflict because people who cannot see one another may say things they would not if they were communicating in person.

In telephone negotiations, the party who places the call has the advantage of understanding what he or she wants to accomplish. A rep who is the receiver of a negotiation call has an immediate disadvantage because the other party has reviewed the facts and planned the call. When caught off guard, a rep may inappropriately yield to demands. Upon receiving an unexpected call from the other negotiating party, a claims representative should postpone the negotiation by offering to review the file and return the call at a mutually agreeable time. A return call gives the claims representative more control, and when a call is scheduled with the other party, both parties can prepare for a productive negotiation.

The online setting adds another aspect to the negotiation. Many claims processes begin online when claimants enter their information through an insurer's online platform or app. Negotiations can also be handled online either by interaction with a live rep or through software that mimics a rep.

Strictly online settlement of claims is usually only appropriate for simple claims, but it can be beneficial by making negotiations less stressful and time consuming and facilitating prompt payment. Insurers should ensure that any interaction with claimants over email or an app is as professional and responsive as a telephone interaction would be.

## Personality

If a rep is self-assured, this trait will likely be apparent in the negotiation, and the claimant may accept a settlement with little or no negotiation. If the rep is arrogant, the claimant may become defensive.

Conversely, if a rep's personality is insecure or submissive, the claimant may try to convince the rep to accept a settlement that is unsatisfactory to the insurer. Thorough knowledge of the facts of the claim can help the rep be more confident and less submissive in the negotiation.

### *Apply Your Knowledge*

Carla is handling a claim in which the claimant, Steve, was injured by an at-fault driver (the insured). Carla has just returned from meeting with another claimant when she receives a call from Steve demanding that they negotiate and settle his claim now. Which one of the following is the best response for Carla?

a. I'd be happy to negotiate your claim now, Steve. I want you to receive a payment promptly.

b. Would you please let me know a time when I can call you back? I'd like some time to thoroughly review your file before we talk.

c. This claim cannot be negotiated or settled until I've decided on an amount. I'll give you a call when I've done that.

d. Would you please send me an email with the amount you want? Unfortunately, I can't disuss your claim right now.

*Feedback*: *b*. Carla should ask Steve if she can call him back after reviewing his file. In this situation, Carla is at a disadvantage because Steve has reviewed the facts and planned the call. Carla should take time to prepare for a productive negotiation.

# OVERVIEW OF CLAIM NEGOTIATION TECHNIQUES

Negotiators tend to use the same techniques repeatedly —particularly strategies and behaviors that have produced successful outcomes. However, negotiators such as claims representatives can increase their chances of success by using a wider variety of negotiation techniques.

Claims representatives (reps) should always consider the party with whom they are negotiating. Some techniques work best when negotiating directly with claimants, and some work well with attorneys or public adjusters (also known as "claimants' representatives").

## Negotiation Techniques Common to All Parties

Two negotiating techniques that can readily be used by all parties to a negotiation are the principle of yes and choicing. Reps may use either or both of these techniques to successfully negotiate claim settlements.

### Principle of Yes

The principle of yes is often used in sales. It is based on the premise that if an individual answers "yes" to a question, he or she is likely to continue to answer "yes" to subsequent questions.

To apply this principle, reps should begin negotiations by asking questions that will generate "yes" answers. Such questions may involve basic facts, including the date of accident, the people involved, and the fact that injury or damage has occurred.

Points on which the parties disagree should be avoided until all points of agreement are established. When parties begin a negotiation with items of disagreement, conflict is almost inevitable and may lead to failed negotiation. See the exhibit "Example of the Principle of Yes."

### Example of the Principle of Yes

| | |
|---|---|
| Claims representative: | Good morning, this is Joe, a claims representative with XYZ Insurance Company. I was hoping that we could discuss settlement of your client's claim. Let's see, this accident happened approximately four months ago, and it is my understanding that our insured struck the rear of your client's auto. Is that correct? |
| Claimant's attorney: | Yes. |
| Claims representative: | It is also my understanding that the damage to your client's auto was paid for by your client's collision insurance coverage. Is that correct? |
| Attorney: | Yes. |
| Claims representative: | I see that you have sent us three different medical bills, one from the emergency room where your client was taken following the accident, one from an orthopedist, and the third from a physical therapist. Are those all of the medical bills? |
| Attorney: | Yes. |
| Claims representative: | So, the only thing left is for us to agree on a settlement value. |

[DA12796]

## Choicing

Choicing is based on the assumption that people feel empowered when given a choice. To use choicing, the rep first presents the choice the other party will find least desirable. This choice becomes a basis of comparison, making the next choice more appealing.

For example, a rep could use choicing to present options for replacing an insured's damaged transmission when the personal auto policy provides actual cash value coverage. See the exhibit "Example of Choicing."

## Example of Choicing

| | |
|---|---|
| Claims Representative: | I just received the appraisal on your car. The transmission is not repairable and needs to be replaced. We have a couple of options for repairing the car, and the choice is yours. |
| *Choice One* | We could pay to put a new transmission in your car. This would cost approximately $4,000, but because your policy provides actual cash value coverage, we will have to depreciate the cost of the transmission. To explain, your car has an anticipated useful life of 120,000 miles and already has 60,000 miles on it, so your transmission is approximately 50 percent worn. Therefore, we will pay only 50 percent of the replacement cost, or $2,000 minus the $500 deductible—$1,500 toward the transmission replacement. |
| *Choice Two* | As another option, I was able to locate a transmission at one of our salvage yards that has only 58,000 miles on it. This transmission is not an original manufacturer's part, but instead it is an LKQ (like kind and quality) transmission. If you agree to this option, you will have to pay only your deductible, $500. We will not subtract depreciation from your claim because this transmission is already depreciated. Which option do you prefer? |

[DA12797]

# Negotiation Techniques for Use With Unrepresented Claimants

When negotiating with unrepresented claimants, reps should keep in mind that making a claim can be a stressful, anxiety-producing experience. Many people have little knowledge of insurance coverage, may not trust insurers, and have limited knowledge of reasonable settlement values. Additionally, attorneys and public adjusters know and understand common negotiating practices that unrepresented claimants do not, such as the need to provide appropriate documentation and the sometimes argumentative nature of negotiations. Certain techniques can help smooth negotiations with unrepresented claimants.

## Collecting and Using Extraneous Information

Claims representatives collect and use extraneous information about the claim, the claimant, and the claimant's wants and needs that help them develop creative settlements. For example, when speaking with a claimant on the phone, a rep may notice the sound of children in the background. The rep may use this information to develop a settlement that meets family needs. If a meeting can be arranged at a claimant's home, a claims representative can make additional observations about the claimant's lifestyle.

Claimants and insureds may reveal personal deadlines for claims resolution. For example, if a claimant says, "I need my car repaired soon because I leave for vacation in two weeks," the rep may propose paying for an upgraded rental vehicle like an SUV during the vacation. This would meet the claimant's needs but also allow time for the claim to be accurately negotiated and settled.

## Using Sales Techniques

Much like real estate agents sell houses and automobile dealers sell cars, claims representatives "sell" settlements. The theories and philosophies used in sales apply to claim settlements, and all sales training courses begin with the same premise: to make a sale, one must first understand the needs and wants of the customer.

The rep bases the negotiation on an understanding of the claimant's wants and needs. Lacking that understanding, reps may develop what they believe is an equitable settlement and then attempt to force it on the claimant.

Another sales technique is mirroring the behavior of the customer. People tend to like other people who are similar to themselves. A rep who mirrors the behavior of the claimant may develop greater rapport, leading to a better relationship and, ultimately, the sale of the claim settlement.

## Using Needs Analysis

Many people have heard of Abraham Maslow's hierarchy of human needs, often represented as a pyramid. The bottom of the pyramid represents basic needs, and the top represents self-actualization needs. According to Maslow, individuals fulfill the most basic needs first and then move to the next need level.

All people operate at various levels of the hierarchy depending on their current situation. Accordingly, money may not be the most important need for all claimants. So it could conceivably be easier to negotiate a claim involving a total-loss house fire than to negotiate one involving a minor burglary.

In the house-fire claim, having lost most of his or her material possessions, a person is operating on a lower needs level and is motivated to conclude the claim. But in the minor burglary case, the claimant may be motivated by a higher needs level (such as the need for esteem) and prefer to get as much money as possible over replacing the stolen items.

## Making the First Offer

Traditionally, the party in a negotiation who makes the first offer is perceived as holding a weaker initial bargaining position, and the party who responds with a counteroffer holds the stronger position because he or she is able to react to the initial offer. However, certain circumstances—such as negotiations with an unrepresented claimant—promote the need to submit an initial offer. This is because unrepresented claimants do not likely know the value of the claim and may suggest an inflated settlement amount.

Newer thinking includes the "anchoring" theory, which says that making the first offer is an advantage because it sets expectations. If the rep uses a fair negotiation range, there is no danger of coming in too high with the first offer, because the range should be within the rep's professional judgment of what is reasonable.

# Negotiation Techniques for Use With Claimants' Representatives

Claims representatives use different techniques to negotiate with attorneys or public adjusters representing claimants because these professionals usually understand the claims process and claim settlement procedures. Public adjusters usually negotiate property claims; attorneys can negotiate any type of claim.

## Using Information Obtained From the Evaluation

A rep's thorough knowledge of the claim is usually a strength in negotiation. Having investigated the loss, the rep usually has more detailed knowledge of the claim than an attorney or public adjuster.

For example, when the claimant's attorney makes a demand in the negotiation, the rep should avoid an immediate reaction. Instead, the rep should ask the attorney to explain how the settlement demand value was determined and then listen carefully to the answer. The answer reflects the extent of knowledge the claimant's representative has about the claim and the level of thought that was put into the evaluation.

Just as with unrepresented claimants, the claims representative should insist that any changes in the settlement offer are justified based on the facts of the case.

## Establishing Strengths and Weaknesses

In any negotiation situation, there are strengths and weaknesses. For example, if a house is uninhabitable after a fire, a rep can use the insured's desire to be back in his or her home as a bargaining tool. As another example, if an insurer and a public adjuster cannot agree on a settlement amount, a rep should suggest an appraisal. The possibility of appraisal may motivate the public adjuster to concede because an adjuster knows that appraisal may result in a lower settlement, which means a lower commission.

## Using Timing in Negotiations

For many claims, the best time to settle with a claimant's attorney is just before the claim becomes a lawsuit. At that point, the attorney has usually spent only a couple of hours working on the claim.

Claimant attorneys typically receive one-third of a settlement as their fee. Once the claim becomes a lawsuit, the plaintiff's attorney must invest much more time in the claim. Even though a higher settlement—and a greater fee—may result from a litigated case, the attorney's fee per hour of work decreases for each hour devoted to the case.

Let's consider an example. A claimant has a bodily injury claim valued at $4,500, and the claimant's attorney will receive a one-third commission. If the attorney spent two hours interviewing the client, requesting and handling lost wage and treatment reports, and negotiating with the claims representative, the attorney's fee of $1,500 would break down to $750 per hour. But if the claim becomes a lawsuit, the attorney must conduct pretrial discovery, requiring significant time to file summons, take depositions, and more.

Assume the claim settles for $6,000 during the pretrial settlement conference, and the plaintiff's attorney spent fifteen hours working on it. The attorney would receive $2,000; however, the hourly breakdown for the work would be $133.33 per hour. Compared with the original $750 per hour, the attorney has an incentive to settle the claim before a lawsuit requires a greater time investment.

## The Initial Offer

As discussed, the party making the initial settlement offer sometimes takes a weaker negotiating position. However, a claimant's representative might make a demand that is higher than the initial offer the claims representative would have proposed. To entice a reasonable demand, the claims representative may begin the negotiation by asking the attorney or public adjuster what fair settlement value would settle the case that day.

For example, if the claims representative's settlement range is $4,000 to $6,500 and an attorney demands $6,500 to settle the claim that day, the rep can respond with a counteroffer that settles the claim, rather than waste time by starting at the low end of the range.

## Making Concessions

In a negotiation, the claims representative should make concessions for only specific reasons:

- New information that affects the claim value has become available—If the facts of the claim change because of new information or because the claimant's condition has changed (usually for the worse), the rep should reevaluate the claim.

- The other party has made a concession—If the claimant lowers the counteroffer, the rep could choose to concede by increasing the insurer's offer in order to reach a settlement.

- A concession by the rep would allow the claim to be settled that day— When there is a compelling reason to settle the claim immediately (such as before the claimant leaves for an extended vacation), the rep may make reasonable concessions to accomplish that settlement.

## Negotiation Techniques Used by Claimants' Representatives

To be prepared for negotiations, claims representatives should be familiar with some techniques commonly used by claimants' attorneys, public adjusters, and other representatives:

- Limited authority negotiations—In some negotiations, one or more parties may have authority to negotiate only up to a limited amount before consulting with some other authority. Car dealers are known for using this technique. With a claim, the claimant's representative can settle a claim legally and ethically only after speaking to the client—and in most cases, the client is not present during the negotiation. This need to contact the claimant leaves the rep waiting, which may induce him or her to offer more money.

- Timing in negotiations—Attorneys are not the only ones who benefit from settling claims before they go into litigation; insurers also benefit by avoiding additional court and legal costs. A claimant's attorney may use that fact to encourage a rep to accept a higher demand.

## CLAIM NEGOTIATION TECHNIQUES TO BE AVOIDED

Some techniques that work well in general negotiations do not work well in negotiations to settle claims and, in fact, may contribute to the failure of the negotiation.

Claims representatives should be familiar with and avoid techniques that do not work well in negotiations. In addition to limited authority negotiation, these techniques include using a first and final offer (Boulwarism) and using decreasing or limited offers.

## Using a First and Final Offer—Boulwarism

Boulwarism, or making a first and final offer, is named after Lemuel Boulware, a former chief executive officer of General Electric Company. When negotiating union contracts with General Electric's labor unions, Boulware would make a single offer, telling the unions that it was the final offer and if they chose not to accept, then they should strike.

This technique is inappropriate for claims representatives. Presented with the first and final offer, the claimant may refuse it, ending the negotiation and possibly resulting in a more costly resolution for the insurer. Boulwarism invites conflict and prevents collaboration. In contrast, other negotiation techniques provide an opportunity for parties to collaborate to achieve a resolution.

## Using Decreasing or Limited Offers

Another negotiation technique that claims representatives should avoid is making decreasing or limited offers. A decreasing or limited offer is an offer that changes simply because time passes. For example, a party to a negotiation may offer $4,000 one day, to decrease by $200 for each day acceptance is delayed. Similarly, a limited offer is withdrawn after the passage of a specified time. For example, the offering party may specify that if the offer is not accepted within forty-eight hours, it will be withdrawn.

Claims representatives should not use decreasing and limited offers. They invite conflict by placing unreasonable constraints on the other party. Once a claims representative makes an offer in a negotiation, it should stand unless a change is warranted by a change in the facts of the claim.

# COMMON PITFALLS IN CLAIM NEGOTIATION

Things can go wrong at any point in the negotiation process. Claim representatives, as well as other negotiating parties, can avoid some of these problems and can conduct more successful negotiations by being aware of some common negotiation pitfalls:

- Allowing personalities to influence the settlement
- Trading dollars
- Bidding against oneself
- Conceding as deadlines approach

## Allowing Personalities to Influence the Settlement

Claim representatives must sometimes negotiate with parties who are difficult to interact with. Personalities can interfere, and the negotiation process can turn into a clash of egos. As emotions rise, rational thought diminishes, and negotiations come to a halt. For this reason, all parties to a claim negotiation should avoid allowing personalities to influence the settlement.

Claim representatives must maintain their focus on resolving the claim and avoid being swayed by the other party's personality. They should object to any form of abuse, but good-faith claim handling precludes retaliation to personal attacks. In response to a personal attack in the negotiation, the claim representative should inform the other party that if the offensive behavior continues, the negotiation will cease until the party is prepared to negotiate in a civil manner. Offensive behavior should never affect the amount of the offer, the claim representative's willingness to negotiate, or any other factor that could prevent a fair claim settlement.

## Trading Dollars

Trading dollars occurs when negotiators barter on the amount in dispute, not considering the facts of the claim. Claim negotiations should focus on the facts of the claim, and not on the offers and demands. If the facts of the claim change, the parties should increase or decrease their offers or demands according to the facts, but the settlement amount should be a byproduct of the negotiation.

## Bidding Against Oneself

Parties to negotiation sometimes inadvertently bid against their own offer; that is, they increase their offer for no reason. For example, a claim representative could say, "We believe that this claim is worth $5,000, but if we settle the claim today, we would increase our offer to $5,500." In this statement, the claim representative has bid against the insurer's offer without any concession from the other party. Such an offer could signal that the claim representative lacks confidence in the claim evaluation or is overly eager to settle the claim. Generally, concessions in a negotiation should be offered only in response to a concession made by the other party and in a good-faith attempt to settle the claim for the appropriate amount.

## Conceding as Deadlines Approach

As deadlines approach in negotiations, the number of concessions usually increases. For example, many union contracts are settled at 11:59 p.m. on the day of a deadline, and, as described previously, many claims settle on the courthouse steps before a trial.

A party can gain significant power in a negotiation by determining any deadlines that may affect the other party. One such deadline for a claim representative to be aware of is the statute of limitations on a claim, which sets the time within which a claimant must file a lawsuit. Other deadlines can be determined through conversation and listening to the other party for such information. Some deadlines, such as impending holidays, may be "soft" deadlines; others, such as a tax deadline for a claimant who needs money to pay the taxes, may be "hard" deadlines.

Claim representatives also have hard deadlines with which they or the insurer must comply and that may increase their motivation to offer concessions. For example, if the insurer gives its claim staff a directive to reduce pending claims by the end of the month, the claim representative may need to settle the claim and report the file closure by that deadline. As the deadline approaches, the claim representative may offer the highest amount in the settlement range in an effort to close the claim by the end of the month. Claim representatives should not make such settlement offers. Instead, their knowledge that a deadline might be imposed should induce them to work more quickly to settle claims sooner and avoid accepting excessive settlements to meet the deadline.

## Apply Your Knowledge

Larry, a new claim representative for XYZ Insurance, was assigned to handle a partial homeowners fire loss claim. The claimant, Tom, was very headstrong and tended to drag out the claim process. Larry and Tom met on two occasions to attempt to negotiate a claim settlement on the loss, but on both occasions, Tom got angry and accused Larry of belittling his claim. Tom then vowed that he would get another estimate to justify his demands. Before the third meeting with Tom, Larry's supervisor told Larry that he really needed to get this claim settled at this meeting or they would need to submit the claim to arbitration. Larry's incorrect perception was that, if the claim was submitted to arbitration, it would indicate that Larry had failed to negotiate properly and it would reflect poorly on his performance as a claim representative. In the third negotiation, Tom became angry again and called Larry derogatory names. This time, Larry gave in to Tom's demanded settlement, even though it exceeded Larry's settlement range by $2,000 and Tom failed to provide any new evidence to support the higher settlement amount.

What two negotiation pitfalls occurred in this case, and how should Larry have avoided them?

*Feedback:* Two negotiation pitfalls that occurred in this case are that (1) Larry allowed personalities to influence the settlement and (2) he conceded as a deadline approached, even though the facts of the case did not warrant any concessions. When Tom became angry, Larry should have told him that they would end the negotiation and reschedule it when they could continue in a civil manner. Larry should have realized that arbitration really is not a deadline but a right guaranteed by the policy for both parties. If Larry was dealing with a genuine deadline, he should have worked more quickly earlier in the claim to avoid any looming deadlines and should not allow deadlines to influence the settlement amount.

# SUMMARY

A negotiation is any discussion designed to produce an agreement among opposing parties. Claims representatives negotiate many claim settlements. Negotiators can adopt one of four different negotiation styles: win-win, win-lose, lose-win, and lose-lose. The choice of style for a given negotiation is determined by the negotiators' concern for obtaining the best outcome and achieving rapport. Whereas the win-win style usually renders more satisfactory, creative claim settlements, claims representatives may sometimes choose to use the win-lose and the lose-win negotiation styles for claim negotiations as the situation warrants. Except in rare circumstances, claims representatives should avoid using the lose-lose style of negotiation.

The negotiation process involves four steps: prepare, develop and evaluate alternative outcomes, identify each party's interests, and make concessions and create appropriate resolutions. The evaluation step should include establishing minimum and maximum settlement amounts acceptable for a claim resolution and developing a BATNA for comparison with other settlement options. Identifying each party's interests is crucial to making concessions and developing appropriate resolutions.

No two claim negotiations are exactly the same. Armed with knowledge of claimants' and claims representatives' negotiating variables, reps can apply a variety of claim negotiation techniques to effect successful claim resolutions.

Many negotiation techniques can be used in claim negotiations. Some techniques, such as the principle of yes and choicing, can work well for all parties. Others apply more specifically to negotiation with unrepresented claimants or represented claimants. Claims representatives should be aware of techniques that claimants' representatives may use, such as limited authority negotiations and the effect of timing.

Claims representatives should avoid some negotiation techniques entirely because they do not produce satisfactory claim settlements for an insurer. Examples of such techniques are using a first and final offer and decreasing or limited offers.

Claim representatives should be aware of common pitfalls in claim negotiations in order to avoid them. These pitfalls include allowing personalities to influence the settlement, trading dollars, bidding against oneself, and conceding as deadlines approach.

# ASSIGNMENT NOTE

1. Judith Gordon, *Organizational Behavior: A Diagnostic Approach* (Upper Saddle River, N.J.: Pearson Education, Inc., 2002), pp. 336–337.

# Direct Your Learning ▶▶

## Litigating Claims

### Educational Objectives

After learning the content of this assignment, you should be able to:

▷ Show how the following concepts apply to both the federal and state court systems:

- Jurisdiction over parties

- Subject matter jurisdiction

- Appellate levels

▷ Examine the claims representative's role in receiving and reviewing a summons and complaint for procedural information.

▷ Evaluate these claims activities in response to lawsuits:

- Referring the lawsuit to defense counsel

- Answering a civil complaint

▷ Demonstrate the five most commonly used methods of discovery.

▷ Assess these aspects of preparing for and participating in a civil trial:

- Preparation activities by defense counsel and the claims representative

- Components of a trial and the claims representative's role therein

▷ Evaluate the role of a claims representative in a civil trial's posttrial activities, such as court-initiated actions, appeals, and judgment enforcement.

▷ Evaluate the role of a claims representative in planning, budgeting, and managing litigation expenses in a civil trial.

# Litigating Claims

## OVERVIEW OF THE CIVIL TRIAL SYSTEM

Although most claims are resolved without litigation, claims representatives are responsible for managing claims that do result in litigation. Therefore, they must have a solid understanding of the civil trial system.

Most lawsuits are initiated on claims that are actively handled by the claims representative. These lawsuits may be filed because the statute of limitations is about to expire or because of unproductive negotiations. The claimant is the plaintiff—the party that files the lawsuit. If the insured is the plaintiff, then the lawsuit is a first-party lawsuit. If someone other than the insured files the lawsuit, it is a third-party lawsuit. The defendant, the party being sued, is usually the insured and/or the insurer, although other parties may also be defendants.

An understanding of the legal process can also help claims representatives avoid errors in handling claims that can lead to bad-faith lawsuits. Claims representatives should recognize that every claim is a potential lawsuit and should remember this potential throughout the claim handling process.

### Civil Trial System

A lawsuit is initiated by a **complaint** and **summons**. It is critical that the claims representative notify defense counsel upon receipt of the complaint and summons because of the time limit to provide an **answer**. Failure to respond to the complaint and summons could jeopardize defense of the lawsuit and result in a bad-faith lawsuit by the insured. A claims representative may be aware that a lawsuit will be filed in a claim before receipt of the formal **pleading**. This informal knowledge of an impending lawsuit can result from unsuccessful settlement negotiations or a statement of intent by the claimant's attorney. When the claims representative knows that a lawsuit will be filed, it can be helpful to select and notify defense counsel. See the exhibit "Process of a Typical Lawsuit."

The **discovery** phase often determines the outcome of a lawsuit. If sufficient evidence refutes all or some of the plaintiff's allegations, the claims representative and defense counsel may reach a successful compromise settlement before trial. The claims representative should provide a copy of the entire claim file, including all investigation results, to defense counsel.

**Complaint**
The allegations made by a plaintiff in a lawsuit.

**Summons**
A document that directs a sheriff or another court-designated officer to notify the defendant named in the lawsuit that a lawsuit has been started and that the defendant has a specified amount of time to answer the complaint.

**Answer**
A document filed in court by a defendant responding to a plaintiff's complaint and explaining why the plaintiff should not win the case.

**Pleading**
A formal written statement of the facts and claims of each party to a lawsuit.

**Discovery**
A pretrial exchange of all relevant information between the plaintiff and defendant.

## Process of a Typical Lawsuit

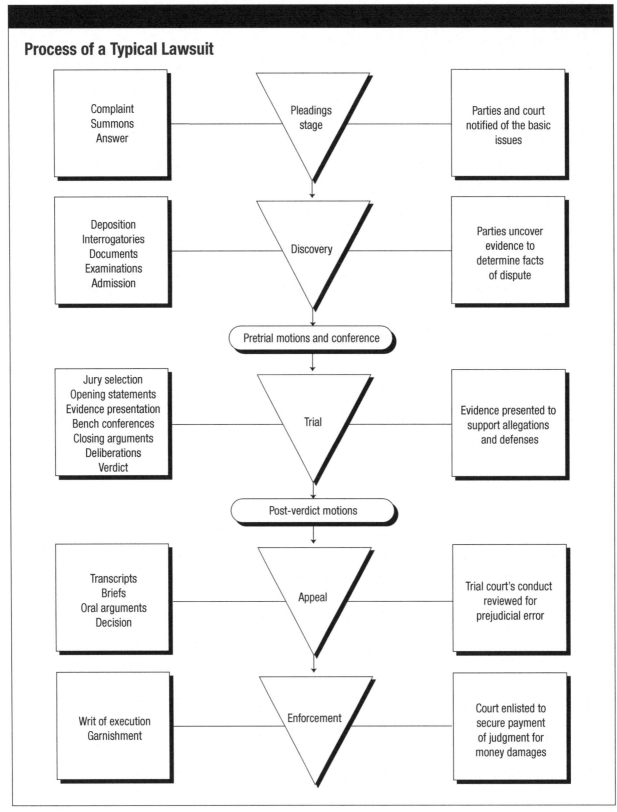

| Complaint<br>Summons<br>Answer | Pleadings stage | Parties and court notified of the basic issues |

| Deposition<br>Interrogatories<br>Documents<br>Examinations<br>Admission | Discovery | Parties uncover evidence to determine facts of dispute |

Pretrial motions and conference

| Jury selection<br>Opening statements<br>Evidence presentation<br>Bench conferences<br>Closing arguments<br>Deliberations<br>Verdict | Trial | Evidence presented to support allegations and defenses |

Post-verdict motions

| Transcripts<br>Briefs<br>Oral arguments<br>Decision | Appeal | Trial court's conduct reviewed for prejudicial error |

| Writ of execution<br>Garnishment | Enforcement | Court enlisted to secure payment of judgment for money damages |

[DA03077]

A significant source of bad-faith lawsuits is an expectation by some plaintiffs and policyholder attorneys that the insurer should settle a claim within policy limits before trial, regardless of the particular facts of the case. Although claims representatives and their insurers want to achieve cost-effective settlements, they must be realistic about the chances of prevailing at trial and the potential for a jury award that exceeds policy limits. Claims representatives should always have a thoughtful discussion with defense counsel about the trial's potential outcome before proceeding.

When a case goes to trial, either party may be dissatisfied with the jury's verdict and award. If there are sufficient legal grounds, either party may appeal the verdict and/or the amount of the award. The appellate process often presents additional opportunities to settle the claim.

If a settlement has not been reached after formal litigation concludes, the insurer must pay the award if the case was decided in favor of the plaintiff. There are time limits for payment, and pre-judgment and/or post-judgment interest may be due on the award depending on policy terms. The claims representative is responsible for timely payment of the appropriate amount owed by his or her insurer. The claims representative may also be responsible for pursuing payment owed to the insurer if the defendant wins the case.

## Jurisdiction and Venue

The claims representative must understand the **jurisdiction** and **venue** for any lawsuit filed and comply with the appropriate state or federal rules of civil procedure. An understanding of United States court systems will help. The U.S. has both state and federal courts. State courts are created by each state's constitution. The single federal court system is created by the U.S. Constitution and acts of Congress.

**Jurisdiction**

A particular court's power or authority to decide a lawsuit of a certain type or within a certain territory.

**Venue**

The locale in which the lawsuit may be brought.

Whether a lawsuit is filed in state court or federal court depends on jurisdiction. Specifically, the court must have jurisdiction over the parties, the subject matter, and the dollar amount.

In state court systems, the courts generally have jurisdiction over parties who reside or do business in that state. Most states also extend jurisdiction over anyone who operates a motor vehicle in the state. For example, a Pennsylvania resident who causes an automobile accident in New York is subject to the jurisdiction of the New York courts.

State court systems are similar to the federal court system, but the court names at various levels may vary among U.S. states and territories. Every state has a trial court level where most litigation starts. General jurisdiction courts have names such as court of common pleas, superior court, and district court. States may also have courts of limited jurisdiction, which hear specific types of cases. Examples are probate courts, which hear estate cases, and municipal or county courts, which typically hear cases involving limited amounts of money.

Additionally, there are administrative court systems that handle certain types of cases, such as workers compensation.

Most states have an intermediate appellate-level court that hears appeals from trial courts. The decisions of a state's appellate-level court can be appealed to the state's highest appellate court. Many states call this court the Supreme Court, while other states use different terms. Claims representatives should be familiar with the names of the courts in which they handle claims. See the exhibit "State Court Systems."

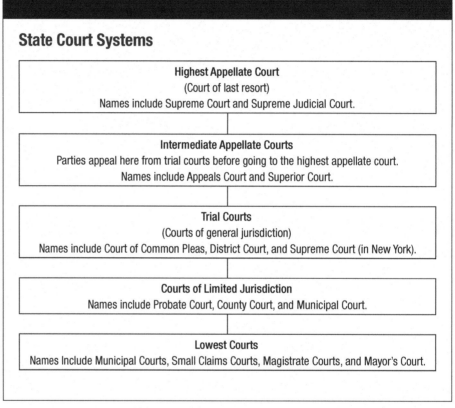

**State Court Systems**

**Highest Appellate Court**
(Court of last resort)
Names include Supreme Court and Supreme Judicial Court.

**Intermediate Appellate Courts**
Parties appeal here from trial courts before going to the highest appellate court.
Names include Appeals Court and Superior Court.

**Trial Courts**
(Courts of general jurisdiction)
Names include Court of Common Pleas, District Court, and Supreme Court (in New York).

**Courts of Limited Jurisdiction**
Names include Probate Court, County Court, and Municipal Court.

**Lowest Courts**
Names Include Municipal Courts, Small Claims Courts, Magistrate Courts, and Mayor's Court.

[DA03072]

In addition to jurisdiction over the lawsuit's parties, courts must have jurisdiction over the lawsuit's subject matter. For example, a federal tax court lacks the subject matter jurisdiction to hear a lawsuit involving an automobile accident. Generally, state courts have subject matter jurisdiction over any legal dispute except those reserved by the U.S. Constitution for federal courts.

The federal court system has trial courts, called U.S. District Courts, and courts of appeal in thirteen multistate judicial circuits. These courts handle lawsuits that deal with federal issues, such as those involving the U.S. Constitution, federal laws, and the U.S. as either a plaintiff or a defendant. In addition, there are special federal courts, such as the U.S. Customs Court and Bankruptcy Court and the Patent Appeals Court, that have specific subject matter jurisdiction. There are also federal administrative courts that handle certain types of cases, such as Social Security appeals. See the exhibit "Federal Court System."

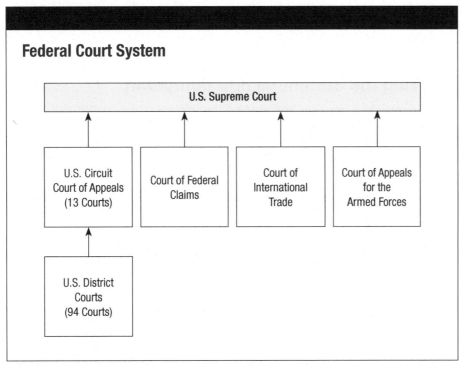

**Federal Court System**

[DA03071]

U.S. district courts also hear lawsuits involving diversity jurisdiction. Diversity jurisdiction is a federal court's authority to hear cases involving parties from different states that involve dollar amounts in controversy over a specified threshold.

A losing party in a lawsuit before a federal district court can appeal to the appropriate U.S. court of appeals if there are legal grounds. The losing party on a court of appeals case can appeal to the U.S. Supreme Court, the country's court of last resort, by filing a petition for a writ of certiorari, which asks the Supreme Court to consider the case. The Supreme Court grants review of a case solely within its discretion and chooses only about 100 cases to review annually.

# STARTING THE CLAIMS LITIGATION PROCESS

An insured or a third-party claimant who is disappointed with a claim decision or settlement offer will often file a lawsuit against the insurer in an attempt to attain a better outcome.

The claims litigation process, which carries forward through discovery, pretrial activities (such as motions to dismiss or requests for summary judgment), trial, and posttrial activities, begins with the receipt of a summons and complaint. It is the claims representative's responsibility to analyze the allegations within the lawsuit, along with the parties, service, statute of limitations, jurisdiction, and venue noted within the complaint, before deciding what course of action to take in response. See the exhibit "The Journey of a Summons and Complaint."

## Receiving the Summons and Complaint

**Allegation**

A claim made in the complaint by the plaintiff, specifying what the plaintiff expects to prove to obtain a judgment against the defendant.

The summons and complaint announcing the initiation of a lawsuit will contain the plaintiff's **allegations**, which serve four functions:

- To give notice—The complaint will summarize who the parties involved are, where the lawsuit was filed, and why it was filed.

- To reveal facts—The facts of the case will be laid out. The claims representative should review them to determine whether the insurance policy in question provides coverage. If not, the insurer may need to issue a reservation of rights letter to the policyholder declaring that the insurer will be providing a defense of the lawsuit, but that coverage could be denied later if warranted. However, before the letter is sent, coverage counsel should be consulted, and the insurer's procedures, such as a managerial review, should be completed. It may be necessary to provide an answer to the complaint or otherwise notify the court of the insurer's decision. If coverage is provided, the claims representative should review the facts to see whether they are supported by the evidence found during the claims investigation.

- To formulate legal causes of action—The complaint will take the facts of the incident at the center of the lawsuit and apply them to a legal cause of action, such as negligence or breach of contract. The claims representative should verify that the cause of action fits the alleged facts and then determine whether coverage is provided.

- To state the damages sought—Complaints generally conclude with a demand for damages. If it appears that the damages could exceed the limits of the insured's policy, the claims representative should notify the insured in an excess letter, which may also serve to inform the insured that he or she has the option of hiring separate defense counsel.

**Service of process**

The delivery of a summons and complaint to a defendant by an authorized person.

A summons and complaint will be delivered via **service of process**. When the insurer receives the summons and complaint, it should go directly to the claims representative handling the claim so it can be processed. See the exhibit "Sample Summons."

Sometimes an insured will receive the summons and complaint, rather than the insurer, and in these cases he or she should deliver it to the insurer or producer as soon as possible. Because the time available to respond is limited, overnight delivery with confirmation of receipt should be used.

## The Journey of a Summons and Complaint

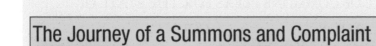

Accidents can be part of life.

Often, each party blames the other for what happened.

Sometimes a claimant retains an attorney to pursue legal action.

In such an instance, the insured is served with a summons and complaint.

The insured then gives the summons and complaint to his agent or insurer.

A claims representative in the office reviews and sends it to defense counsel.

The defense attorney and claims rep collaborate on the defense plan and budget.

Next, the attorneys engage in discovery to reveal the facts of the accident.

The attorneys may make pretrial motions and attend conferences.

If the case is not settled privately, the matter will go to trial.

In some cases, the insured will prevail.

In some cases, the claimant will prevail.

[DA08635]

## Sample Summons

### IN THE COURT OF COMMONS PLEAS FOR THE STATE OF

### IN AND FOR _____ COUNTY

Name (s)                                               )
                                                       )
                                                       )
                        Plaintiff (s),                 )
         V.                                             ) Civil Action No.
                                                       )
                                                       )
Names (s)                                              )
                        Defendant (s).                 )


TO THE SHERIFF OF                              COUNTY,
YOU ARE COMMANDED:

To summon the above named defendant(s) and serve upon said defendant(s) a copy of this summons and complaint.

TO THE ABOVE NAMED DEFENDANT(S):

Within twenty (20) days after you receive this summons, excluding the day you receive it, you must file an Answer to the attached Complaint if you want to deny the allegations. The original of your answer must be filed with the Clerk's Office of the Court of Common Pleas, _____ _____ , Delaware and must include proof that a copy of the Answer was served on the plaintiff or his/her attorney who is named on this Summons.

Failure to file an answer denying the allegations will result in a judgment against you, and action may be taken by the plaintiff or his/her attorney to satisfy the judgment.


DATED: _____   _____
                                                                    Clerk

Plaintiff's Attorney Name
Address
Telephone Number

In the Court of Common Pleas of _____ County, Delaware
Civil Division

Plaintiff's name,                                        )
                        Plaintiff,                       )
                                                         )
            v.                                           )
                                                         )
Defendant's name,                                        )
                        Defendant.                       )


Complaint


        AND NOW comes Plaintiff _____, by its undersigned attorneys, and brings this civil action against (defendant's names), Defendants, of which the following is a statement:

1.  Plaintiff, _____ is a resident of the state of _____.

2.  Defendant, _____ is a resident of the state of _____.

3.  On or about March 31, 200X Defendant _____ did negligently operate her vehicle in such a manner as to strike the vehicle of Plaintiff _____.

4.  The accident occurred at the intersection of Main Street and Roosevelt Boulevard, in _____.

5.  As a result of the negligence of the Defendant, _____ Plaintiff, _____ suffered serious bodily injury and damage to property.

6.  At the present time the value of the property damage is $10,000.

7.  The Plaintiff, _____ seeks damages in the amount of 1 million dollars for the bodily injury sustained.

WHEREFORE, Plaintiff, _____ seeks judgment for the property damage and bodily injury sustained and costs of this action, together with reasonable attorney's fees.


                                    Name of Plaintiff's Law Firm

                                    By _____
                                         Signature of Lawyer

[DA03070]

### Apply Your Knowledge

If the allegations in the complaint do not appear to be covered under the applicable policy, the claims representative should:

a.   Issue a letter of denial.

b.   Discuss the coverage issue with coverage counsel.

c.   Issue a reservation of rights letter.

*Feedback: b.* The claims representative should discuss coverage issues with coverage counsel before taking any action and should also follow any insurer procedures, such as discussion with a manager.

## Reviewing the Summons and Complaint

After receiving a summons and complaint, the claims representative should follow this procedure:

• Identify the parties in the complaint

• Check how service was accomplished

• Determine the time available to answer

• Determine whether a statute of limitations applies (and, if so, whether it expired)

• Verify that the jurisdiction and venue are correct

Because an insurer's duty to defend is broader than its duty to pay damages, it is usually obligated to defend the insured against any allegations that could potentially be covered by the policy, even if they are frivolous or fraudulent. If the insurer believes coverage for the allegations may not exist under the policy in effect, it can issue a reservation of rights letter stating that it will provide a defense only until it can establish that there is no coverage for the allegations.

Under some circumstances, however, an insurer can deny coverage and refuse to provide any defense. Examples of such instances are claims in which the allegations involve an event that occurred outside the policy period, or the named defendant is not an insured, or the allegations are obviously not covered by the policy.

### Identify the Parties in the Complaint

Complaints usually identify the parties to a lawsuit by name and address, while also providing the name and address of the plaintiff's attorney. Once the claims representative is aware of the party named as a defendant in the lawsuit, he or she should verify that the defendant is an insured under a policy with the insurer. For matters involving personal insurance, such as an auto policy, this can be straightforward, but it can become complicated with a commercial policy. For example, if a general contractor has an insurance policy that covers various subcontractors by endorsement, the claims representative would have to review all of the endorsements to determine whether coverage applies to any subcontractors named in the complaint.

## Check How Service Was Accomplished

State and local laws often determine who can be served with legal papers and how that service is required to be accomplished. (The **Federal Rules of Civil Procedure** outline similar rules for the service of federal lawsuits.) The claims representative should determine whether the appropriate party was served and that the manner of service was correct by becoming familiar with the rules that apply in the jurisdiction of the lawsuit. If it appears that service was improper, the claims representative should advise defense counsel, who may then file motions with the court or assert the improper service as a defense in the lawsuit.

Although **actual service** is the preferred method of delivery for legal papers, **substituted service (constructive service)**, such as publishing a notification in a local newspaper, may be permitted.

## Determine the Time Available to Answer

When reviewing a summons and complaint, the claims representative needs to take note of the deadline for filing an answer or appropriate motion. If the deadline passes, there could be severe consequences for the insured and insurer, including the loss of any opportunity to defend themselves against the allegations. The deadline to file an answer can vary, but it is often twenty days from the date the summons and complaint was received by the party being served.

## Determine Whether a Statute of Limitations Applies

In some instances, a statute of limitations provides a time limit to file a lawsuit after the originating event occurs. The claims representative should check the complaint for the date of the alleged offense and compare the amount of time that has passed to any statutes of limitations that might apply. If an applicable statute of limitations has expired, defense counsel should be advised because he or she may be able to file a motion to dismiss the lawsuit.

## Verify That the Jurisdiction and Venue Are Correct

Jurisdiction is the power of a court to decide cases of a certain type or within a specific territory. Venue determines in which city, county, or state the lawsuit will be heard. State and federal rules of civil procedure determine each, and the claims representative should review the summons and complaint carefully to make sure both comply with any laws that apply. It may be beneficial to have defense counsel perform a review as well, because an attorney can seek

**Federal Rules of Civil Procedure**

A set of rules established to ensure that civil actions and procedures move through the United States district courts as quickly as possible.

**Actual service**

Hand delivery of a summons and complaint to a defendant.

**Substituted service (constructive service)**

Any method of notifying a defendant of a lawsuit other than personal delivery of a summons and complaint.

to have a case dismissed if the chosen court does not have the jurisdiction to hear it.

If a case's amount of damages in question is over $75,000 and the parties to the case reside in different states, a federal court may opt to hear a case instead of a state court, through what is known as diversity jurisdiction. For example, if a resident of Pennsylvania files a lawsuit against a citizen of New Jersey for $80,000, the case would be eligible for diversity jurisdiction. If the Pennsylvania resident were suing both a New Jersey resident and a Pennsylvania resident, though, the case would no longer be eligible.

When several different courts meet the requirements of jurisdiction and venue, the plaintiff's attorney will usually choose the court that is most likely to render a favorable verdict. Although that is an accepted practice, some plaintiffs' attorneys engage in a questionable practice called forum shopping, in which the facts of a case are manipulated to take advantage of a favorable venue. Occasionally, a defendant can successfully file a motion to transfer the suit to a venue that is more appropriate under all of the circumstances. See the exhibit "Example of Forum Shopping."

---

### Example of Forum Shopping

West Virginia is frequently chosen as a venue for asbestos lawsuits because West Virginia law allows claims from all over the country to be litigated there. Litigating an asbestos claim in West Virginia typically adds $1 million to the baseline award.

Michelle J. White, "Asbestos Litigation: The Problem of Forum Shopping and Procedural Innovations, and Potential Solutions," http://econ.ucsd.edu/~miwhite/Manh-Inst-talk.pdf (accessed July 24, 2018). [DA08606]

---

If the claims representative doubts the validity of the chosen venue, the defense counsel should be advised in case it is possible to have the lawsuit moved to a more appropriate location.

---

### *Apply Your Knowledge*

Clarita, a claims representative, happens to be walking past her company's near-forgotten fax machine when she realizes an insured has faxed a copy of a summons and complaint. What is the first thing Clarita should do?

a.   Verify that the jurisdiction is correct

b.   Review the occurrence date with the policy effective dates

c.   Determine the date a response is due

d.   Determine whether a statute of limitations applies

*Feedback: c.* Clarita should first determine the date a response is due.

---

# DEFENSE COUNSEL AND CIVIL COMPLAINTS

Although a claims representative's (rep's) key responsibility after receiving a summons and complaint is to refer the lawsuit to defense counsel quickly, the rep should also remain alert while investigating the claim for any possible defenses to be used in the case.

Reps should have a fundamental understanding of the civil trial system and litigation process. Beyond referring a lawsuit to defense counsel, they should approach claim investigations by seeking evidence that supports potential responses to the lawsuit. Further, the rep should always be mindful of newly discovered factors that may lead to a reevaluation of the insurer's position.

## Referring a Lawsuit to Defense Counsel

Referring a lawsuit to defense counsel is not a one-step process. Although timing is important because of court-imposed deadlines, a claims representative should make sure the referral is completed properly, to the greatest benefit possible for the insured.

### Defense Counsel Selection

The process of selecting defense counsel varies by insurer. Defense counsel may be selected by the claims representative or by a litigation specialist or claims manager—often from an insurer's approved panel.

Many insurers use a stable of law firms to act as defense counsel for their cases, periodically reviewing their performances in areas such as legal expense, outcomes, and length of litigation. Other insurers have attorneys on staff, providing a dedicated source of defense counsel. Some insurers will use a combination of the two, relying heavily on in-house counsel while using outside law firms for specialized defenses, to handle overflow cases, or for conflicts of interest arising when more than one insured is a defendant in a case.

In some instances, even if an insurer has its own in-house defense attorneys, it may need to hire outside counsel. For example, with coverage issues, the insurer may appoint and pay for independent defense counsel for the insured to avoid the appearance of a conflict of interest. Additionally, certain insureds, such as large commercial accounts with significant deductibles or loss-sensitive programs, may have the contractual right to help select defense counsel.

The expertise and experience of the attorney chosen should match the type of case that is being assigned. For example, an attorney who specializes in commercial auto liability would probably not be the best choice to handle the defense of a product liability claim. He or she must also be able to work with the rep and insured, especially when the insured is closely involved in the claim. Although the attorney may have specialized knowledge and skills, the rep and insured should be included in and informed about the litigation process.

## Transmittal Form Completion

Once counsel has been selected, the rep will share a set of instructions, along with the summons and complaint and a copy of the claim file. If the lawsuit is the first notice of the claim, the lawsuit transmittal letter informs defense counsel of how the claims representative plans to investigate the allegations.

Although lawsuit transmittal documents vary by insurer, they should contain these elements:

- Case caption
- Title of the court in which the lawsuit is filed, along with the court's location
- Court claim number
- Insurer's name and claim number
- Date of loss
- Name and address of the plaintiff's attorney
- Plaintiff attorney's claim number, if applicable
- Details of service of process
- Name and address of the insured
- Identity of all defendants to be defended by the appointed attorney, along with any relevant information regarding defendants in the lawsuit not to be defended by the counsel
- Policy number and policy type
- Policy limit
- Deductible, if applicable
- Presence of demand in excess of policy limits
- Results of investigation conducted to date
- Additional planned investigation
- Details of any settlement negotiations conducted
- Billing guidelines, if not already provided
- Litigation reporting schedule by defense counsel, if not already provided
- Request for liability analysis
- Request for litigation plan

In addition to this information, the rep should prepare the claim file for transmittal. Many insurers send the file electronically, while others may send a physical copy of the file to the attorney with the summons and complaint. Whatever form of the file is provided, the claims representative should ensure that it contains all documents pertinent to the claim, including copies of email messages and activity notes. In most cases, a copy of the applicable insurance policy should also be included.

## Insured Notification

Once an attorney has been selected, either the claims representative or defense counsel should notify and provide contact information to the insured. (If the claims representative sends the notification, a copy should be provided to defense counsel with the transmittal letter.) At the same time, the insured should be instructed not to discuss the case with anyone other than the claims representative, defense counsel, or persons authorized by the claims representative or attorney.

## Assisting Counsel

The rep's responsibilities in handling the claim continue after the claim has been referred to defense counsel. The rep should be involved in all aspects of the defense, including assessment of coverage, investigation of liability and damages, claim evaluation, and attempts to resolve the claim.

Communication between defense counsel and the rep throughout the litigation process is essential. The rep should promptly forward copies of investigative reports and other relevant documents. Defense counsel should contact the rep after depositions of witnesses, motion hearings, and other litigation activities.

## Litigation Plan

After defense counsel analyzes the lawsuit and the claim file, the attorney and claims representative should work together to develop a litigation plan and budget. The plan should also outline the roles and responsibilities of the attorney and the rep.

Generally, litigation plans outline a strategy to reach one of these objectives:

- Defend the lawsuit at trial
- Settle the lawsuit
- Conduct additional investigation to decide on the goal

Litigation plans should be adjusted as additional information is obtained. If the plan is to investigate further, a timeline should detail when a decision will be made. The plan's objective does not have to be permanent, however. For example, an objective of settling the lawsuit may be changed to defending at trial if a witness provides new information indicating that the insured was not responsible for the damages or if the plaintiff's attorney will not reduce an unreasonable demand in negotiations.

### Apply Your Knowledge

Paul is a claims representative who receives a summons and complaint alleging that an insured was at fault in an auto accident that resulted in serious injury to the plaintiff. Paul received the claim assignment a week before receiving service of the lawsuit. He has not yet received the police report and has no medical records regarding the alleged injury to the plaintiff. Paul refers the lawsuit to Beth, staff counsel, as soon as he receives the summons and complaint. Which one of the following litigation goals is Paul and Beth likely to select?

a. Defend the case at trial

b. Settle the claim

c. Conduct additional investigation before deciding on a goal

*Feedback: c.* Paul and Beth are likely to select the litigation strategy of conducting additional investigation before deciding on a goal. They will want to receive the police report and as much additional information as possible, including information about the alleged damages, before deciding whether they plan to defend the case at trial or settle the claim.

# Answering a Civil Complaint

The initial response to a complaint's allegations, referred to as an answer, will often deny many of the plaintiff's factual allegations. There are other possible responses, however, including these:

• Affirmative defenses

• Counterclaim

• Cross-claim

• Third-party claim

## Affirmative Defenses

**Affirmative defense**

A legal defense arguing that even if the plaintiff's factual allegations are correct, there are overriding reasons the defendant should not have to pay damages.

The answer offers an opportunity to present **affirmative defenses** to the allegations. As opposed to negative defenses, which seek to disprove a plaintiff's allegations, affirmative defenses present new information in an attempt to have the lawsuit dismissed in the defendant's favor. Reps should be aware that precise definitions for these defenses may vary by jurisdiction.

Examples of affirmative defenses are asserting that the lawsuit was not filed within the appropriate statute of limitations, that the court in which the lawsuit was filed lacks jurisdiction, and that the venue is incorrect.

## Counterclaim

There is also an opportunity for the defense counsel to file a **counterclaim** in the answer. For judicial economy, courts usually hear both the original claim and the counterclaim simultaneously. For example, if the plaintiff claims the defendant negligently damaged the plaintiff's car, the defendant can counterclaim that the plaintiff negligently damaged the defendant's car and that the defendant's actions were in response to the plaintiff's irresponsible driving.

Counterclaim

A complaint brought by the defendant against the plaintiff.

## Cross-Claim

Defendants can also file cross-claims against other defendants in a case. A defendant's cross-claim, which is often heard simultaneously with the original lawsuit, alleges that another defendant should be at least partially responsible for any liability that may be imposed on the cross-claiming defendant.

For example, in an indemnity contract with a general contractor, a subcontractor assumes responsibility for any damage that occurs while the subcontractor is working on the project. After an accident at the worksite, the customer sues for damages and names both the general contractor and the subcontractor as defendants in the suit. If damages are awarded against the general contractor, it would file a cross-claim against the subcontractor to argue the subcontractor should pay the general contractor's damages because of the indemnity contract in effect.

## Third-Party Claim

Another way a defendant can bring a third party into a lawsuit is by filing a third-party complaint. In doing so, the defendant alleges that the third party should bear some or all of the responsibility for the occurrence. In the example of the general contractor and subcontractor, if the subcontractor was not named as a defendant in the plaintiff's lawsuit, the general contractor defendant could file a third-party claim against the subcontractor. Courts usually hear third-party complaints simultaneously with the original lawsuit.

While defense counsel will decide when to use a counterclaim, cross-claim, or third-party complaint, the claims representative should be alert for facts in the claim that may lead to these types of legal actions. Those facts can then be discussed with defense counsel as a litigation strategy is developed.

It is critical to answer the complaint promptly or obtain an extension of time to do so to avoid a **default judgment**. Default judgments automatically give the plaintiff all the damages asked for in the complaint. If an insured was served a summons and complaint that was not properly forwarded to the insurer, a default judgment may be the insurer's first notice that a lawsuit has been filed, Although it may be possible to have a default judgment vacated (withdrawn), this outcome is not guaranteed.

Default judgment

An automatic judgment against a party to a lawsuit who fails to appear in court or to answer a pleading.

### Apply Your Knowledge

Lance, a claims representative, receives a summons and complaint alleging that an insured failed to stop at a stop sign and caused a motor vehicle accident in which the plaintiff was injured. During the investigation, Lance discovers that an overgrown hedge on the property of a shopping mall obscures the stop sign. Which one of the following types of litigation strategies might Lance and defense counsel discuss for this claim?

a.  Counterclaim

b.  Cross-claim

c.  Third-party claim

d.  Affirmative defenses

*Feedback: c.* Lance and defense counsel may discuss filing a third-party claim against the owner and/or maintenance contractor regarding the overgrown hedge that obscured the stop sign.

# DISCOVERY IN THE CLAIMS LITIGATION PROCESS

Discovery is the stage of a lawsuit in which the opposing legal teams obtain any relevant evidence that is not privileged (such as attorney-client communications) or otherwise protected (such as an attorney's or insurer's work product prepared in anticipation of trial). It can narrow the issues of the lawsuit, which may lead to an earlier resolution.

**Rules of civil procedure**

The conventions that govern the litigation process and the form and substance of all documents that must be filed with the court.

A court's **rules of civil procedure** govern permissible discovery methods, the definitions of each method of discovery, deadlines for exchange of discovery information, and penalties for noncompliance. The litigation plan devised by the defense counsel and claims representative will outline which particular methods of discovery they will use. These are the five most commonly used methods of discovery:

•  Requests for production of documents

•  Interrogatories

•  Depositions

•  Physical or mental examinations

•  Admissions of facts not in dispute

Attorneys can use discovery methods in any order, but they generally use them in the order listed because the information gathered in one method is used in the next method. For example, produced documents and answers to interrogatories provide information that forms the basis of the questions asked in depositions.

## Requests for Production of Documents

Discovery usually begins with a **request for production of documents**. This sort of tangible evidence includes video, diagrams, photographs, electronic records, and records in any other medium used to transmit or preserve information. Any of the requested documents that a party possesses or can obtain must be produced unless the document is privileged. To withhold a document as privileged, the party must identify the document, the parties communicating in the document, and the basis for exercising the privilege. Attorneys may contest which types of documents are subject to privilege, but state statutes define privileged evidence and relationships.

**Request for production of documents**

A request made by either the plaintiff or defendant in a lawsuit to the opposing side to provide all the documents and other tangible evidence it has in its possession relating to the facts of the case.

## Interrogatories

After receiving and reviewing the requested documents, the attorney creates **interrogatories**. In some cases, the interrogatories may be sent with a request for production of documents. Interrogatories allow each side to discover the other side's position about the facts of the case and the applicable law. Because written answers offer no opportunity for follow-up questions, interrogatories are best used to identify specific facts and sources of information.

**Interrogatories**

Specific written questions or requests raised by one party to a lawsuit that the opposing party must answer in writing.

Failure to answer all interrogatory questions completely precludes the responding party from subsequently relying on undisclosed information. If, for example, a defendant withheld information about why he detained the plaintiff after an alleged shoplifting, the defense would not be able to use that unrevealed information later.

Defense attorneys may request that claims representatives help answer interrogatories, especially when the plaintiff raises issues about the claims process. The claims representative should respond promptly because deadlines for answering interrogatories are usually short, and failure to meet filing requirements can result in sanctions, such as fines or a finding in favor of the interrogating party. See the exhibit "Sample Interrogatory."

## Depositions

Attorneys often use the answers to interrogatories and information obtained through other evidence as the basis for deposition. Because the testimony at a deposition is either typed by a court reporter or recorded, depositions can be used as evidence at trials.

Depositions have two purposes. First, they allow each party to the lawsuit to discover what the other party's witnesses know about the facts of the matter or the opinions of physicians or other expert witnesses. Second, because the testimony is transcribed, it can be used to challenge any conflicting testimony given by the same witness at trial. Such a challenge can discredit the witness and, in some cases, expose the witness to a perjury charge.

## Sample Interrogatory

SUPERIOR COURT OF

DAWSON COUNTY

COMMONWEALTH OF PENNSYLVANIA

CIVIL ACTION NO. 1-77804

James A. Dermont

Plaintiff

v.                                    INTERROGATORIES

Hamilton W. Grind

Defendant


TO: HAMILTON W. GRIND

Please take notice that the plaintiff, James A. Dermont, demands answers to the following interrogatories under oath within 30 days from the time service is made upon you.

Question No. 1: Was the defendant legally intoxicated at the time of the accident?

Question No. 2: Did the defendant fail to stop at a stop sign?

Question No. 3: What physical evidence will the defendant present?

Question No. 4: State the names and addresses of all the witnesses that the defendant will use to testify on behalf of the defendant in the trial of the case.


s/s Jerry R. Fleetwood

Jerry R. Fleetwood

Attorney for Plaintiff

1200 Audubon Street

New Haven, Pennsylvania

Date: 10/15/20X5

[DA03074]

Attorneys can depose two types of witnesses: party witnesses and nonparty witnesses.

Party witnesses are parties to the suit, such as the plaintiff or the defendant. When a corporation is a party to a lawsuit, a representative or an employee acts as the party witness. Prior to the deposition, a party witness and his or her attorney usually review anticipated questions. Attorneys may not always know the name of a corporate representative with the relevant information. In such cases, the attorney may request a deposition from the person with the most knowledge about the allegations in the complaint and answer.

Nonparty witnesses include anyone else with knowledge of the case. Nonparty witnesses may be eyewitnesses to an accident, expert witnesses, or record custodians who can testify to the validity of certain records.

During a deposition, opposing counsel should display professional courtesy. Harassing or intimidating a witness or asking irrelevant questions will likely lead to an objection on the record by the other party's counsel. However, attorneys can ask questions out of order, rephrase previous questions, and use other tactics to catch the deposed person off guard and reveal contradictions in his or her testimony. Observing witnesses during a deposition also helps lawyers evaluate how they will testify in court.

When a claims representative is deposed, he or she should prepare by reviewing the claim file and notes and discussing the purpose of the deposition and potential questions with defense counsel. Courts differ on whether a claims representative is required to produce claims notes, but defense attorneys should object to the production of the claims representative's notes as privileged or protected work product.

## Physical or Mental Examinations

Information obtained through discovery may lead defense counsel to request a mental or physical examination of the opposing party. Requests for independent medical examinations (IMEs) are most common in claims for bodily injury and psychological injury and are usually initiated by the defendant to assess the physical or mental injuries claimed by the plaintiff.

Generally, the rules of civil procedure require the injured party to submit to an examination. The claims representative and the defense attorney decide when an IME is needed, and the claims representative usually makes the necessary arrangements with a medical practitioner the claims representative and defense counsel selected.

## Admissions of Facts Not in Dispute

After receiving the information compiled through the other methods of discovery, one or both parties to the lawsuit may decide to request **admissions**. Admissions can reduce the number of facts to be decided at trial. Facts that are usually admitted by the parties before trial include the names and addresses of the parties, dates of certain incidents, and similar facts that are not disputed but would otherwise need to be proven at trial.

**Admissions**
Factual statements that, unless denied, bind the party at trial.

Whether each party admits certain facts is up to the respective attorneys. When the defense receives a request for admissions, the attorney may send it to the claims representative for review. Although some attorneys may not want to admit any facts, such an approach can unnecessarily prolong litigation. For example, if the complaint alleges that the insured owns a 2018 Toyota Camry and the insured does own such a vehicle, this fact should be admitted.

After the completion of discovery, the claims representative and defense counsel should review their litigation plan to determine whether the information obtained requires a change in strategy.

### Apply Your Knowledge

Janice, a claims representative, is working with a defense attorney on a case involving an insured accused of being at fault in an auto accident. The lawsuit is currently at the pretrial phase. During which part of the discovery process should Janice (in conjunction with the insured and defense attorney) provide prompt responses because of the stiff penalties that could be imposed if she misses a deadline to answer?

a.   Giving a deposition

b.   Answering interrogatories

c.   Submitting to mental examinations

d.   Submitting to physical examinations

*Feedback: b.* Janice should respond promptly to interrogatories because the deadlines are usually short, and failing to meet one can result in sanctions, such as fines or a finding in favor of the interrogating party.

# THE CIVIL TRIAL PROCESS

Before a trial begins, claims representatives must gather information to aid the defense counsel. Their responsibilities do not end when the trial starts, however.

Claims representatives should work closely with defense counsel while preparing for trial. They should be aligned on defense strategy and level of investigation needed. Once a trial begins, claims representatives may need to file reports about it, so they should have an understanding of the trial process.

## Preparing for a Civil Trial

Four key activities are involved in preparing for a civil trial:

• Trial strategy

• Pretrial motions

• Pretrial conferences

• Additional investigation

These aspects often overlap. For example, a motion to dismiss may be filed while the defense attorney is still developing the trial strategy. Or, while discussing the trial strategy, the defense attorney and claims representative could decide that additional investigation is needed.

## Trial Strategy

As preparation for trial begins, defense counsel will create a trial strategy and communicate it to the claims representative, usually in the form of a pretrial report outlining the strengths and weaknesses of the defendant's and plaintiff's cases. The report may include a synopsis of applicable law and a range for settlement and/or probable jury awards.

The defense attorney may research court decisions in similar cases to find a favorable precedent for the defense's position based on the principle of **stare decisis**, which is translated as "stand by that which has been decided." Attorneys also work on distinguishing their cases from unfavorable precedents or on finding ways to apply precedents that are less directly related.

Although precedents can strengthen a legal argument, they are not always set in stone. Court decisions based on precedents can be reversed on appeal if a higher court rules that the precedent used has become obsolete because of changes in statutory law, technology, or society in general. See the exhibit "An Example of Obsolete Precedent."

**Stare decisis**
The principle that lower courts must follow precedents set by higher courts.

### An Example of Obsolete Precedent

The 1999 United States Supreme Court case *Sutton v. United Air Lines* decided that an employee whose health condition could be mitigated by medication was not considered disabled. However, the ADA Amendments Act of 2008 changed statutory law so that such employees may still be considered to have a disability.

That 2008 act rendered *Sutton* obsolete and left court decisions based on *Sutton* vulnerable to being overturned.

[DA12794]

Defense counsel often includes citations for precedent cases in their pretrial reports or case analyses. These citations allow readers to find the original court opinions, which are chronicled in publications referred to as reporters or in online legal databases. See the exhibit "How to Read a Case Citation."

Published court decisions usually start with a short case synopsis and a summary of the court's decision, followed by a full account of the court's decision and any concurring and dissenting opinions, as applicable. Claims representatives may find it helpful to stay abreast of changes in case law that affect the claims they handle in addition to reading the court opinions relevant to a particular claim in litigation.

## How to Read a Case Citation

Case citations provide this information:

- Name of the case
- Volume number, name of the reporter, and page number where the case can be found
- Court that decided the case
- Year the case was decided

Courts publish their written opinions in official case reporters. Each state and level of court may have its own reporter, the names of which are abbreviated in the case citation. The reporters have tables listing the abbreviations and the full names of the volumes. Commercial entities such as Westlaw or LexisNexis also publish compiled cases, and case law is available on the internet at many different commercial, educational, and judicial websites.

*Brown v. Board of Education*, 347 U.S. 483, U.S. Supreme Court (1954)

| Plaintiff | Defendant | Volume | Reporter | Page | Court | Year |

[DA03075]

## Pretrial Motions

After reviewing the trial strategy and case analysis, the claims representative and defense attorney should agree on any pretrial motions. Common issues are whether certain evidence can be admitted at trial, certain persons can be called as witnesses, and sufficient legal grounds exist for the case to proceed.

Motions are governed by the rules of civil procedure, which designate when and why a motion can be brought, what must be included in a motion, and when opposing counsel must respond to a motion. Claims representatives should be familiar with three common pretrial motions:

- Motion to dismiss
- Motion for summary judgment
- Motion *in limine*

**Motion to dismiss**

A request that a court terminate an action because of settlement, voluntary withdrawal, or procedural defect.

A **motion to dismiss** could be filed early in the proceedings for several reasons, including a defective complaint or the plaintiff's failure to state a legally recognized cause of action.

Before the trial, but after discovery, which is the period of time during which both sides of the case gather as much information as possible, either the plaintiff or defendant can file a **motion for summary judgment**. In most cases, the other party responds to this motion and can also file its own motion, using the same facts as the first party, but arguing for a different interpretation of the law.

Any party to the lawsuit may file a **motion in limine** ("in limine" translates to "at the threshold"), in an effort to exclude evidence that is harmful to their case. For example, if the plaintiff offers photographs showing bloodstains on a vehicle involved in an accident, defense attorneys may attempt to exclude them for these reasons:

- They are highly prejudicial. (Bloodstains tend to influence jurors, whether or not they help determine fault.)

- They are cumulative. (Other available photographs show the damage to the vehicle without including the bloodstains.)

- The fact confirmed by the photos is not in controversy. (The defendant admits that the car was damaged.)

After motions and responses are filed, the court may hold a hearing to question the attorneys about the bases of their respective motions or their opposition. In considering a motion, the judge assumes that all of the pleadings of the party opposing the motion are true.

## Pretrial Conferences

Pretrial conferences are called at the judge's discretion to settle the case or resolve certain issues. The judge may ask whether any possibility of settlement exists or may wish to limit the issues presented at trial.

Claims representatives may be asked to attend a pretrial conference by either the court or defense attorney. Before the conference, the claims representative and defense counsel should agree on the conference's expected outcome and the claims representative's role, if any, in the conference. For example, they should be ready for the possibility that the judge may attempt to persuade the claims representative to participate in settlement negotiations.

## Additional Investigation

As part of trial preparation, the claims representative may gather additional information, such as more photos of the accident scene or medical records. Claims representatives may also help maintain a chain of evidence—a record showing who has possession of or access to the evidence and when. Keeping track of this information can come into play in a claim against a potentially responsible third party, because an insurer could be denied the ability to recover damages if evidence has been lost or destroyed.

Similarly, an insurer defending a first-party coverage lawsuit could be found liable if evidence is intentionally or negligently lost or destroyed. The claims

**Motion for summary judgment**
A pretrial request asking the court to enter a judgment when no material facts are in dispute.

**Motion in limine**
A pretrial request that certain evidence be excluded from the trial.

representative shares responsibility for preserving evidence with the property owners, the defense attorney, and any expert given access to that evidence.

### *Apply Your Knowledge*

Which one of the following is not a common issue for a court to rule on in pretrial motions?

a.  Whether certain evidence can be admitted at trial

b.  Whether certain persons can be called as witnesses

c.  Whether any possibility of settlement exists

d.  Whether there are sufficient legal grounds for the case to proceed

*Feedback*: c. Whether any possibility of a settlement exists is often dealt with in a pretrial conference, not in a pretrial motion.

## The Civil Trial Process

The litigation reports most insurers ask claims representatives to file during a trial inform various parties associated with the insurer, such as the underwriter and home office Claims Department, about the progress and outcome of the case. To prepare these reports, and to be able to participate in a meaningful way during the trial, claims representatives should be familiar with components of the trial process:

*   Nonjury and jury trials
*   Jury selection
*   Opening statements
*   Introduction of evidence
*   Trial motions
*   Summations
*   Jury instructions
*   Verdicts

## Nonjury and Jury Trials

A trial can be a jury trial or a nonjury trial. A jury is a group of people who hear and consider the evidence of a case and decide which facts are true. In a jury trial, the jury decides all questions of fact, and the judge decides all questions of law. A jury may have six to twelve members, including alternate jurors who hear the evidence but do not deliberate, or provide input on the verdict, unless another juror is unable to serve throughout the trial. In a nonjury trial, the judge decides all questions of both fact and law.

The right to trial by jury, as well as the number of jurors on a given jury, may depend on the dollar amount in dispute or on the particular area of law that applies to the facts of a case. In a civil trial, the plaintiff and defendant may agree to have a case heard by a judge rather than a jury, which is called a bench trial, or trial by court or judge. In cases in which the type of trial can be selected, claims representatives should discuss with defense counsel the better option for the facts of the case.

## Jury Selection

Jurors are selected from a jury pool. Potential jurors are questioned by the judge and/or attorneys about their knowledge or opinion of the parties to the litigation and the issues to be decided in the case. During this **voir dire** (from French, meaning "to speak the truth") process, attorneys attempt to select jurors that they believe would be favorable to their clients.

Depending on the statute or a court rule, attorneys for each party are given a set number of **peremptory challenges**. After using the allotted peremptory challenges, attorneys must state a reason for excluding potential jurors.

In third-party lawsuits against insureds, jurors are not informed of insurer involvement in the case. This is so the jury is not affected by the fact that an insurer will have to pay the judgment or is providing the insured's defense. The trial should be conducted as if no insurers are involved, even when it is apparent that they are. For example, it is common knowledge that parties involved in an automobile accident are likely to have insurance. Nevertheless, any mention by a party that an insurer is involved could be grounds for a mistrial.

In cases with great significance, financial or otherwise, for the insured and/ or the insurer, a jury consultant may be hired to assist with jury selection. Along with defense counsel, the claims representative should be involved in deciding whether to hire such a consultant, setting a budget, and choosing the consultant.

## Opening Statements

Once the jury is assembled, the trial begins with attorneys' opening statements. An opening statement does not introduce evidence but provides a summary of the case and of the proof the attorney *intends* to present. Because the plaintiff has the **burden of proof**, the plaintiff's attorneys go first. They usually summarize the facts of the case and the issues the jury will decide. The jury is generally told which witnesses will testify, how this testimony relates to the issues it will decide, and why it should rule in the plaintiff's favor.

Rather than immediately following the plaintiff's attorneys' opening statement, attorneys for the defendant can opt to postpone, or reserve, their opening statement until after the close of the plaintiff's case. Whether the

**Voir dire**
The process of examining potential jurors about their possible interest in the matters presented at trial, their ability to decide the case fairly and without prejudice, and their overall competence to serve as jurors.

**Peremptory challenge**
A lawyer's ability to object to a potential juror's placement on the jury without having a specific reason.

**Burden of proof**
In a trial, the duty of a party to prove that the facts it claims are true.

defendant's attorneys reserve the opening statement is a matter of strategic planning and personal preference.

## Introduction of Evidence

The plaintiff's attorneys then introduce evidence by calling witnesses and questioning them to establish the plaintiff's case. To satisfy their burden of proof, plaintiffs must generally prove all the essential elements of their case by a **preponderance of evidence**.

**Preponderance of evidence**

Evidence supporting the jury's decision that is of greater weight than the evidence against it.

For a judge or jury to determine preponderance of evidence, the basis and extent of witnesses' knowledge, the type and quality of information they possess, and their manner of testifying are more important than the number of witnesses. Determining preponderance of evidence is a subjective judgment and is a much lower standard of evidence than what is used for criminal trial, where guilt can only be determined by evidence beyond a reasonable doubt (in other words, there is no other reasonable explanation for what happened other than that the accused party committed the crime).

The defendant's attorney is entitled to cross-examine the plaintiff's witnesses. Cross-examination is essential because it allows opposing attorneys to test the truth of a witness's testimony; to further develop the testimony; or to question a witness for other purposes, such as to elicit additional evidence. Successful cross-examination can discredit testimony or reduce the weight a jury may give to the evidence.

After the plaintiff's attorneys have presented their case, the defense follows the same procedure, presenting an opening statement if it did not do so previously and then calling defense witnesses to testify. The plaintiff's attorney may cross-examine defense witnesses.

Witnesses may be lay witnesses—people who have no special expertise in the matters about which they testify but have firsthand knowledge of those matters, based on observation—or expert witnesses, who have specialized knowledge in a particular field. Whether a witness is qualified to be an expert is determined by the judge presiding over the trial. Often, both parties will produce expert witnesses in the same field who testify with different opinions about the same facts. Expert witnesses can include doctors, engineers, accountants, psychologists, and economists. Occasionally, an expert is required in an unusual field of expertise, such as identifying artistic forgeries.

As the trial moves along, claims representatives may need to produce physical evidence and locate witnesses, as well as assist with their attendance. If witnesses have moved or are otherwise difficult to locate, claims representatives may need to hire private investigators to help find them. They may also help choose expert witnesses.

## Trial Motions

Motions can be made during the course of the trial. After the plaintiff's case has been presented, defense attorneys can move for a **directed verdict**, asking the court to dismiss the case because the plaintiff has failed to prove its allegations. If this motion is granted, the verdict favors the defendant, and the trial concludes. Directed verdicts are rarely granted—and when they are, they are often appealed. Names and standards for various trial motions that can conclude a case vary by jurisdiction, and a claims representative should become familiar with relevant local court procedures.

Motions regarding the evidence presented can also be made during trial. For example, a motion can be made to strike evidence from the record or to request that the judge instruct the jury to disregard a portion of a witness's testimony. Motions for a mistrial may be made if a particularly damaging piece of evidence is introduced that opposing counsel believes is highly prejudicial and was improperly introduced or if there are factors that seem to prevent a fair and impartial trial.

**Directed verdict**

An order to the jury from the presiding judge to return a specific verdict.

## Summations

After all evidence has been presented, attorneys for each side are given an opportunity to address the jury through closing arguments. Each attorney typically summarizes the facts presented in a light most favorable to his or her client.

At any point throughout the trial process, cases can be settled. Claims representatives should discuss any settlement possibilities that arise with defense counsel and weigh those opportunities against the cost of continuing the litigation and the probability of a favorable outcome.

## Jury Instructions

After closing arguments, the judge instructs the jury about the law to apply in deciding the case. For example, in an automobile accident trial, the judge instructs the jury in the principles of negligence and fault and explains which party has the burden of proof.

Attorneys usually submit written proposals for instructions, but it is the judge's choice whether to incorporate these proposals into the jury instructions. A losing party may appeal a case on the grounds that the judge incorrectly instructed the jury.

## Verdicts

After receiving the judge's instructions, the jury retires to the jury room to decide the case. The deliberations have no time limit and continue until a verdict is reached or until the jury decides, with the judge's involvement, that it is impossible to reach a verdict. In some jurisdictions, a verdict does not have to be unanimous as long as a quorum, or a set number, is reached.

After reaching a verdict, the jury returns to the courtroom, and the verdict is read in open court.

### Apply Your Knowledge

Ida is a claims representative who is helping move one of her claims through the trial process. The defense counsel worked with her to establish a trial strategy, and all of the pretrial motions and conferences have come to a conclusion. Now that the trial is about to begin, how should Ida expect to be part of the process?

*Feedback:* As the trial moves along, Ida may need to produce physical evidence and locate witnesses, as well as assist with their attendance. If witnesses have moved or are otherwise difficult to locate, she may need to hire private investigators to help find them. She may also help choose expert witnesses and will have to file litigation reports to inform various parties associated with the insurer, such as the underwriter and home office Claims Department, about the progress and outcome of the case.

# POSTTRIAL ACTIVITIES

Although a trial concludes with the verdict, the same cannot be said for the claims representative's and defense counsel's responsibilities.

Three major activities can occur after the conclusion of a trial:

- Court-initiated actions
- Appeal of verdict
- Judgment enforcement

## Court-Initiated Actions

At the conclusion of a trial, several actions are available to the court. Most often, the court will accept the jury's verdict and enter a judgment to that effect. However, on rare occasions, the court can act on its own initiative or on a motion of the losing party and enter a **judgment notwithstanding the verdict (judgment n.o.v.).**

For example, if a jury finds a defendant liable for the plaintiff's injuries without evidence to support that verdict, the court can enter a judgment for the defendant, notwithstanding the verdict. Sometimes the losing party must file a motion for a directed verdict before a judge can grant a judgment n.o.v.

The court also has the option of granting a new trial on its own initiative or on the losing party's motion. Typical grounds for a new trial include insufficient evidence, erroneous rulings on instructions, newly discovered evidence,

**Judgment notwithstanding the verdict (judgment n.o.v.)**

A judgment in favor of one party even though the jury's verdict favored the other party.

or a verdict contrary to the judge's instructions. However, trial judges seldom grant new trials.

Another option the court has at the conclusion of a trial is to adjust the damages awarded by the jury if the judge considers the jury award excessive or insufficient. This typically happens when a jury awards an extraordinarily high judgment that is disproportionate to the damages.

## Appeal of Verdict

Either party can appeal a court verdict to a higher court, although it is usually the losing party that does so. Appeals courts hear no new evidence from witnesses and do not consider whether the finder of fact (the judge or the jury) in the lower court was correct in determining the facts, but rather limit their opinions to a review of the application of law to the facts decided by the judge or jury.

The distinction between the facts and the law can be subtle. For example, if the trial court found a motorist drove thirty-five miles per hour in a twenty-five-mile-per-hour zone, an appeals court would not review that finding. However, the appeals court might review whether the judge gave correct instructions to the jury on the law of negligence as applied to the fact that the motorist was speeding.

Appeals are most commonly based on matters of evidence, meaning that a party may appeal a verdict on the grounds that the judge's decision to admit or exclude certain evidence altered the outcome of the trial. Appeals could also be made based on instructions the judge may have given the jury or a judge's error in stating the law.

The appeals process can be lengthy. After the parties file briefs, a hearing is held. The attorneys for each party argue for or against the appeal and answer questions raised by the appellate justices. Generally, the decision of a state's highest appeals court is final and concludes the matter, unless an appeal is attempted to the United States Supreme Court based on an issue related to the U.S. Constitution. However, the U.S. Supreme Court chooses the cases it will hear, and it selects for review only the cases it finds to be most important.

Because of the cost and time involved in appeals, insurers typically have an internal review process under which one or more managers approve the appeal of a verdict that was unfavorable to an insured. There are time limits to file an appeal, and the claims representative must work closely with defense counsel in following the insurer's procedures to advance a timely appeal when appropriate.

## Judgment Enforcement

Once a judgment is final, the plaintiff moves to enforce the judgment. In most cases, the defendant arranges to pay the plaintiff, if necessary. In some cases, an insurer may owe prejudgment and/or postjudgment interest, depending on the terms of the policy. Claims representatives are usually responsible for managing payment of judgments owed by the insurer, and they should be certain they understand the court's order and any applicable laws or rules regarding how and when payment should be made. Penalties may apply for failing to properly pay an award.

---

### Apply Your Knowledge

Certain limitations are placed on appellate courts regarding what they may base their decisions on. Explain what those limitations are.

*Feedback:* Appeals courts hear no new evidence from witnesses and do not consider whether the finder of fact (the judge or the jury) in the lower court was correct in determining the facts, but rather limit their opinions to a review of the application of law to the facts decided by the judge or jury.

---

# MANAGING LITIGATION EXPENSES

Failure to manage litigation expenses properly can lead to adverse financial consequences for both the insured and the insurer; therefore, managing those expenses is a critical aspect of the claims representative's role in litigation management.

Claims representatives who use a litigation plan, a litigation budget, and legal bill audits and who evaluate defense counsel's performance can contribute to an effective defense of the insured at a reasonable cost.

## Creating a Litigation Plan

By working with defense counsel to establish a litigation plan, the claims representative fosters a sound relationship with counsel. Continual review and updating of the plan will ensure that the claims representative and defense counsel are always aware of major activity associated with the litigation.

Activities related to discovery constitute a large portion of the litigation plan, and the claims representative and the defense attorney will need to agree on who will perform the necessary discovery. For example, medical records may be sufficient to provide needed information, rather than a deposition of a doctor. If the defense attorney agrees, the claims representative can obtain the medical records more cost-effectively than the defense attorney simply because the attorney bills for the activity.

Claims representatives should never hinder an attorney's representation of a client by refusing to allow a deposition, research, or any other activity the attorney deems necessary. However, defense counsel should be able to explain why a given activity is required to provide the insured with a sound defense and how that activity fits into the overall litigation plan. He or she should also be able to estimate the cost of the activity.

## Creating a Litigation Budget

In tandem with establishing the litigation plan, the attorney and the claims representative should create a litigation budget. The budget will depend on the type of fee arrangement the attorney has with the client/insurer. The most common fee arrangement is an hourly charge, but others can be used, such as **flat fee** or **phased fee** arrangements. Most insurers have agreements with the attorneys they frequently retain in litigation about how fees are to be handled, which relieves the claims representative from having to negotiate the type of fee arrangement.

When establishing a litigation budget, the claims representative and the attorney should consider the activities that must occur to provide the best defense. These activities can be broken down into several categories and should be recorded in a budget:

- Case review, including initially reviewing material from the claims representative and interviewing the insured and other parties involved

- Legal research

- Initial pleadings, including drafting an answer to the complaint, and cross-claims or counterclaims

- Discovery, including drafting interrogatories, answering the opponent's interrogatories, preparing for and attending depositions, and complying with document production requests

- Locating and retaining experts

- Motions

- Negotiations and conferences

- Trial

Each task listed in the budget should include the name of the party assigned to perform it. The claims representative should determine which people on the attorney's staff will actually work on the case. It is often cost-effective to have an associate or a paralegal perform some tasks rather than the defense attorney.

The budget should include a time estimate for each task, and an additional column may show the cost estimate. This estimate may be a simple calculation of the number of hours multiplied by the hourly rate, or it may be a "not to exceed" estimate, which places a limit on the amount the attorney can spend without first discussing it with the claims representative. Legal research often uses a "not to exceed" figure.

**Flat fee**

A fee arrangement in which the attorney agrees to handle the case from start to finish for a specified amount.

**Phased fee**

A fee arrangement in which the attorney agrees to handle each phase of litigation for a specific fee.

# Auditing Legal Bills

Most insurers have attorney billing guidelines that usually require a detailed, itemized record of work performed that includes the task, how long the task took in tenth-of-an-hour increments, the name of the attorney or paralegal who performed the activity, and any expense associated with the task. The billing guidelines may also specify the hourly rate to be charged by each attorney and paralegal; travel expenses allowed; and associated expenses, such as overnight mailing or photocopying charges, that can be charged to the case.

Many insurers have designated staff, usually attorneys, to review legal bills. Insurers may also use outside bill auditing firms, except in states that prohibit such arrangements. In either case, the claims representative should carefully review legal bills for compliance with agreed-upon fees and guidelines. Any bill that does not provide sufficient information for review or does not comply with the billing guidelines should be returned to the attorney for explanation. See the exhibit "Checklist for Reviewing Legal Bills."

---

### Checklist for Reviewing Legal Bills

- Dates of the major activities on the bill should correspond with dates of the same activities in the claim file. For example, if the bill lists a thirty-minute phone call with the claims representative on a specific date, the claims representative should have a corresponding entry in the claim activity log.

- Only the work of parties (partner, associate, paralegal) agreed to in advance by the handling attorney and the claims representative should be included on the bill.

- Mathematical computations should be checked for accuracy. Despite law firms' use of computerized billing systems, errors do occur.

- Only authorized investigative activity should be included on the bill.

- Only authorized attorneys should have appeared at depositions, hearings, motions, or trials. Billing for any additional attorneys or legal staff should be questioned.

- Itemized incremental billing should be based on a reasonable time for the specific activity billed. Attorneys bill in tenth-of-an-hour increments, so 6 minutes equals 0.1 hour, 12 minutes equals 0.2 hour, 18 minutes equals 0.3 hour, and so on. For example, unless a letter is extremely long, it usually does not take someone 18 minutes to review it.

- Absent a compelling reason, most attorneys should not bill more than 10 hours per day.

- Administrative costs, such as general postage, local travel, word processing, and other items of overhead, should not be billed unless specifically agreed to, either in the billing guidelines or by the claims representative.

- Airfare, hotel, and meal charges should comply with the billing guidelines.

[DA03345]

When a claims representative believes a portion of a legal bill should be challenged, he or she should be prepared to explain the concerns to the attorney and suggest an appropriate amount to be paid. To determine a figure, the claims representative should carefully weigh the merits of the particular item, the associated fee, and any circumstances that may affect the fee.

After reviewing a legal bill and determining the amount that should be paid, the claims representative should make every effort to ensure that the bill is paid promptly, which helps maintain a good relationship with counsel. If payment will be delayed for a specific reason, the claims representative should advise the attorney.

### Apply Your Knowledge

As the claims representative working on a case that is going to trial, Antonia has been asked to create a litigation budget. How should she approach this task?

*Feedback*: Antonia should work with defense counsel to consider the activities that must occur for the best defense to be provided. These activities can be broken down into several categories and should be recorded in a budget, with a cost projected for each. Each task listed in the budget should include the name of the party assigned to complete it. Antonia should determine which people on the attorney's staff will actually work on the case. Often, it is more cost-effective to have an associate or a paralegal perform some tasks rather than the defense attorney. The budget should also include a time estimate for each task, along with the expected monetary total.

# Evaluating the Litigation Plan and Counsel Performance

Once a claim in litigation has been resolved, the claims representative may evaluate the litigation plan and the attorney's performance on the case. These questions may be helpful to the claims representative in the evaluation:

- Was the final outcome of the case satisfactory?
- Was the case's final outcome the one that was specified in the plan at the beginning of the case? If not, why?
- Was the original plan realistic, given the facts known at the time?
- Was the plan revised in a timely manner to reflect changes in facts as they became known?
- Were the plan and any subsequent revisions agreed on by both the claims representative and the attorney, or were changes made unilaterally?

- Did the attorney adhere to the plan?
- Were any expenses incurred that were unanticipated by the plan and the budget? If so, how could this be avoided in the future?

Although a case may be resolved satisfactorily even if the litigation plan is not followed, adhering to a plan can usually reduce the overall cost, duration, and stress of the case.

The claims representative should share the results of the performance evaluation with the attorney. Some insurers may have a formal means of providing this feedback, such as a mid-year and annual review process. Others may have the claims representative provide the feedback directly, shortly after the case has been resolved. Most attorneys welcome the feedback because they want to have a good working relationship with their clients.

# SUMMARY

Because any claim can result in a lawsuit, claims representatives should be familiar with the civil trial system. They need to understand the civil litigation process and be aware of the time limits for each stage. Claims representatives should also know the different types of U.S. courts and how jurisdiction and venue are determined, and they should be familiar with the court systems in the states where they handle claims.

The claims litigation process begins with the receipt of a summons and complaint. It is the claims representative's responsibility to analyze the allegations within the lawsuit, along with the parties, service, statute of limitations, jurisdiction, and venue noted within the complaint, before deciding what course of action to take in response.

When referring a lawsuit to defense counsel, a claims rep selects the appropriate attorney, completes the lawsuit transmittal form, notifies the insured, assists counsel, and develops a litigation plan with the assigned attorney. In addition to being aware of facts and evidence that support a denial of a plaintiff's allegations, reps should be aware of facts that may support affirmative defenses, a counterclaim, a cross-claim, or a third-party claim.

The five methods of discovery are requests for production of documents, interrogatories, depositions, physical or mental examinations, and admissions of facts not in dispute. Claims representatives should work with defense counsel on producing and obtaining information throughout the discovery process, then reevaluate the litigation plan after discovery concludes.

After discovery, when the defense attorney and claims representative decide to proceed to trial, the defense attorney develops a trial strategy for review by the claims representative. Preparation for trial often includes pretrial motions, pretrial conferences, and additional investigation for trial evidence. Because claims representatives are responsible for preparing litigation reports and might participate in various trial activities, they should understand the components of the trial process: nonjury and jury trials, jury selection, opening statements, introduction of evidence, trial motions, summations, jury instructions, and verdicts.

Claims representatives should be familiar with posttrial activities—such as court-initiated actions, appeals of verdict, and judgment enforcement—and their associated responsibilities, such as obtaining management approval for an appeal or having payment issued for an award.

Managing litigation includes managing its costs. For each case, the claims representative and the attorney prepare a budget that works in conjunction with the litigation plan. During and after the case, the claims representative reviews the legal bills submitted to ensure that they adhere to billing guidelines. Any part of a legal bill that is in question should be addressed with the attorney. Once the case has been resolved, the claims representative should evaluate the success of the litigation plan, budget, and performance of the attorney.

# 9

# Good-Faith Claims Handling

## Educational Objectives

After learning the content of this assignment, you should be able to:

▷ Determine how the law of bad faith relates to an insurer's duty of good faith and fair dealing.

▷ Evaluate the legal rights of these plaintiff types in a bad-faith claim:

- Insureds

- Claimants

- Excess insurers

▷ Examine these bases of bad-faith claims:

- Claim or coverage denial

- Excess liability

- Statutory bad faith

- Unfair claim settlement practices acts

▷ Describe the damages that can be awarded for bad faith or extracontractual liability.

▷ Examine the defenses available to an insurer in a bad-faith claim.

▷ Examine the elements of good-faith claims handling.

# Good-Faith Claims Handling

## LAW OF BAD FAITH

A primary function of insurers is to pay valid insurance claims. Claims representatives should strive to handle claims with utmost good faith and in an ethical and professional manner. Because interactions with claims representatives are often the only personal contacts that the general public has with an insurer, the claims representative's actions may be closely scrutinized and are often criticized. These criticisms, whether or not legitimate, can result in bad-faith allegations against an insurer.

To avoid bad-faith allegations, claims representatives must understand the law of bad-faith claims. Bad faith law evolved from the special relationship between insurers and insureds based on the implied duty of good faith and fair dealing.

No single widely accepted definition of bad faith exists. *Black's Law Dictionary* defines "bad faith" in insurance as:

> An insurance company's unreasonable and unfounded (though not necessarily fraudulent) refusal to provide coverage in violation of the duties of good faith and fair dealing owed to an insured. Bad faith often involves an insurer's malicious failure to pay the insured's claim or a claim brought by a third party.

Although some state laws define bad faith differently or more specifically, the Black's definition is useful for discussion of the issue because it is broad enough to encompass actions that courts nationwide have determined to constitute bad faith.

### Development of the Law of Bad Faith

The law of bad faith developed in response to the perception that insurers were placing their own interests ahead of their insureds' interests. In some cases, insureds became personally liable for losses or damages they believed were covered by their insurance, and they sued their insurers for breach of contract. The insureds alleged that, by wrongfully denying or mishandling their claims, the insurers had failed to fulfill their contractual promise.

In some of these cases, breach of contract remedies were perceived to be inadequate. The legal remedy for breach of contract is damages in amounts up to the contract's terms, or the policy limits. Consequently, if an insurer wrongfully denied or mishandled a claim, the policyholder would have to go through the expense, stress, and delay of a lawsuit to get the insurer to pay what it should have rightfully paid under the policy. Furthermore, if the insurer's actions caused the insured to be liable to a third party for damages above the policy limits, the insured would be responsible for those damages as well.

Because contract remedies were considered inadequate in such cases, insureds brought lawsuits against insurers for alleged torts, such as fraud and intentional infliction of emotional distress. However, such cases often failed because of the difficulty of proving in court that an insurer's behavior was either fraudulent or outrageous enough to award damages for emotional distress.

Eventually, some courts decided that insurers have an implied duty of good faith and fair dealing when settling claims. Insurers' failure to comply with this duty can result in a **bad-faith claim**.

Insureds and claimants continue to seek new bases for bad-faith claims, such as invasion of privacy, defamation, libel, or slander based on letters or documents in the claims files. In addition, the standard of conduct for proving bad faith continues to evolve.

**Bad-faith claim**

A claim that implies or involves actual or constructive fraud, a design to mislead or deceive another, or a neglect or refusal to fulfill some good-faith duty or some contractual good-faith obligation.

# Duty of Good Faith and Fair Dealing

Most bad-faith claims for breach of the implied duty of good faith and fair dealing arise under insurance-related contracts rather than other types of contracts. Why have bad-faith claims developed to such an extent in insurance? Insurance contracts involve the public interest and require a higher standard of conduct because of the unequal bargaining power between the parties. The insured has less "bargaining power" than the insurer because the insurer not only dictates the terms of the contract (the policy), but also usually controls the claim investigation, evaluation, negotiation, and settlement.

## Public Interest

States regulate insurers to protect consumers against illegal business practices and against insurer insolvency because it is in the best interest of the public for insurers to have the financial resources to pay claims. Courts also want to protect the public interest by ensuring that insurers pay claims they owe. In cases in which insurers have acted in bad faith and have harmed the public interest, courts require them to pay damages beyond their contractual obligations.

## Higher Standard of Conduct

In comparison to other contracts, insurance contracts require a higher standard of conduct—utmost good faith. Because of the nature of insurance contracts, both the insured or applicant and the insurer must disclose all pertinent facts. The insurer must disclose all the terms of the insurance policy, and the applicant must disclose all the information needed to accurately underwrite the policy.

The parties to insurance contracts have unequal bargaining power. Insurers are often perceived as powerful corporations with vast resources. Even if the insured is a large, financially strong corporation, insurers are considered to have greater bargaining power because they develop the insurance contract and settle the claims. When individual consumers purchase an insurance policy, they generally must accept the policy terms written by the insurer.

In addition, many insurance policies specifically state that the insurer controls the investigation and settlement of a claim. For example, Section II—Liability Coverages of Insurance Services Office's (ISO's) homeowners policy states the following: "We may investigate and settle any claim or lawsuit that we decide is appropriate."[1] Because insurers control how claims are resolved, courts reason that insurers should be responsible for the outcome of their claims handling if they have acted in bad faith. Thus, courts hold insurers to a higher standard of conduct to discourage insurers from abusing their position of power.

To conclude that an insurer has acted in bad faith, courts must determine the standard of conduct to which the insurer should be held. Can an insurer be guilty of bad faith for unintentional mistakes or errors in judgment? Or, must an insurer's behavior be intentional, wanton, or reckless to constitute bad faith? Courts differ about whether bad faith should be based on negligence or on gross or intentional misconduct. In many cases, the results are the same regardless of the standard because insurers' actions can be considered both negligent and reckless or intentional.

Some courts use a negligence (sometimes called due care) standard in determining whether a claims representative's (and, by extension, the insurer's) actions constitute bad faith. Some courts may use negligence as a basis to award compensatory damages but award punitive damages only when the insurer has exhibited gross misconduct.

Many courts have rejected a negligence standard for bad faith. They hold insurers liable only if their behavior is found to be intentional or to constitute gross misconduct. To prove intentional misconduct, a complainant must show that the claims representative intended both the misconduct and the consequences, for example, denying coverage with the knowledge that coverage applies under the policy.

When applying a gross misconduct standard, courts have historically looked for signs of "dishonest purpose, moral obliquity, conscious wrongdoing … some ulterior motive or ill will partaking of the nature of fraud."[2] Bad faith may fall somewhere between simple error and outright fraud. Other courts have used terms such as "arbitrary, reckless, indifferent, or intentional disregard"[3] of a party's interests to describe bad-faith behaviors. Because these behaviors are judged on a subjective basis, courts attempt to determine the claims representative's state of mind at the time that bad-faith acts are alleged to have occurred.

Claims representatives should understand the subjective interpretation of negligence and gross misconduct. The difference between negligence and gross misconduct is determined by the court's or jury's interpretation of the facts. For example, a claims representative issues a coverage denial after performing an incomplete investigation. One court might consider the incomplete investigation to be the result of an oversight or of mere negligence. Another court might conclude that deciding coverage without being fully informed is clearly reckless and arbitrary and, therefore, constitutes gross misconduct on the part of the claims representative. Although the standard of care required varies by jurisdiction, some areas of bad faith, such as the parties to a bad-faith claim, are typically the same.

---

### Apply Your Knowledge

Maryam is a claims representative for Great Insurance Company. She is handling a claim for a large retail account. The claimant alleges that she was improperly detained on suspicion of shoplifting, and her arm was injured while she was being led into a small detention room. Gary, the account's risk manager, requests that Maryam deny the claim. He says that the claimant has shoplifted at the store previously. Maryam obtains a background check on the claimant and finds that she was arrested once on a misdemeanor shoplifting charge five years ago, and the charge was dismissed. How should Maryam handle this claim in order to avoid an allegation of bad faith?

a.   Maryam should deny the claim on the basis of the insured's word.

b.   Maryam should deny the claim because of the claimant's arrest record.

c.   Maryam should conduct a complete, thorough investigation of the claim.

d.   Maryam should give the claimant the benefit of the doubt and accept the claim.

*Feedback:* c. Maryam should conduct a complete, thorough investigation of the claim. Great Insurance has a good-faith duty to make fair claim decisions. The insurer could potentially face bad-faith allegations from either the claimant or the insured unless there is a complete and well-documented investigation.

---

# PARTIES TO A BAD-FAITH CLAIM

Various types of plaintiffs can bring bad-faith claims—allegations that an insurer has neglected to fulfill its duty—and lawsuits against an insurer. Each type of plaintiff has unique legal rights that dictate how the bad-faith claims process will proceed. Understanding the rights of the parties involved in bad-faith claims helps claims representatives and insurers protect themselves.

The insurer is usually the **defendant** in a bad-faith lawsuit. Most states do not allow bad-faith claims against claims representatives because they are not parties to the contract. However, some states allow claims representatives to be held personally liable for fraud, conspiracy, or other torts. Insureds, claimants, and **excess insurers** are the **plaintiffs** in bad-faith claims. State laws may vary on who can sue an insurer for bad faith.

# Insureds

In a claims context, insureds can allege bad-faith through first-party lawsuits or third-party lawsuits.

## First-Party Lawsuits

In a first-party bad-faith lawsuit, the insured sues his or her own insurer for bad faith in handling a claim involving the insured's personal loss, such as property damage.

Let's take a look at an example: An insured, a long-haul trucker, was involved in an accident that damaged his tractor-trailer. His insurance policy covered the $30,000 collision damage, payable within sixty days after the insurer received a proof of loss or a damage appraisal. The trucker submitted the proof of loss but did not receive payment for almost nine months. The delay occurred because of a series of mistakes and inattention on the insurer's part, not through any fault of the insured. Because the trucker could not have his truck repaired during that time, he was unable to work and lost seniority status with his employer. He sued his insurer for negligent claims handling, breach of contract, and unfair and deceptive practices. He was awarded $70,000 in damages. The court stated that insurers have a duty to act "in good faith to effectuate prompt, fair, and equitable settlements of claims in which liability has become reasonably clear."[4]

## Third-Party Lawsuits

In a third-party bad-faith lawsuit, the insured sues his or her own insurer for bad faith in handling a third-party claim. For example, the insurer may have inadequately defended the insured in a lawsuit brought by a third party (the claimant), or the insurer may have conducted an inadequate investigation. If the insured is found liable for a judgment in excess of the policy limits because of these actions, the insured can bring a bad-faith lawsuit against the insurer to try to hold it liable for the excess judgment. Sometimes, the insured might give the third-party claimant the right to file this lawsuit against the insurer. Only certain states allow claimants who are not insureds to sue the insurer directly.

For example, Pedro is involved in a car accident with Miu. Pedro is insured by Insurance Company. The facts of the accident clearly show that Pedro is at fault. Miu has suffered serious injuries as a result of the accident. Pedro has

**Defendant**

The party in a lawsuit against whom a complaint is filed.

**Excess insurer**

An insurer that provides coverage for losses above an attachment point, below which there is usually another insurance policy or a self-insured retention.

**Plaintiff**

The person or entity who files a lawsuit and is named as a party.

a $300,000 auto policy limit, and Miu's attorney offers to settle the case for $300,000. However, Insurance Company only offers a $50,000 settlement. Miu sues Pedro for negligently causing the accident and wins a $1 million judgment. As Pedro only has a $300,000 policy limit, he is now responsible for the remaining $700,000; therefore, Pedro sues Insurance Company for a bad-faith failure to settle Miu's claim within policy limits after the original offer. At trial, the court holds that Insurance Company's failure to respond to settle for the policy limit was bad faith because Insurance Company did not give the insured's interests as much consideration as its own.

## Claimants

Can a claimant sue an insurer for bad faith when the claims representative acted in bad faith? Because the contract between the insured and the insurer is the basis for the implied duty of good faith and fair dealing, a claimant who is not a party to the insurance contract generally cannot sue an insurer for bad faith. There are exceptions, however.

For example, an insured can assign rights against the insurer to the claimant. The insured may do this to avoid paying the claimant. In exchange for this assignment, the claimant generally signs a covenant (an agreement) not to pursue recovery of the excess judgment from the insured. Essentially, the claimant assumes the insured's rights to sue the insurer for bad faith for the excess judgment, and in return the insured protects its personal assets from the claimant.

In addition, a few states have unfair claims settlement practices acts that allow claimants to sue insurers. Case law has evolved to permit claimants to sue insurers for bad faith in some states.

---

### Apply Your Knowledge

Ann is severely injured in a car accident. Aleski, who was responsible for the accident, has a $100,000 auto policy limit. Ann's attorney offers to settle for the policy limit, but the insurer offers only $65,000. This takes place in a state in which third-party claimants cannot directly sue insurers. What is a way in which Ann can sue Aleski's insurer, rather than Aleski?

*Feedback:* If Aleski assigns his rights against the insurer to Ann, Ann can sue the insurer for bad faith.

---

## Excess Insurers

Excess insurers write policies, such as umbrella policies, that provide coverage over the limits of the insured's primary policy. Excess insurance does not pay until the loss amount exceeds the underlying policy limits or the drop-down coverage for certain losses. If a claimant wins a judgment in excess of the underlying policy limits, the excess insurer must pay the excess up to its policy limits—meaning that excess insurers have an interest in how primary insurers handle claims. An excess insurer can pursue a bad-faith claim against a primary insurer through equitable subrogation or through a direct action.

With equitable subrogation, an excess insurer has the same rights as an insured to bring a claim against an insurer after being harmed by a judgment in excess of the primary policy limits. For example, a homeowners policy has a liability limit of $300,000, and the excess policy provides another $1 million of coverage above the $300,000 limit, meaning that the insured has $1.3 million in total coverage. There is a covered bodily injury claim against the homeowner, and the primary insurer refuses an offer to settle within policy limits for $300,000. The claimant sues the homeowner and wins an $800,000 judgment. While the excess policy covers this amount, the excess insurer could sue the primary insurer because it did not originally settle for $300,000.

Some courts have ruled that excess insurers may bring direct actions against insurers for bad faith. These courts reason that an insurer should not be allowed to take chances with the excess insurer's money by risking an excess judgment. By imposing on primary insurers a duty of care toward the excess insurer, courts encourage settlements, keep the premiums for excess insurance low, and create no extra burden for the primary insurer, who is already under an obligation to settle the claim in the insured's interests.

Claims representatives who discover that excess insurance could apply to a loss should document that information in the claims file and follow notice and reporting procedures associated with the excess policy.

## BASES OF BAD-FAITH CLAIMS

While the majority of insurance claims do not result in allegations of bad faith, those that do are troublesome and controversial for insurers and claims representatives (reps). Understanding the limited bases on which a bad-faith lawsuit can be brought can help reps avoid and handle these allegations.

An insurer's claims practices can be used as grounds for a bad-faith claim, and the use of good-faith claims handling practices can help reduce the frequency and severity of an insurer's exposure. Generally, bad-faith claims arise from several bases:

- Claim or coverage denials
- Excess liability claims
- Statutory bad faith
- Unfair claim settlement practices acts

## Claim or Coverage Denial

When insureds file claims, they expect their policies to provide coverage for losses. A rep must thoroughly investigate a claim and determine whether the claim is covered. Sometimes after such an investigation, the rep finds that no coverage applies and denies the claim entirely. In other claims, the rep may find that part of a claim is covered and deny only a portion of it.

If a claim is either fully or partially denied, the insured or claimant may retain an attorney to pursue coverage. This increases the possibility of a bad-faith claim because lawyers have a better understanding of actions (such as inappropriate claims denials) that can be the basis for a bad-faith claim. However, reps who follow good-faith claims handling practices should not be overly concerned by an attorney's involvement.

In some jurisdictions, if an insurer denies coverage and a court finds that coverage does in fact apply, the insurer is liable for the full judgment, regardless of having complied with good-faith claims handling practices. Reps should carefully document their reason for fully or partially denying a claim because either action can trigger a bad-faith lawsuit.

## Excess Liability Claims

Bad-faith claims can also be based on excess liability. For an excess liability claim to be filed, a final judgment or settlement must have been entered against the insured, and the amount of the judgment must be in excess of the insured's policy limit. The insured is not required to have paid the judgment before bringing suit; the judgment alone is enough for a bad-faith claim to be pursued.

Rather than waiting for a final judgment, some courts allow a settlement in excess of the policy limit to be the basis of the claim. For example, if an insurer refuses to settle a claim, the insured can settle with the claimant, and the settlement may be in excess of the policy limits. The insured can then sue its insurer for the settlement amount, including the amount above the policy limits. If the insured can produce evidence that the claimant would have settled the claim within the policy limits if the insurer had properly handled the claim, a court can find the insurer liable for the entire amount, including the amount in excess of the policy limits, even though the settlement was not fixed by a judgment. See the exhibit "Sources of Excess Liability Claims."

## Statutory Bad Faith

Some states have statutes that specifically define what constitutes insurers' bad faith and that allow a bad-faith cause of action. Under those statutes, plaintiffs have the right to pursue claims against insurers if they fall within the statutory definition of bad faith. For example, Pennsylvania has a statute providing for recovery of punitive damages, interest, attorneys' fees, and costs

---

### Sources of Excess Liability Claims

Excess liability claims can arise from several situations, including these:

- The insurer refuses the opportunity to settle within policy limits—Before an insurer can be faulted for this, some states require that the claimant offer to settle within the policy limits. However, other states hold the insurer responsible for exploring whether settling within policy limits is likely or reasonable.

- The insurer refuses to pursue settlement—An insurer can wrongfully refuse to pursue settlement of a claim by denying liability or being negligent. When handling a claim, insurers should use a standard of care that a reasonable person would use in managing his or her own affairs.

- The insurer is subject to strict liability—Under strict liability, the insurer is liable for any excess settlement or judgment even though the insurer is not at fault. But in reality, only one state has imposed strict liability on insurers for rejecting a reasonable written offer within policy limits;[5] other courts place burdens that have some aspects of strict liability on insurers. Claims representatives should be familiar with the laws and decisions made in the states where they work.

[DA12795]

when an insured can prove bad faith.[6] Colorado's bad-faith statutes allow an insured to recover two times the delayed or denied claim settlement plus attorneys' fees and costs.[7]

In many states, the criteria for bad-faith liability require more than mere negligence on the part of the insurer. In jurisdictions with bad-faith statutes, claims representatives should pay particular attention to the criteria outlined in the statute and the case law interpreting the statute.

# Unfair Claim Settlement Practices Acts

Many states have unfair claim settlement practices acts, which specify what a claims representative can and cannot do when handling a claim. Such statutes may also require claims representatives to be licensed if they handle claims in that state. Claims representatives should be familiar with the provisions of the acts in any states where they handle claims.

While the acts vary by state, many states base their unfair claim settlement practices laws on the Unfair Claims Settlement Practices Act, a model act developed by the National Association of Insurance Commissioners (NAIC).[8] This act outlines the activities that are considered unfair claim settlement practices.

## Provisions of the NAIC Model Act

The NAIC model act specifies wrongful claim settlement practices. Some provisions apply to first-party claims only, and others apply to third-party claims.

Violations of the model act are those "committed flagrantly and in conscious disregard of the Act" or "committed with such frequency to indicate a general business practice." Therefore, a single instance of carelessness or indifference typically does not violate the act. To comply with the model act, reps should treat both insureds and claimants with respect and professionalism.

Some of the actions defined as unfair claims practices relate to failure to act with promptness—for example, in acknowledging claims-related communications, providing forms necessary to present claims (required within fifteen days of a request), investigating and settling claims, and affirming or denying coverage after completion of an investigation. Others relate to failure to adopt and implement standards

Additional unfair claims practices defined in the act include misrepresenting relevant claims-related facts or policy provisions, failing to settle claims fairly and in good faith, failing to investigate a claim before denying it, offering unreasonably low settlements, delaying investigation or payment by requiring extra paperwork, and failing to provide a reasonable and accurate explanation for claims denial or offers to compromise.

## Enforcement

The NAIC model act specifies that its provisions are to be enforced by state insurance departments. The stated purpose of the act is not to punish insurers and claims representatives, but to elevate the standard of conduct for claims handling by insurers for the benefit of all involved and to avoid bad-faith claims. However, state insurance commissioners can issue statements of charges or violations against insurers, require hearings on those charges, and impose appropriate penalties if the charges are proven.

The NAIC model act allows regulators to impose one or more of these penalties and sanctions on insurers found guilty of violating the act:

- Fines
- Interest on an overdue claim payment
- Payment of other fees and costs
- Injunctions or cease-and-desist orders
- Suspension of a claims representative's or insurer's license
- Revocation of a claims representative's or insurer's license

The act sets fines of up to $1,000 per violation and up to $100,000 in the aggregate. For example, if a claims representative violates several different provisions of the act in the same claim, each violation may be subject to a fine (assessed against the insurer, not the rep) up to the aggregate limit. If a violation is considered flagrant or in conscious disregard of the act, fines may reach $25,000 per violation and $250,000 in the aggregate.

Insurers pay fines to the state department of insurance, not to the insured. Suspension and revocation of licenses are extreme penalties and are usually imposed only after other penalties have proved ineffective. An insurer can appeal an insurance commissioner's decision through either an administrative board or the court system. Generally, insurers who have been penalized or sanctioned take corrective action to prevent further violations.

## State Provisions

Most states have incorporated some or all of the model act's fourteen provisions into their state insurance codes. Some states have fewer provisions, and others have added additional provisions. Regardless, the goals of their provisions support promptness, honesty, responsiveness, fair-mindedness, and even-handedness.

Claims representatives should keep these goals in mind to avoid exposing themselves or their employers to bad-faith claims.

## Bad-Faith Lawsuits Under the Model Act

Some states allow insureds and claimants to bring lawsuits against insurers for violating the state version of the model act, while other states allow only insureds to bring such suits.

Many state laws either specifically prohibit bad-faith lawsuits based on violations of unfair claim settlement practices acts or are silent on the issue. If the law is silent, lawyers pursue bad-faith claims and ask courts to decide.

Violations of the model act are damaging even in states that do not allow them to be used as the basis for a bad-faith lawsuit. Evidence of behavior that violates an act is likely also evidence of the malice, reckless disregard, or bad faith necessary for bad-faith lawsuits.

## Other Bases for Bad Faith

Insureds may use violations of other statutes or regulations as evidence of alleged bad faith and/or alleged extracontractual liability against an insurer.

Bad-faith claims are sometimes based on fraud, deceit, conspiracy, defamation, libel, and slander. For example, an insured may bring a bad-faith lawsuit against an insurer because the claims representative told the insured's creditors that the insured had committed fraud, without having sufficient information to support this allegation. In addition, bad-faith allegations are sometimes made for violations of privacy rights.

Bad-faith claims are not the only risk insurers face from improper claims handling. They may also face extracontractual liability claims—that is, claims for damages outside the insurance policy, such as punitive damages, or in excess of the insurance policy. Such claims can be made as part of a bad-faith claim or arise under other state and federal statutes and regulations.

### *Apply Your Knowledge*

Ananya is a claims representative handling a homeowners coverage claim for Chris, an insured. After carefully reviewing the policy, Ananya finds that Chris does not have coverage for his property damage. She lets him know promptly with a carefully worded claims denial letter. A few days later, Chris calls Ananya to let her know he has hired an attorney. Should Ananya worry that her actions will lead to a bad-faith claim against the insurer?

*Feedback:* While an attorney's involvement increases the possibility of a bad-faith claim, Ananya should not be overly concerned as long as she has followed good-faith claims handling practices. Ananya fully documented the reason for the coverage denial, and this documentation may be important in a lawsuit.

# DAMAGES FOR BAD FAITH OR EXTRACONTRACTUAL LIABILITY

In addition to bad-faith claims arising from improper claim handling, insurers may also face extracontractual liability claims, that is, claims for damages outside the insurance policy.

Insurers found liable for bad faith or responsible for extracontractual liability are required to pay damages to the harmed party. Damages in bad-faith or extracontractual lawsuits may be based on common-law or statutory provisions, and they vary by jurisdiction. If a plaintiff wins a bad-faith or extracontractual lawsuit, the insurer may be required to make these payments to the plaintiff:

- Compensatory damages
- Punitive damages
- Lawyers' fees and court costs
- Prejudgment interest

## Compensatory Damages

Compensatory damages are a monetary compensation to a victim for harm actually suffered. Compensatory damages can include contractual damages, consequential damages, and/or emotional distress damages, which are damages for mental suffering without physical injury.

**Contractual damages** are the amounts payable under the contract according to the contract's terms. For example, in a coverage lawsuit, contractual damages are the full amount of coverage up to the policy limits.

**Contractual damages**

The amounts payable under the contract according to the terms of the contract.

**Consequential damages** are damages awarded by a court to indemnify an injured party for losses that result indirectly from a wrong such as a breach of contract or a tort. They can be out-of-pocket expenses that can be quantified and itemized, such as these:

- Amount of an excess verdict over policy limits
- Verifiable business losses
- Expenses associated with filing the lawsuit and participating in the litigation process
- Interest or other statutorily prescribed damages for delay
- Lawyers' fees

In some jurisdictions, these expenses may not be considered consequential damages but instead may be prescribed by statute or common law.

In states that regard bad faith as a tort, courts may award emotional distress damages as part of compensatory damages. But courts have used different standards to determine when emotional distress is sufficient to incur damages. For example, some courts award damages if the insured suffers a property loss or an economic loss that causes emotional distress, even if the emotional distress is not severe. Some courts award damages when the insured suffers emotional distress, even when the insurer does not intend to cause the distress. Other courts award emotional distress damages only if a physical injury results or if the insurer's misconduct was intentional, malicious, or willful.

## Punitive Damages

Punitive damages, which are damages imposed in order to punish the wrongdoer, can result in very large monetary awards. Many bad-faith claims include a demand for punitive damages because the potential awards can be lucrative for both the claimant and the claimant's attorney. However, punitive damages are not always awarded in bad-faith claims. The standard for awarding punitive damages varies by jurisdiction but generally requires proof of insurer behavior that is worse than ordinary wrongdoing, such as malicious, fraudulent, or oppressive behavior. Some states require proof that the insurer's conduct was intentional, reckless, gross, wanton, or recklessly indifferent for punitive damages to be awarded.

When evaluating a claim for punitive damages, courts ask questions such as these:

- Did the insurer intend to harm the insured?
- Did the insurer substantially harm the insured?
- Was the insurer's conduct so blatant that a reasonable person would foresee the harm to the insured?

**Consequential damages**
A payment awarded by a court to indemnify an injured party for losses that result indirectly from a wrong such as a breach of contract or a tort.

- Does the insurer have substantial net worth?
- Do state laws influence when and what amount of punitive damages are allowed?

The amount of a punitive damage award can be influenced by a variety of factors. One factor may be the insurer's compensation or bonus plan. For example, if claim representatives receive incentive-based compensation to close claims quickly or to reduce claim payments, the insurer may run a greater risk of a punitive damage award, because this conduct may be contrary to public interest. Another factor that can influence a punitive damage award is an insurer's reaction to a bad-faith claim. A court may not look favorably on an insurer that shows no remorse for serious claim handling deficiencies. Candor in admitting mistakes and an open and honest approach to dealing with complaints can help insurers reduce their exposure to punitive damages.

Insurers generally support limits on punitive damages:

- Punitive damages should not exceed the amount of compensatory damages awarded except in unusual cases.
- Higher punitive awards are appropriate only in cases in which the plaintiff has not received a substantial award of compensatory damages and the defendant's conduct is outrageously reprehensible.
- Evidence supporting punitive damages must be specific to the harm suffered by the plaintiff and should not be based on misconduct occurring in other jurisdictions or at other times.

## Lawyers' Fees and Court Costs

Among the types of consequential damages commonly imposed in bad-faith or extracontractual liability cases are lawyers' fees and court costs. Insureds or claimants incur lawyers' fees in bringing bad-faith lawsuits. In addition, if the insurer has refused to defend the underlying claim, insureds and claimants may incur lawyers' fees to defend the underlying lawsuit. In some states, statute or common law allows recovery of such lawyers' fees as part of damages in bad-faith cases. Even in states without such laws, individual courts may allow recovery of lawyers' fees as part of consequential damages resulting from the insurer's conduct. Those courts reason that when the insured must hire a lawyer to obtain the benefits the insurer wrongfully refused to provide, the lawyer's fees are an economic loss and are recoverable as consequential damages. Similarly, courts may allow the insured or claimant to recover court costs. However, some courts have refused to award attorneys' fees and costs if the claimant would have incurred the fees and costs regardless of the outcome of the suit.

## Interest

If an insured pays an excess judgment and then wins a bad-faith lawsuit against the insurer to recover the payment of the excess judgment, the insurer may have to pay the insured the statutory interest rate on that excess judgment amount. Some courts award interest on the claimed damages because the insured was deprived of the money while the insurer had the money to earn interest. Some states' laws allow interest and penalties to be assessed against an insurer solely because of its failure to promptly pay a claim. In addition, some courts have allowed an excess insurer to claim prejudgment interest if the primary insurer was found to have negligently refused to settle.

The amount of damages resulting from a bad-faith or extracontractual liability claim can be sizeable because of all the different types of damages allowed. Claim representatives should be aware of these and other potential consequences of bad faith as they handle claims. Despite their best efforts to handle claims with good faith, bad-faith allegations will still be made, so the claim representative and the insurer must be prepared to defend against these claims.

# DEFENSES TO A BAD-FAITH CLAIM

Insurers faced with bad-faith lawsuits have many defenses. Understanding these defenses can increase claims representatives' awareness of how to avoid actions that could result in bad-faith claims.

An insurer faced with a bad-faith lawsuit has a choice of several defenses—some that provide a total defense of the claim and some that provide only a partial defense. An insurer that can assert more than one defense is more likely to defeat a bad-faith claim or reduce the amount of damages awarded. Each defense must be analyzed in relation to a specific lawsuit to determine whether it can be used. See the exhibit "Defenses to Bad-Faith Claims."

---

**Defenses to Bad-Faith Claims**

**Defenses That Result in Dismissal of Lawsuit**

- Statutes of limitations
- Lack of right to sue (lack of standing)
- Reliance on lawyers' advice
- Insured's collusion with the claimant
- Debatable reasonable basis
- Statutory defenses
- Fair dealing and good documentation
- Comparative bad faith

**Defenses That Reduce Damages**

- Comparative bad faith
- Contributory negligence

---

# Statutes of Limitations

**Statute of limitations**

A law that stipulates the length of time after an event during which legal proceedings (such as a lawsuit or criminal charges) may be initiated.

**Statutes of limitations** apply to bad-faith claims. A court will dismiss a bad-faith lawsuit if the time limit specified in the statute of limitations has expired.

Statutory periods vary depending on whether the alleged bad faith is considered a breach of contract or a **tort**. Statutory periods also vary by state, generally ranging from two to six years from the date the bad faith occurs. The claims representative and the insurer's defense lawyer should check state law to determine the statute of limitations that applies to a particular bad-faith lawsuit.

**Tort**

A wrongful act or an omission, other than a crime or a breach of contract, that invades a legally protected right.

Another common issue is starting date of the statutory period. Courts have differed on whether the statutory period for a bad-faith lawsuit begins on the date the insurer denies the claim or otherwise wrongfully withholds benefits or whether it begins on the date the damages are ascertainable. For example, in excess liability cases, the statute begins when a final judgment in excess of the policy limit is awarded. For a bad-faith claim based on an insurer's refusal to defend an insured, the statute begins when the insurer refuses to defend.

# Lack of Right to Sue (Lack of Standing)

State laws vary on which parties have the right to sue (also called standing to sue) an insurer for bad faith. Insureds, claimants, and excess insurers all may have standing, depending on state law. The lack of right to sue can be a defense for an insurer if, for example, a claim has been brought by an excess insurer in a state that does not give excess insurers the right to sue.

**Tortfeasor**

A person or an organization that has committed a tort.

Several states allow a claimant to bring a bad-faith action directly against the insurer of a **tortfeasor**. In these states, a claimant who has been injured in an auto accident caused by another driver, for example, could sue the insurer of the at-fault driver for bad faith in handling the claim. Claims representatives should check with defense lawyers to determine whether the states in which they handle claims allow direct actions for bad-faith claims.

A claimant or an excess insurer that has no standing to sue under state law may still bring suit if the policyholder assigns the right to sue. In such cases, defense lawyers should ascertain whether the assignment is legal; an illegal or improper assignment can be a valid defense.

# Reliance on Lawyers' Advice

An insurer can base its defense against a bad-faith lawsuit on its reliance on the opinions and advice of competent, independent lawyers. This is called the advice of counsel defense, and it can be used to indicate that the insurer acted reasonably and with proper consideration in handling the insured's claim. For the defense to be successful, some courts require proof of these assertions:

- The insurer disclosed all the facts to the lawyer.
- The insurer acted or relied on the lawyer's advice in good faith.

Proof that the insurer followed a lawyer's advice may be effective in reducing or eliminating punitive damage awards. A court may reason that an insurer's good-faith reliance on a lawyer's advice eliminates the elements of oppression, fraud, or malice required for punitive damages. However, this defense may waive attorney-client privilege, meaning the insured can review the file of the insurer's attorney.

## An Insured's Collusion With the Claimant

Another defense that can lead to dismissal of a bad-faith claim is collusion between the insured and the claimant. For example, an insured and claimant may conspire to help the claimant recover an excess judgment and agree to split the proceeds. This type of collusion is more likely when the insured and the claimant have a business or personal relationship.

Collusion can also occur after a court has awarded damages above the policy limits, if the claimant agrees not to collect the judgment from the insured's personal assets. Courts carefully scrutinize any such agreements before honoring them.

Another potential opportunity for collusion arises from coverage issues. The insured may share the insurer's reservation of rights letter with the claimant and coach the claimant on how to describe a claim so that it is paid by the insurer and not the insured. Claims representatives should look for indicators of possible collusion. For example, the insured's attitude toward the claimant may suddenly become more favorable. Or the insured may become uncooperative and exhibit lack of concern about possible personal excess exposure. A claims representative who suspects collusion should immediately alert claims management because of potential conflicts of interest between the insurer and insured, as well as of coverage issues requiring special handling.

## Debatable Reasonable Basis

In a lawsuit for bad-faith refusal to pay a claim, the insurer's defense may be that it had a reasonable basis for questioning whether a claim was covered.

For example, a claims representative makes a good-faith investigation and determines that a claim is not covered. The insured disagrees and sues for coverage, alleging bad faith in the original coverage determination. A court can find that the claim is covered and still find that no bad faith was involved because there was a reasonable basis for the original coverage denial.

Some courts have held that a claim is "fairly debatable" if a reasonable insurer would deny or delay payment of a claim with the same facts and circumstances. To use the debatable question defense, insurers must show that they had reasonable justification in law or fact for denying or delaying payment of the claim.

In a bad-faith claim based on denial of coverage, an insured may file for summary judgment (meaning the case would be decided without a trial taking place) on the grounds that the policy covers the claim and that no factual issues need to be decided by the court. The court's refusal to grant a summary judgment indicates that factual issues of coverage remain in dispute—in other words, that debatable questions exist. By attempting to resolve this question before making payment, the insurer would not, then, have acted in bad faith.

## Statutory Defenses

Federal and state statutes designate other defenses insurers can use to seek dismissal of a bad-faith lawsuit. For example, some states require insurers to report suspected insurance fraud to the state attorney general's office.

Obviously, there should be no bad-faith claim against the insurer for reporting suspected fraud in good faith if the suspicion is reasonable, so most states offer the insurer immunity from related lawsuits.

## Fair Dealing and Good Documentation

Good-faith claims handling practices and supporting evidence can help defend bad-faith lawsuits by establishing that insurers have dealt fairly with the insureds and claimants. Documentation in each claims file demonstrates how insurers conduct the claims investigation, evaluate claims, and negotiate claims.

Activity logs, correspondence, and documentary evidence, such as police reports, damage estimates, and medical bills, can indicate that claims representatives, supervisors, and managers are doing their jobs properly, which is part of a successful defense strategy for a bad-faith claim.

Before denying a claim, claims representatives should have thorough documentation. Investigative attempts should be documented regardless of the results for the insurer. Fair dealing practices and good documentation can also help claims representatives explain and correct errors. When an error is discovered, a sincere apology and quick action to correct it can help in avoiding and defending bad-faith claims.

Claims representatives should follow their company's best practices in documenting files, which they should assume will be read to a jury. In addition to requiring thorough documentation, these best practices often include avoiding derogatory comments and showing only analyses that are supported by facts.

## Comparative Bad Faith

The duty to act in good faith applies to both the insurer and the insured. So, in a few jurisdictions, evidence that an insured has acted in bad faith may allow the insurer to use the defense of comparative bad faith in a bad-faith lawsuit. The comparative bad-faith defense permits dismissal or reduction of a bad-faith claim if an insured failed to deal fairly with the insurer by breaching one or more implied duties.

For example, an insured delays reporting an accident in which he or she is at fault and also fails to cooperate in the accident investigation. If the insured later sues the insurer for bad faith in handling that claim, evidence demonstrating that the insured's actions prevented the insurer from properly handling or settling the claim may establish comparative bad faith as a defense.

## Contributory Negligence

Another defense that may be used in a bad-faith lawsuit is contributory negligence. In some states, proof of any contributory negligence by the insured prevents recovery. However, most states use a comparative negligence approach, reducing the amount of damages that may be awarded.

If the insured contributed to the damages, the insurer's bad-faith damages are reduced by the percentage that the insured contributed. Generally, a contributory negligence defense is available only in states that permit negligence as a basis for a bad-faith claim.

### Apply Your Knowledge

Josh is a claims representative handling a claim for an insured, Ava. Ava was issued a traffic violation for an improper lane change in an auto accident that severely injured the other driver, Tahir. Tahir's attorney is requesting a settlement amount exceeding Ava's policy limits, based on the long-term nature of his injuries.

Since the beginning of the claims process, Ava has insisted that Tahir was speeding and that she is not solely responsible for the accident. She has urged Josh to resist settling the claim. Josh calls Ava to update her on the claim and inform her that it seems likely the case will go to court. He is surprised when she suddenly seems disinterested in the claim settlement and is sympathetic to the claimant.

Which one of the following should Josh be on the lookout for, especially if Ava later files a bad-faith claim?

a. Lack of standing

b. Collusion

c. Immunity

d. Attorney-client privilege

*Feedback: b.* Josh should be on the lookout for collusion. Indicators of collusion include the insured's attitude toward the claimant suddenly becoming more favorable and the insured becoming uncooperative and exhibiting lack of concern about possible personal excess exposure.

# ELEMENTS OF GOOD-FAITH CLAIMS HANDLING

Good faith in claims handling requires an insurer to demonstrate, at minimum, an equal amount of consideration for the insured's interests as its own. Because this broad concept provides courts with a lot of leeway in deciding what constitutes good faith in a given situation, the claims representative must use common sense and good judgment to minimize the potential for bad-faith claims.

These are some of the primary elements of good-faith claims handling:

- Thorough, timely, and unbiased investigation
- Complete and accurate documentation
- Fair evaluation
- Good-faith negotiation
- Regular and prompt communication
- Competent legal advice
- Effective claims management

## Thorough, Timely, and Unbiased Investigation

Investigations that are thorough, timely, and unbiased are the foundation of good-faith claims handling. If claims representatives investigate claims adequately, they will have sufficient evidence of their good-faith efforts to conclude claims. That evidence is helpful in defending bad-faith lawsuits.

### Thorough Investigation

Claims representatives should collect all relevant and necessary evidence. Investigation should continue as long as new facts develop or become available. Claims representatives should develop the information and documentation necessary to determine liability and damages and should make decisions once they believe they have sufficient information to do so. In a thorough investigation, the claims representative is alert for new information that may change the course of the claim.

For example, a homeowner files a claim for an injury to a visitor who fell on his front step. This may appear to be a simple claim. However, the claims representative discovers from the homeowner's statement that the visitor was on the premises as a business customer, and coverage may therefore be excluded under the homeowners policy. Without the additional investigation, the claims representative might have paid a claim that was not covered by the policy.

Claims representatives use their own judgment to determine when an investigation is sufficiently thorough. For example, even if an insurer's claims handling guidelines offer guidance about which claims require statements and from which parties, a claims representative may decide that an additional statement is necessary for a specific claim.

Many insurers hire experts to assist in the investigation of the cause of loss and the amount of damages. How an insurer selects such experts and uses the information they provide can have bad-faith implications. Insurers must make a good-faith effort to find experts who are reputable within their profession and who will provide unbiased evaluations. Insurers may face bad-faith claims for failing to consider an expert's opinion in denying a claim or for failing to ascertain the unreliability of an expert's opinion and act on it.

## Timely Investigation

An insured who makes a claim expects prompt contact from the claims representative. Most insurers have guidelines requiring the claims representative to contact the insured and the claimant within a specific period, such as twenty-four hours after the claim has been submitted.

Timely contact with the parties to the claim benefits the insurer in several ways. First, parties are more likely to remember the details of the loss accurately. Memory fades quickly over time; therefore, claims representatives are most likely to get complete, accurate information from insureds and claimants if they contact them promptly. Second, the parties are more likely to share information if contacted promptly; prompt contact reassures insureds and claimants that their claims are important and makes them less likely to accept the advice of others who may encourage them to retain a lawyer or pursue unnecessary litigation.

Documentation of timely contact in the claim file can help prove an insurer's use of good-faith claims handling procedures.

## Unbiased Investigation

Investigations should seek to discover the facts and consider all aspects of the claim in order to reach an impartial decision. Claims representatives should pursue all relevant evidence, especially evidence that establishes the claim's legitimacy, without bias. They should avoid asking misleading questions that slant the answers toward a particular outcome, such as "The light was red when you saw it, wasn't it?" In addition, claims representatives should work with service providers that are unbiased and have no conflict of interest. Courts and juries may not look sympathetically on medical providers or repair facilities that always favor insurers.

While striving for impartiality, claims representatives must still be alert to indicators of possible fraud and investigate them thoroughly. Even if the evidence is not sufficient to bring criminal charges, in some states a preponderance of evidence that fraud was committed may be sufficient to defeat a claim. Some states allow claims representatives to seek waivers or extensions of statutory deadlines for accepting or rejecting claims so that they can investigate suspected fraud; in such cases, the suspicions must be based on evidence and clearly documented in the file.

## Compliance With Federal Statutes

When conducting a good-faith claim investigation, claims representatives must comply not only with state unfair claims practices acts, but also with federal statutes. These statutes, designed to ensure the privacy of confidential information, include the Health Insurance Portability and Accountability Act, which deals with the disclosure of private health information; the Gramm-Leach-Bliley Act, which seeks to protect the security and confidentiality of customers of financial institutions; the Sarbanes-Oxley Act, which imposes financial disclosure requirements on publicly traded companies; and the Fair Credit Reporting Act, which promotes the accuracy and privacy of personal information assembled by credit reporting agencies.

## Complete and Accurate Documentation

A common saying among claims representatives is that if an activity, action, or event is not recorded in the claim file, it did not happen. A claim file must provide a complete and accurate account of all the activities of and actions taken by the claims representative.

Claims representatives should be aware that many people, each with a different purpose, may read a claim file. A supervisor or manager may read the file to monitor performance or provide guidance. A home-office examiner or an auditor may review the file for compliance with claims handling guidelines. Claims department peers may review the file as part of a roundtable discussion of reserving. The underwriter, the agent, or the broker may review the file to determine whether the coverage determination or valuation is appropriate. A state insurance department representative may review the file in response to a complaint or during a market conduct study. Defense counsel, and maybe even the claimant's counsel, will review the claim file during the course of litigation. Mediators and arbitrators may review the file as part of a dispute resolution process. Claim files should provide complete information for all of these purposes.

## Fair Evaluation

Fair evaluations are based on facts, not opinions. Claims representatives determine a range of claim amounts based on the facts of the claim, the credibility of the evidence, and applicable laws. File documentation showing that the claims representative used best practices to evaluate a claim is evidence of good-faith claims handling.

Fair evaluation is particularly important in liability claims, which may result in damages that exceed policy limits. By evaluating liability claims as if no coverage limit existed, claims representatives can avoid the mistake of unfairly attempting to settle a claim for less than the policy limit when it may be worth more.

A crucial element of fair claim evaluation is promptness. Evaluation usually takes place at the conclusion of the investigation, when the claims representative has received all supporting documentation. Compliance with statutory time limits for completion of evaluations of coverage and damages can help reduce the insurer's exposure to bad-faith claims.

Promptness is also important in responding to the claimant, the insured, or their respective lawyers' demands. If a letter specifies a time limit for reply, the claims representative should make every effort to respond within that limit. If more time is needed, the claims representative should arrange for an extension by telephone, confirm it promptly in a follow-up letter or e-mail, and document it in the claim file.

A prompt reply is particularly important to a communication that contains a demand for settlement that is at or near the policy limits. The lawyer may contend that the case is worth much more than the policy limits but that the client will accept the policy limits if the claim is settled quickly. If the claims representative has properly evaluated and documented the claim file, this time demand should pose no problem.

Fair evaluations result from thorough, timely, and unbiased investigation and from an understanding of the laws of the jurisdiction in which the claim is brought. For assistance in making evaluations, claims representatives can consult with sources inside and outside the insurance company, including co-workers, supervisors and managers, defense lawyers, people who represent a typical jury, and jury verdict research companies.

Many insurance companies use claims evaluation software to determine a claim's worth. The extent to which an insurer uses claims evaluation software should be balanced against the insurer's duty of good faith and fair dealing, which requires that each claim be analyzed on its own merits.

## Good-Faith Negotiation

Good-faith negotiations flow naturally from thorough, timely, unbiased investigations and prompt, fair evaluations.

Although claims representatives must make realistic offers and carefully consider all demands, lawyers are not held to the same standard. They can make exaggerated demands in a vigorous representation of their clients, and their clients often expect them to do so, in the hope of obtaining the best settlement possible. Claims representatives should respond to such demands by offering a settlement that is consistent with the evidence and documentation in the claim file. They should not trade unrealistic offers and demands with lawyers, as such behavior may result in an unrealistic settlement. Every demand should be documented in the file, along with reasons for accepting or rejecting it.

To resolve disputes over settlement amounts, claims representatives should use policy provisions, such as arbitration clauses, when applicable. An insurer that adheres to policy provisions and pays the amount determined through arbitration is in a better position to defend a bad-faith lawsuit. Claims representatives should consider all possible forms of voluntary alternative dispute resolution, including mediation or a series of face-to-face negotiations, to resolve claims.

## Regular and Prompt Communication

Communicating with all parties to a claim (for example, the insured, the defense attorney, and the excess insurer) is a crucial aspect of good-faith claims handling and resolving claims. Keeping insureds informed is especially important because they expect it, they are most likely to make a bad-faith claim, and they may have the most important information about an accident. Regular and prompt communication allows the insured to participate in the defense and in discussions about the possibility of settlement. Correspondence with the insured provides important documentation for the file that can serve as evidence of the insurer's good-faith claims handling.

The claims representative has a duty to inform the insured of policy provisions that apply to the claim, rights under the policy, and steps to be taken to get maximum benefits. Additional questions from the insured should be answered clearly and promptly. The duty to inform stems from the insurer's duty of utmost good faith under the insurance contract and is also required under many states' unfair claims practices acts.

Communication by and with attorneys in the case is also important. The defense attorney should regularly and promptly inform the insured of all major events in the defense. Any request by an insured not to be informed of these events should be confirmed in writing. Claims representatives and lawyers should document telephone and personal communication in writing and confirm information from such communications that is crucial to the claim.

If defense lawyers fail to communicate promptly and regularly, claims representatives should contact them to solicit information and correct any misunderstandings. Claims representatives cannot delegate claims to defense lawyers and still meet good-faith claims handling standards.

If the insured has excess insurance, the claims representative should notify the excess insurer of the claim and provide the insured with copies of all communications. The excess insurer may request a copy of the claim file and may or may not want to be actively involved in the claim thereafter to protect its interests. Additionally, if the insured hires a lawyer, that lawyer will want to be kept advised of significant claim activity.

An insurer's internal organization can influence the efficiency and effectiveness of communication between claims representatives and parties to a claim, attorneys, and others. If an insurer centralizes call-handling by using customer service representatives to field telephone calls, it should allow call center staff to access claim files so that they can respond to specific questions. Claims representatives should be informed of calls relating to the claims they handle and should be allowed to contact insureds and claimants directly. Insurers that use mail centers must ensure that correspondence from insureds, claimants, or attorneys is delivered to the appropriate claims representative.

## Competent Legal Advice

Following the advice of competent lawyers can be considered evidence that an insurer acted in good faith. Lawyers who defend the insured should be selected based on their experience, knowledge of the law, and success in the courtroom. Lawyers have an ethical obligation to be loyal to the insured first and the insurer second, because the insured is the lawyer's client, regardless of who is paying the lawyer's fees. Defense lawyers who are overly optimistic about their chances of successfully defending a case may not be good choices, because their optimism may be unproved and can expose the insured and insurer to an excess verdict. Claims representatives should provide lawyers with all information and documentation necessary to reach a complete and accurate opinion and should avoid any attempts to influence the lawyer's independent judgment.

When resolving a coverage question, insurers should avoid conflicts of interest by using lawyers other than the defense lawyers hired to defend an insured. Asking a lawyer who defends an insured a coverage question creates an ethical dilemma for that lawyer because the answer may not be in the insured's best interest. Insurers that use in-house or staff lawyers (lawyers who are the insurer's employees) to defend insureds should be especially sensitive to the possibility of a conflict of interest and, if any appearance of such a conflict exists, should use outside lawyers.

Insurers often request independent opinions on claim-related issues from attorneys not involved in the claim. Such opinions can provide impartial analysis of an issue and research about approaches other courts have taken regarding similar issues.

## Effective Claims Management

An insurer's claims management directly affects a claims representative's ability to handle claims in good faith. Claims management in this context refers to how claims departments are managed by claims supervisors and managers. Claims management involves many duties. Especially crucial to good-faith claims handling are consistent supervision, thorough training, and manageable caseloads.

Supervisors and managers are responsible for ensuring that claims are investigated, evaluated, and resolved promptly and accurately and that claims representatives follow proper claims handling practices. Managers develop guidelines for claims handling and are ultimately responsible for ensuring that the guidelines are followed.

Insurers should provide continuous and consistent training for claims representatives relating to all necessary claims handling procedures and best practices as well as to good-faith claims handling. Training is essential when a claims representative handles a new type of claim or a more complex, serious claim for the first time.

Supervisors and managers must monitor the number of claims assigned to each claims representative to ensure that the work is manageable. To ensure good-faith claims handling, they should identify potential caseload problems and reassign claims or provide additional support when necessary.

Many insurers hire management or strategic consultants to improve the efficiency of claims handling. In selecting such consultants, the insurer must make certain that the consultant is aware of the special requirements of the insurance industry.

## SUMMARY

Insurers and the claims representatives who work for them have a duty of good faith and fair dealing in claims handling. This requirement is imposed on insurers and claims representatives because of (1) the public interest in ensuring that insurers have the financial resources to pay claims and that they pay claims fairly and promptly, (2) the unequal bargaining power of the parties to the insurance contract, and (3) the insurer's control over the investigation and resolution of the claim.

Bad-faith claims or lawsuits are usually brought by the insured against the insurer over the handling of the insured's first-party claim or of a third-party claim against the insured. If the insured assigns the right to sue his or her insurer for bad faith to a claimant, the claimant can sue the insurer for bad faith. Bad-faith claims can also be brought against an insurer by an excess insurer that has had to pay a claim because of the insurer's bad faith.

Bad-faith claims usually result from a claim or coverage denial, a verdict in excess of the policy limit, or a violation of a state statute or of an unfair claim settlement practices act. The Unfair Claims Settlement Practices Act, a model act developed by the NAIC, lists practices that are generally accepted as unfair claim settlement practices. Most states have adopted some or all of the model act's provisions.

Damages resulting from bad faith or extracontractual liability can vary by jurisdiction. Generally, they can include compensatory damages, emotional distress damages, and punitive damages. Among compensatory damages are lawyers' fees, court costs, and interest.

Insurers and claims representatives have several defenses available to combat bad-faith claims or reduce the amount of damages awarded. These include statutes of limitations, lack of right to sue (lack of standing), reliance on lawyers' advice, an insured's collusion with the claimant, debatable reasonable basis, statutory defenses, fair dealing and good documentation, comparative bad faith, and contributory negligence.

To defend themselves against most bad-faith claims, insurers must be able to show that their claims personnel acted in good faith. The claim file must contain documentation of a thorough investigation; a fair, prompt, and knowledgeable evaluation of the claim; and a documentation of good-faith negotiation. The file should reflect prompt and adequate communication among the parties to the claim, the insurer's consideration of legal advice, and adherence to the insurer's claims management practices. The file should also show compliance with applicable federal statutes.

# ASSIGNMENT NOTES

1.  Form ISO HO 00 03 05 01, Copyright ISO Properties, Inc., 1999.

2.  Slater v. Motorists Mut. Ins. Co., 174 Ohio St. 148, 187 N.E.2d 45 (1962).

3.  Commercial Union Ins. Co. v. Liberty Mutual Ins. Co., 393 N.W.2d 161, 164 (Mich. 1986).

4.  Pickett v. Lloyd's, 621 A.2d 445, 451 (N.J. 1993).

5.  LexisNexis Legal Newsroom Insurance Law, "Bad Faith in Liability Insurance—New Appleman on Insurance Law Library Edition, Chapter 23," August 11, 2010, www.lexisnexis.com/legalnewsroom/insurance/b/applemaninsurance/archive/2010/08/11/bad-faith-in-liability-insurance-new-appleman-on-insurance-law-library-edition-chapter-23.aspx (accessed August 1, 2018).

6.  42 Pa. C.S.A. § 8371.

7.  Jonathan Bukowski and Larry Bache, "Calculating Damages Under Colorado's Bad Faith Statute," October 16, 2017, Property Insurance Coverage Law Blog,

www.propertyinsurancecoveragelaw.com/2017/10/articles/bad-faith/calculating-damages-under-colorados-bad-faith-statute/ (accessed August 1, 2018).

8.    National Association of Insurance Commissioners, Unfair Claims Settlement Practices Act, NAIC Model Laws, Regulations and Guidelines, vol. VI, NAIC (Kansas City, Mo: NAIC, 1984–2011), pp. 900-2–900-3, https://www.naic.org/store/free/MDL-900.pdf?94 (accessed August 1, 2018).

# Index

Page numbers in boldface refer to pages where the word or phrase is defined.